THE
INTERIOR CASTLE
OR
THE MANSIONS

ST. TERESA OF JESUS
1515-1582

THE INTERIOR CASTLE

CASTLE

OR

THE MANSIONS

By

St. Teresa of Avila

Translated from the Autograph of St. Teresa of Jesus by
The Benedictines of Stanbrook

Revised, with Notes and an Introduction, by the
Very Rev. Fr. Benedict Zimmerman, O.C.D.
PRIOR

TAN BOOKS AND PUBLISHERS, INC.
Rockford, Illinois 61105

Nihil Obstat: Dom Michael Barrett, O.S.B.
                Censor Deputatus

Imprimatur: ✠ Edward
                Apostolic Administrator
                Birmingham, Oscott.
                February 24, 1921

This translation first published in approximately 1912. This edition published in 1997 by TAN Books and Publishers, Inc., by arrangement with the Benedictines of Stanbrook, being photographically reproduced from the "Third Edition with Additional Notes" published by Thomas Baker, London, in 1921.

Library of Congress Catalog Card No.: 97-60909

ISBN 0-89555-604-9

Cover illustration: Contemporary portrait of St. Teresa of Avila by Fray Juan de la Miseria, Discalced Carmelites, Seville.

Printed and bound in the United States of America.

TAN BOOKS AND PUBLISHERS, INC.
P.O. Box 424
Rockford, Illinois 61105
1997

DEDICATED TO

The Martyred Daughters of St. Teresa,
The Blessed Martyrs of Compiegne, France,
by the Descendants of Their Fellow Prisoners.

Stanbrook Abbey
Day of the Beatification
May 27, 1906

NOTE

IN this new edition the wording has been revised and condensed, chiefly with a view to rendering the translation more pregnant. Only one passage (VI. Mansion, ch. v. 13) has been substantially changed, in conformity with an explanation received from a high authority. It is admittedly a very difficult passage which appears to have been misunderstood by nearly all translators; but it is gratifying to notice that the new French translation by the Carmelite nuns of Anderlecht agrees with our interpretation. The editor is under an obligation to that translation for several interesting facts embodied in the Introduction and in the notes to the text.

B. Z.

WINCANTON
December 25. 1911

CONTENTS

5

THE FIFTH MANSIONS

THE SIXTH MANSIONS

THE SEVENTH MANSIONS

THE
INTERIOR CASTLE
OR
THE MANSIONS

The Benedictines of Stanbrook desire to express their gratitude to the Very Rev. Benedict Zimmerman for having kindly revised the translation of the 'Interior Castle' and also for the Introduction, Notes, and Index which he has added to the book.

INTRODUCTION

SAINT TERESA began to write the *Interior Castle* on June 2, 1577, Trinity Sunday, and completed it on the eve of St. Andrew, November 29, of the same year. But there was a long interruption of five months,[1] so that the actual time spent in the composition of this work was reduced to about four weeks—a fortnight for the first, and another fortnight for the second half of the book. The rapidity with which it was written is easily explained by the fact that the Saint had conceived its plan some time previously. On January 17, 1577, she had written to her brother, Don Lorenzo de Cepeda, at Avila: 'I have asked the bishop—Don Alvaro Mendoza—for my book (the *Life*) because I shall perhaps complete it by adding those new favours our Lord has lately granted me. With these one may even compose a new work of considerable size, provided God grants me the grace of explaining myself; otherwise the loss will be of small account.'[2] She never asked for permission to write anything, but waited until she received a command from her superiors, which, in this case, came from

[1] *Castle*, Mansions v. ch. iv. 1.
[2] *Letters of St. Teresa*, Vol. II.

Father Jerome Gracian, superior of the Discalced Carmelites of the Provinces of Andalusia and Castille, and from Don Alonso Velasquez, canon of Toledo, afterwards bishop of Osma.[3] The Saint was not in good health at the time; she repeatedly complains of noises in the head and other infirmities, but, worst of all, she was weighed down by troubles and anxieties resulting from the action of the superiors of the Order and of the Papal Nuncio against the nuns and friars of the Reform. Matters became even more serious when, in October, the nuns of the Incarnation of Avila proceeded to the election of a new prioress. Notwithstanding the prohibition of the provincial, fifty-five electors recorded their votes in favour of the Saint and were immediately declared excommunicated. The whole work of the Reform seemed on the brink of ruin, the Saint, as well as all her friends, was in disgrace, subject to obloquy and ill-treatment.

No trace of these trials is to be found in the *Interior Castle*. Saint Teresa possessed the power of concentration of thought in a marvellous degree. The early mornings and late evenings were devoted to the composition of the book, while the rest of the day was taken up by the affairs of the Order. Mother Mary of the Nativity, a member of the

[3] The French Carmelite nuns in their new translation, *Œuvres complètes de Sainte Thérèse*, t. vi, Introduction, p. 5, quoting the *Año Teresiano*, t. vii ad 7 July, and Father Gracian's *Dilucidario*, as well as his additions to Ribera, show the exact share of Fr. Gracian and Dr. Velasquez in the preliminaries of this work.

community of Toledo, where the book was begun, declared afterwards,[4] that she often saw her writing, generally after Holy Communion, her face resplendent, with such rapidity and so absorbed in her occupation that she seemed undisturbed by, and in fact quite unconscious of, any noise that was made. Mother Mariana of the Angels[5] reports having heard from the same witness, that entering her cell one day to deliver a message, the holy Mother was just beginning a new sheet of her book. While taking off her spectacles to listen to the message she was seized by a trance in which she remained for several hours. The nun, terrified at this, did not stir, but kept her eyes steadily on the Saint. When she came to, it was seen that the paper, previously blank, was covered with writing. Noticing that her visitor had discovered it, Saint Teresa put the paper quietly in the box.

[4] Fuente, *Obras de Santa Teresa de Jesus*. Edit. 1881, Vol. vi, p. 278.
[5] *Ibid.* p. 178. A somewhat similar incident is reported by Mother Anne of the Incarnation (*Ibid.* p. 213), but it appears to be wrongly brought into connection with the composition of the *Castle*. The nun in question had belonged to the convent of St. Joseph at Segovia at an earlier period, but there is no evidence that St. Teresa visited this place in the course of the six months during which she composed this work. The Bollandists, indeed, maintain that it was commenced at Toledo, continued at Segovia and completed at Avila (n. 1541), but their sole authority for including Segovia is the passage in question, which, however, must refer to some other work of the Saint. The sister, passing St. Teresa's door, saw her writing, her face being lit up as by a bright light. She wrote very fast without making any corrections. After an hour, it being about midnight, she ceased and the light disappeared. The Saint then knelt down and remained in prayer for three hours, after which she went to sleep.

Another nun, Mary of St. Francis, left the following declaration: 'I know that our holy Mother wrote four books, the *Life*, the *Way of Perfection*, the *Foundations*, and the *Mansions*, which I have seen her writing. Once, while she was composing the last-named work, I entered to deliver a message, and found her so absorbed that she did not notice me; her face seemed quite illuminated and most beautiful. After having listened to me she said: "Sit down, my child, and let me write what our Lord has told me ere I forget it," and she went on writing with great rapidity and without stopping.'[6]

Mary of St. Joseph says she heard from Mary of the Nativity that Father Jerome Gracian commanded the Saint to write the *Mansions*; she, however, begged to be excused, because so many books having been written by holy and learned men, there remained nothing for a woman to write. At length she yielded under obedience. This nun (Mary of the Nativity) was frequently in the Saint's cell while she was writing and she noticed her resplendent face and the almost preternatural velocity with which her hand travelled over the paper.[7]

Writing to Mother Mary of St. Joseph, Prioress of Seville, November 8, 1581, St. Teresa gives her a message for Father Rodrigo Alvarez, S. J.: 'Our Father (Jerome Gracian, then provincial) tells me that he has handed you a book written by me,

---

[6] Fuente, p. 223.   [7] *Ibid.* p. 255.

which perhaps you do not feel inclined to read yourself. Kindly read to Father Rodrigo Alvarez, at his next visit, the last Mansion, but under the seal of confession, as he asks this in his superior wisdom. This is only for you two. Tell him that the person he knows has arrived at this Mansion and enjoys the peace there described; that she is entirely at rest, and that some grave theologians have assured her that she is on a safe road. In case you could not read these pages to him do not send him the book, for it might lead to unpleasantness. Until I have his answer on this matter I will not write to him. Give him my compliments.'

At the end of the original manuscript, before the epilogue (marked with Ihs.) there is a notice in Father Alvarez' hand-writing to this effect: 'The Mother Prioress of the convent of Seville has read to me this seventh Mansion, whither a soul may arrive in the present life. Let all the saints praise the infinite goodness of God, Who communicates Himself to His creatures so that they truly seek His glory and the salvation of their neighbour. What I feel and judge of this matter is, that everything that has been read to me is conformable to Catholic truth and in accordance with Holy Scripture and the teaching of the Saints. Whosoever has read the doctrine of the Saints, such as the books of St. Gertrude, St. Catharine of Siena, or St. Bridget of Sweden, and other saints and spiritual writers, will clearly understand that the spirit of Mother Tireza *(sic)* of Jesus is true, since it leads to the same effects as are to be found in the saints; and because this is in truth my judgment and opinion, I have hereunto set my name, this, the 22nd day of February, 1582. P. Rodrigo Alvarez.'[8]

The work was copied, probably under the supervision of the Saint, who introduced many changes; when completed the original was handed to Father Jerome Gracian and to the Dominican, Fray Diego de Yanguas, for approval. Both, particularly the former, made numerous corrections, which Fuente, not without reason, calls impertinent, scratching out whole sentences and adding others. The book thus revised must have enjoyed a certain celebrity, though not to the same extent as the *Life*, to which St. Teresa herself preferred it. Scarcely a week after its completion she wrote to Father Salazar, S.J.: 'If Señor Carillo [Salazar himself] came, the person in question [the Saint] thinks he would find another jewel which in her opinion is superior to the former [the *Life*]. This one reflects nothing foreign to itself, but is resplendent in its own beauty. It is enriched with more delicate enamels than the former, the workmanship, too, is more perfect. For, as the person in question says, the jeweller was less experienced when he fashioned the previous one. Moreover, the gold of the new

[5] Autograph, fol. cx.

one is of better quality than that of the former, though the precious stones are not so well set. It has been done, as might be expected, according to the designs of the Jeweller Himself.'[9] Later on she wrote to Father Jerome Gracian: "The book I have written since seems to me superior [to the *Life*]; at least I had more experience when I wrote it.'[10]

One day, speaking with Mother Mary of Jesus on spiritual matters, she said that our Lord had communicated so much to her since she had reached what she described in the seventh Mansion,—the spiritual Marriage,—that she did not consider it possible to advance further in this life, in the way of prayer, nor even to wish to do so.[11]

The book was eagerly read by those who were able to obtain copies. At the archiepiscopal Seminary at Salamanca it was read publicly after dinner; the students, contrary to custom, sacrificing the recreation rather than miss so edifying an instruction. The result was that several entered the religious life, one becoming a Franciscan, two others, who had already taken their degrees, joining the Discalced Carmelites.[12] We also know of a lady who became a Poor Clare through reading the *Interior Castle*.[13] The process of Beatification contains the following evidence of Don Francisco de Mora, architect to Philip III: 'The same prioress (of a

[9] December 7, 1577. *Letters* Vol. II.
[10] Jan. 14, 1580. *Letters* Vol. IV:
[11] Fuente, *Obras. l.c.* p. 275. [12] *l.c.* p. 217. [13] *Ibid.* p. 227.

convent of Dominican nuns) being concerned about my salvation gave me a book in manuscript, called *The Mansions*, by Mother Teresa, hoping I should derive some benefit from it. I fear this was not the case, but it made me acquainted with Teresa of Jesus, the foundress of the Discalced Carmelite nuns, of whom I had not yet heard, but for whom I now felt devotion.'[14]

In August 1586 it was decided to print Saint Teresa's works, the Augustinian Fray Luis de Leon being selected as editor, as he was unconcerned in the quarrels raging round the Reform. Accordingly, the manuscript of the *Interior Castle* was handed to him. On the first leaf he wrote the following note:

'Many passages of this book written by the holy Mother have been scored through, other words being substituted or notes being added in the margin. Most of these corrections are badly done, the original text being much better. It will be noticed that the holy Mother's sentences are superior and agree with the context, which is not the case with the corrections. These improvements and glosses may therefore be dispensed with. Having myself read and considered everything with great care, it appears to me that the reader, too, should have before him the words of the author who knew best what to say; for this reason I have left out the additions, and have restored what has been changed, excepting only a

[14] Fuente, *Obras.* p. 190.

few corrections made by the writer herself. I beg of the reader that he would in charity reverence the words and even the letters traced by so holy a hand, and strive to understand what has been written. He will then see that there was no need for corrections; should he fail to understand her, let him believe that the writer knew what she said, and that her words cannot be tampered with if they are not to lose their meaning; otherwise what was to the point will seem out of place. This is how books become corrupted, useless, and are finally lost.'[15]

When Luis de Leon undertook the editing of St. Teresa's writings he received a long letter from Don Diego de Yepes, afterwards Bishop of Tarazona, a former friend and confessor of the Saint, in which he records his personal recollections. I shall only insert here what he says about the *Interior Castle*:

'This holy Mother desired to see the beauty of a soul in the state of grace, a thing greatly to be coveted both for the sake of seeing and of possessing it. While this desire lasted, she was commanded to write a treatise on prayer, of which she had much personal experience. On the eve of the Blessed Trinity, while considering what subject to choose for this treatise, God, Who disposes everything in due season, fulfilled her wish and furnished a suitable subject. He showed her a most beautiful globe

[15] Autograph. fol. 1.

of crystal, in the shape of a castle, with seven rooms, the seventh, situated in the centre, being occupied by the King of glory, resplendent with the most exquisite brilliancy, which shone through and adorned the remaining rooms. The nearer these lay to the centre, the more did they partake of that wondrous light. It did not, however, penetrate beyond the crystal, for everything round about was a mass of darkness and impurity, full of toads and vipers and other venomous animals.

'She was still admiring this beauty which, by the grace of God dwells in the soul, when, lo! the light suddenly disappeared, and the crystal, wherein the King of glory was still residing, became opaque and as dark as coal, emitting an intolerable odour; the venomous animals, formerly held in check outside, obtained admittance into the castle. The holy Mother wished that every one should behold this vision, for she thought that no one having seen the beauty and splendour of grace, which is forfeited by sin and replaced by such repulsive misery, would ever dare to offend God.

'She told me this vision on the same day, for in this as well as in other things she was so communicative that on the following morning she said to me: "How I forgot myself yesterday! I cannot think how it could have happened. Those high aspirations of mine, and the affection I have for you must have caused me to go beyond all reasonable limits. God grant I may have derived some profit therefrom." I promised her to say nothing about it during her life-time, but since her death I should like to make it known to all men. From this vision she learnt four important matters.

'First, she came to understand this axiom, which in this form she had never heard of in her life,[16] that God is present in all things by His essence, presence, and power. As she was deeply humble and submissive and obedient to the doctrine of the Church and the teaching of the learned ministers of God, she never rested until her revelations had been approved of by her superiors and by theologians, and were shown to be conformable to Holy Scripture. She went so far as to say that if all the angels of heaven said one thing, and her superiors another, though she could not doubt that the former were true angels, yet she would hold what was told her by her superiors, because faith comes through these and there remains no room for deceit, whereas revelations coming from angels might be illusionary.

'With such regard for obedience, she asked me one day at Toledo—probably at the time when she saw the vision of the Castle—whether it was true that God was in all things by His power, presence,

[16] See *Life*, ch. xviii. 20. *Mansions* v. ch. i. 9. The ignorance of the priest who had told her that God was only present by His grace, made a lasting impression on St. Teresa. She was first undeceived by a Dominican.

and essence, to which I replied in the affirmative, explaining it as best I could on the authority of St. Paul, particularly where he says "the sufferings of this time are not worthy to be compared with the glory to come that shall be revealed in us,"[17] Laying stress on these words, "shall be revealed in us," she was so overjoyed that I was quite astonished. Though in a way it seemed to me a kind of curiosity, I could not help thinking there was some mystery about it, for she said: "This is the very thing."

'Secondly, she was greatly surprised at the malice of sin, since, notwithstanding the presence of God in these various ways, it prevents the soul from partaking of that powerful light.

'Thirdly, she derived such humility and self-knowledge from this vision, that from that moment she never thought of herself in all the good she was doing; for she learnt that all the beauty of the soul emanates from that resplendent light, and that the powers of the soul and of the body are enlivened and strengthened by the Power established in the centre, whence comes all our good, so that we have but a small share in our good works. All the good she did, she from this moment referred to God as its principal author.

'Fourthly, she derived from it the subject of the book she was ordered to write on prayer, comparing

[17] Rom. viii. 18.

the seven rooms of the Castle with as many degrees of prayer, whereby we enter within ourselves and draw nearer to God. So that, penetrating to the depths of our soul and gaining perfect self-know-ledge, we reach the seventh room where God Himself dwells, with Whom we become united by as perfect a union as is possible in the present life, being made partakers of His light and love.

'I will say no more of this vision and the *Mansions*, because your Reverence must by now have seen this admirable book, and must know with what accuracy, with what majestic doctrine, with what lucid examples she describes the pro-gress of the soul from the gate to the very centre. It is clearly seen in this treatise how she communi-cated with our Lord, and how His Majesty vouch-safed to place her in the centre and to unite her with Himself, as she puts it, by the bonds of marriage and an inseparable union.'[18]

After the publication of the *Interior Castle*, in 1588 at Salamanca, it became not only more widely known, but also more and more appreciated. Francis Suarez, the great theologian of the Society of Jesus, says in his deposition in the process of Beatification that he had read some of St. Teresa's works, par-ticularly the *Mansions*, which contain an absolutely safe doctrine and give proof of a wonderful spirit of prayer and contemplation.[19]

[18] Fuente, pp. 131-133.   [19] *l.c.* 184.

Thomas Hurtado, professor of theology at Seville, speaks as follows:

'As often as I read the books of the holy Mother, I admire the wonderful manner in which God instructed her in mystical theology for the sake of souls giving themselves truly to familiar intercourse with His divine Majesty. But where I most regret my inability of expressing in fitting terms my sentiments towards this excellent teacher is when I look at, and refresh myself in that Castle with its seven rooms; for there is seen the effect of infused knowledge such as St. Denis received from St. Hierotheus[20] and both from St. Paul, and which has been committed to writing in the famous book of *Mystical Theology*. Hence comes, as from a fountain-head, notwithstanding the obscurity (to our manner of thinking) of its language, the doctrine of the great masters of the spiritual life such as Hugh of St. Victor, St. Bernard, Ruysbroek, Tauler, Gerson, and many others whom I pass by.

'Nevertheless, I will boldly say that no one has given us water more limpid from that Apostolical and Areopagitical well than the holy Mother Teresa, who, in her books, but chiefly in the *Mansions*, has cleared up in simple language the most difficult questions of this divine theology, and has brought forth light from darkness, as it is

---

[20] Allusion to the famous *Mystical Theology* attributed to Dionysius the Areopagite, and long considered the chief authority on this subject.

written: (He) commanded light to shine out of darkness.'[21] Who has ever been able to show as clearly as our Saint how God takes possession of the soul, how He unites Himself with its substance, whence comes to the intellect the light of faith, to the will the ardour of love, and to the senses the jubilation over His works? No one has ever turned theory into practice in a more convincing or more catholic manner. The most profound secrets of this supernatural wisdom are here treated with such ease, so amiably, so delightfully, they are illustrated by such nice and homely examples, that instead of awe-inspiring obscurity, we find lovely flowers and the sweetness of love, through which, as through an avenue, the soul passes onwards. When God made known His exalted doctrine to St. Dionysius and other mystical writers, He made use of their own language and pen. But St. Teresa in the *Mansions* is like the light of dawn whose rays are not intercepted by the clouds of this world; like a soft rain from above, whereby the soul grows and profits by its communications with God. Until the teaching of this great doctor became known it seemed as though God were inaccessible, being surrounded by darkness, through which Moses and some other persons had to pass when approaching Him;[22] but they neither ex-

[21] 2 Cor. iv. 6.

[22] The example of Moses is scarcely to the point (cf. Exod. xxxiii. 11, and Num. xii. 7, 8).

plained the manner nor showed the way whereby they came to the enjoyment of the sweetness of the Spouse. Now, however, this way is clear and patent to all, having been pointed out in the *Mansions*, in language so straight and so methodical, and no longer such as could not be understood, or required further explanation. In my opinion this holy writer derived not only the substance of her teaching from infused knowledge, but even the words with which she explains it.'[23]

Likewise Don Alvaro de Villegas, canon of Toledo, expressed his opinion that the *Way of Perfection* and the *Interior Castle* contain 'heavenly doctrine.' The weight of the subject-matter, the propriety of the comparisons, the force of the expressions, the consistency of the teaching, the sweetness of her well-chosen, vivid words, the clearness of the arguments, all this proves that she was guided by her heavenly Spouse, in Whom are hidden the treasures of the wisdom of God; and that the Holy Ghost, Who more than once was seen resting on her head like a dove, was dictating these works. Villegas does not believe that any one could read them, as such books ought to be read, without becoming himself a master of the spiritual life. For they are like heavenly dew, rendering the soul fruitful in the matter of prayer.[24]

[23] Fuente, pp. 330-332.
[24] *l.c.* p. 334. These testimonies could be easily multiplied.

It would be a mistake to consider the *Interior Castle* a complete treatise of mystical theology. Like St. Teresa's other works, it is intensely personal: she describes the road by which she has been led, being well aware that others may be led in a different way. In the heavenly Father's house there are many mansions, not only seven, and many paths lead to them. What gives the work such high value is, that it is the result of a most searching inquiry into the various phases whereby a soul is gradually transformed into the likeness of God Himself. Here St. Teresa is always at her best. She takes nothing for granted, even her own personal experiences are admitted only after having been fully investigated and found to be consistent one with the other, and conformable to the teaching of the Church and the words of Holy Scripture.

Mystical theology is generally divided into three parts, respectively called the purgative, the illuminative, and the unitive life. In the first, man is cleansed from sin and habitual imperfection by the use of the sacraments and by voluntary mortification of the passions. The mind is purified by sedulous meditation on the last end and on the Life and Passion of Christ, which must ever be the great model of the Christian. This first portion of the way to heaven can be covered by the help of the ordinary means of grace, without any direct and extraordinary intervention of divine power.

The second part differs in many ways from the first. It comprises the passive purification of the soul and the passive enlightenment of the mind. By sending it keen interior and exterior trials and sufferings, God completes the cleansing of the soul in a manner far surpassing any voluntary effort of man. By raising it to the stage of contemplation He gives it fresh light on the mysteries of our Redemption. The mind is then no longer compelled to strain the memory, the reason, and the will, in order to dwell upon the great truths of religion and to derive some personal benefit therefrom, for these truths are now more or less permanently before it and fill it with holy thoughts, sometimes giving it consolation in trouble, at other times striking a warning note against imperfection. Again, the subtraction of sensible consolation, and the interior aridity arising therefrom, leave a terrible blank in the soul, showing it that, without God's help, it is mere nothingness. This apparent estrangement from God is the keenest trial that can befall a soul, but also the most powerful means of cleansing it from the least, the most subtle imperfections.

Emerging from this state of probation, the soul enters upon the third stage, in which, though perhaps in the midst of severe suffering and sharp persecution, it knows itself to be a chosen child of God, to Whom it is united by perfect conformity of the will. Such phenomena as revelations, visions, locutions, and even more wonderful manifestations, like the wound of love, spiritual betrothal and nuptials, are incidental rather than essential to the second and third stages. Some great contemplatives have never experienced anything of the kind, while, on the other hand, some of these occurrences may sometimes have been merely the work of an exuberant imagination, or even the result of diabolical illusion. They should therefore never be wished for, or cherished, but rather shunned and ignored, in as far as that is possible. If they are real and come from God, they will do their work without the co-operation of the soul. The danger of self-deception is so great that a person labouring under such phenomena should offer every resistance, and the spiritual director should exercise the utmost vigilance. St. Teresa is very eloquent on this point, and undeceived many would-be contemplatives, while her disciple, St. John of the Cross, is even more thorough-going in the deprecation of spiritual favours. Among the numerous marks whereby the trained theologian may discriminate between real and imaginary phenomena, there is one about which Saint Teresa speaks with wonderful clearness. If they proceed from hysteria the imagination alone is active and the higher powers of the soul are torpid; if, however, they come from God, the intellect and the will are so intensely active, that the lower powers and even the body lose all strength for the time being.

It will be noticed that the first two Mansions belong to the purgative life, the third and fourth to the illuminative, and the remaining three to the unitive life. Compared with similar works, the treatment of the first stage must be called meagre. True, in her *Life* and in the *Way of Perfection* St. Teresa has dealt with this subject somewhat more fully.   Indeed, the last-named work was designed as a treatise on Christian Ascetics, dealing with the purgation of the soul by mortification and the enlightenment of the mind by meditation. There, too, appears the first idea of the *Mansions*,[25] and Fuente remarks that the passage in question may be taken for the parting of the ways between the two works. However, this is not the only, nor, indeed, the chief reason why St. Teresa is so reticent about the preliminary stage of the contemplative life. The fact is that she herself did not pass through these experiences. By God's grace she was preserved from childhood from grievous sin and gross imperfection. Though she never grows tired of bewailing her faults and unfaithfulness, these avowals must be taken *cum grano salis*. While yet a child, she sometimes gave way to vanity in dress and wasted her time in reading romances. As a young religious, she was sought after by friends and relatives who

[25] *Way of Perf.* ch. xx. 1

took pleasure in her attractive conversation. This proved further loss of time and caused distractions. Owing to acute suffering, she for some years left off the practice of mental prayer, though she faithfully performed all her religious obligations, as far as her weak state of health allowed. This is all. The war of the flesh against the spirit, the insubordination of the lower parts of nature, the fickleness of the will, which so often thwart the most noble aspirations of a soul, were unknown to her. Under these circumstances, we cannot be surprised to find her entering upon the journey towards God at a point which in many cases marks but the closing stage.

As to the remaining parts of this book, it will be seen from the parallel passages that they cover much the same ground as her *Life* and the *Relations*. With her singular gift of introspection and analysis, the Saint studied her own case from every point of view, so as to make sure that her extraordinary experiences were due to no illusion, and offered no obstacle to the safety of her soul. Although the *Interior Castle* contains little that we do not already know from her other works, it is superior to them by reason of its logical order and the masterly treatment of the most recondite matters of mystical theology. While ostensibly dealing with general facts, St. Teresa in reality records her personal experiences. How definite these were, how little room there remained for the freaks of the imagination, will appear from the fact that she nearly always repeats the very words she had used in her *Life* and in the other reports of her interior progress, although she did not have these writings before her eyes, nor had she ever seen them since they first left her hands. Every one of her experiences must have produced a profound impression to be remembered so minutely after an interval of years.

There is that in the *Interior Castle* which reminds one of Dante's *Paradiso*. In the one and the other, the soul, purified from earthly dross, is gradually being invested with new and glorious qualities, and is being led through regions unknown until it arrives at the very threshold of the throne of God. Not even the boldest imagination could have designed so wonderful a picture of a soul adorned with graces at once so varied and so true. In one case we know, the poet has drawn abundantly from the treasury of the Angelical Doctor, putting in verse the conclusions of the scholastic theologian. In the other case we can follow, chapter by chapter, the influence of the teaching of St. Thomas Aquinas. St. Teresa had never studied it herself, but her directors and confessors were deeply versed in it and solved her doubts and perplexities on the lines of the greatest of the schoolmen. The *Interior Castle* might almost be considered a practical illustration of certain parts of the *Summa theologica*,[26]

[26] S. Theol. 2da 2dæ, qq. 171-184.

as it describes the progress of the soul through every stage of perfection. When we have reached the second chapter of the seventh Mansion, there remains but one thing: the Beatific Vision, and this is reserved for the next life.

After the publication of the *Interior Castle* by Luis de Leon, the manuscript came into the possession of Father Jerome Gracian, who, after having made a copy of it which is still extant, presented the original, on the occasion of a visit to the convent of Seville, to Don Pedro Cereso Pardo, a great friend of the Saint, and a benefactor to the convent. When his only daughter took the habit there, the precious manuscript was part of her dowry. Doña Juana de Mendoza, Duchess of Beguiar, a novice in the same convent, had it bound in silver and precious stones. It is still there,[27] and the present writer had the privilege of seeing it. It comprises a hundred and thirteen leaves in folio, but originally there must have been some more leaves which at a later period were torn out. These, it is presumed, contained the headings of the chapters. Unlike the *Life* and the *Foundations*, the text of the *Castle* is divided only by figures, without indication of the contents of each chapter, but the arguments which have come down to us are so entirely similar to those of the two works

[27] Bollandists, *Acta*, n. 1495. See also *Impressions in Spain*. By Lady Herbert. London, 1867, p, 171.

named, that it is impossible to consider them otherwise than the genuine work of the author. In the present translation they have been inserted in their proper places.

On the occasion of the ter-centenary of Saint Teresa's death, a photo-lithographic edition of the original was published under the direction of Cardinal Lluch, Carmelite of the old observance, Archbishop of Seville:

El Castillo Ynterior ó Tratado de las Moradas, escrito por Sta. Teresa de Jesús.
Litografia de Juan Moyano (Seville) 1882.

The present translation, the third in English,[28] has been made directly from this autograph edition. It has been thought advisable that, as far as the genius of the language allows it, the wording of the author should be strictly adhered to, and that not even a shade of her expression should be sacrificed. For Teresa is not only a saint whose

[28] The first translation is to be found in the *Works of the Holy Mother St. Teresa of Jesus* (third part). Printed in the year MDCLXXV, pp. 137-286. It bears the title: *The Interiour Castle: or, Mansions.* As to the authors of this translation—Abraham Woodhead and another, whose name is not known—see my book *Carmel in England*, p. 342, note. It is stated there that the third part, containing the *Way of Perfection* and the *Castle*, has no title-page. This is true with regard to the copy I had before me when writing that book. The one I have now is more complete.

The second translation, by the Rev. John Dalton, appeared in 1852 and has been repeatedly reprinted. It was dedicated to Bishop Ullathorne.

Of foreign translations it will be sufficient to mention the one by Cyprien de la Nativité, in *Œuvres de la Sainte Mère Térèse de Jésus*, Paris, 1657, and the new one in *Œuvres* already mentioned.

every word is telling, but she is a classic in her own language who knows how to give expression to her deepest thoughts. Having compared word for word the translation with the original, I am in a position to affirm that this programme has been faithfully carried out. For the foot-notes—with few exceptions—as well as for the Index, I am responsible. It seemed to me important to point out all the parallel passages from the various works of the Saint. Only by this means can it be seen how consistent Saint Teresa is in all her writings.[29] It would have been easy to multiply quotations from the works of other writers on mystical theology. Thus, the influence of the *Imitation of Christ* and of the *Life of our Lord* by Ludolphus the Carthusian can be distinctly traced in the *Interior Castle*. Both these works, as well as some Spanish books, were held in such esteem by St. Teresa, that she ordered the prioress of each convent to keep them at the disposal of the nuns. As there is a limit to footnotes, I have contented myself with such references as seemed to me conducive to the elucidation of the doctrine laid down in this treatise.

In conclusion I venture to express the hope that

[29] The present translation ought to dispose of the reservations expressed by an able critic in his otherwise valuable appreciation of the works of the Saint. See *Santa Teresa*, by the late Alexander Whyte, D.D. London, 1898, p. 32.

Criticisms which have appeared in various papers, or have been privately conveyed, have been gratefully received and acted upon in the second and the present edition.

this new translation will be found helpful by those who feel called to a higher life.

BENEDICT ZIMMERMAN,

Prior, O. C. D.

St. Luke's Priory,
Wincanton, Somerset.
July, 1, 1905, and *December* 25, 1911.

THE INTERIOR CASTLE
OR THE MANSIONS
BY ST. TERESA

IHS

THIS TREATISE, STYLED THE INTERIOR CASTLE, WAS WRITTEN
BY TERESA OF JESUS, NUN OF OUR LADY OF CARMEL, FOR HER
SISTERS AND DAUGHTERS, THE DISCALCED CARMELITE NUNS.

RARELY has obedience laid upon me so difficult a task as this of writing about prayer; for
one reason, because I do not feel that God has given
me either the power or the desire for it, besides
which, during the last three months I have suffered
from noises and a great weakness in my head that
have made it painful for me to write even on
necessary business.[1]

However, as I know the power obedience has
of making things easy which seem impossible, my
will submits with a good grace, although nature
seems greatly distressed, for God has not given me
such strength as to bear, without repugnance, the
constant struggle against illness while performing
many different duties. May He, Who has helped

[1] 'I am always suffering from my head.' Letter of June 28, 1577.
Letters. VOL. II.

me in other more difficult matters, aid me with His grace in this, for I trust in His mercy. I think I have but little to say that has not already been put forth in my other works written under obedience; in fact, I fear this will be but repetition of them. I am like a parrot which has learnt to talk; only knowing what it has been taught or has heard, it repeats the same thing over and over again. If God wishes me to write anything new, He will teach it me, or bring back to my memory what I have said elsewhere. I should be content even with this, for as I am very forgetful, I should be glad to be able to recall some of the matters about which people say I have spoken well, lest they should be altogether lost. If our Lord will not even grant me this, still, if I weary my brains and increase my headache by striving to obey, I shall gain in merit, though my words should be useless to any one. So I begin this work on the Feast of the Blessed Trinity in the year 1577, in the Convent of St. Joseph of Carmel at Toledo, where I am living, and I submit all my writings to the judgment of those learned men by whose commands I undertake them. That it will be the fault of ignorance, not malice, if I say anything contrary to the doctrine of the Holy Roman Catholic Church, may be held as certain. By God's goodness I am, and always shall be, faithful to the Church, as I have been in the past. May He be for ever blessed and glorified. Amen.

He who bids me write this, tells me that the nuns of these convents of our Lady of Carmel need some one to solve their difficulties about prayer: he thinks that women understand one another's language best and that my sisters' affection for me would make them pay special attention to my words, therefore it is important for me to explain the subject clearly to them. Thus I am writing only to my sisters; the idea that any one else could benefit by what I say would be absurd. Our Lord will be doing me a great favour if He enables me to help but one of the nuns to praise Him a little better; His Majesty knows well that I have no other aim. If anything is to the point, they will understand that it does not originate from me and there is no reason to attribute it to me, as with my scant understanding and skill I could write nothing of the sort, unless God, in His mercy, enabled me to do so.

THE FIRST MANSIONS

CHAPTER I.

THIS CHAPTER TREATS OF THE BEAUTY AND DIGNITY OF OUR
SOULS AND MAKES A COMPARISON TO EXPLAIN THIS. THE
ADVANTAGE OF KNOWING AND UNDERSTANDING THIS AND
THE FAVOURS GOD GRANTS TO US IS SHOWN, AND HOW PRAYER
IS THE GATE OF THE SPIRITUAL CASTLE.

1. Plan of this book. 2. The Interior Castle. 3. Our culpable self-ignorance. 4. God dwells in the centre of the soul. 5. Why all souls do not receive certain favours. 6. Reasons for speaking of these favours. 7. The entrance of the Castle. 8. Entering into oneself. 9. Prayer. 10. Those who dwell in the first mansion. 11. Entering. 12. Difficulties of the subject.

1. WHILE I was begging our Lord to-day to speak for me, since I knew not what to say nor how to commence this work which obedience has laid upon me, an idea occurred to me which I will explain, and which will serve as a foundation for that I am about to write.

2. I thought of the soul as resembling a castle,[1] formed of a single diamond or a very transparent crystal,[2] and containing many rooms, just as in

[1] *Way of Perfection*, ch. xxviii, 9.

[2] In her *Life* St. Teresa likened God to a diamond (ch. xl, 14); and elsewhere (ch. xi, 10) the soul to a garden wherein our Lord takes His delight.

heaven there are many mansions.[3] If we reflect, sisters, we shall see that the soul of the just man is but a paradise, in which, God tells us, He takes His delight.[4] What, do you imagine, must that dwelling be in which a King so mighty, so wise, and so pure, containing in Himself all good, can delight to rest? Nothing can be compared to the great beauty and capabilities of a soul; however keen our intellects may be, they are as unable to comprehend them as to comprehend God, for, as He has told us, He created us in His own image and likeness.[5]

3. As this is so, we need not tire ourselves by trying to realize all the beauty of this castle, although, being His creature, there is all the difference between the soul and God that there is between the creature and the Creator; the fact that it is made in God's image teaches us how great are its dignity and loveliness. It is no small misfortune and disgrace that, through our own fault, we neither understand our nature nor our origin. Would it not be gross ignorance, my daughters, if, when a man was questioned about his name, or country, or parents, he could not answer? Stupid as this would be, it is unspeakably more foolish to care to learn

[3] St. John xiv. 2: 'In domo Patris mei mansiones multæ sunt.' St. John of the Cross uses the same comparison : 'If the soul shall overcome the devil in the first combat, it shall then pass on to the second; and if it shall be victorious there also, it shall then pass on to the third; and then through the seven mansions, the seven degrees of love, until the Bridegroom shall bring it to the "cellar of wine" of perfect charity.' (*Ascent of Mount Carmel,* bk. ii. ch. xi. 7.)

[4] Prov. viii. 31: 'Deliciæ meæ esse cum filiis hominum.'

[5] Gen. i. 26: 'Faciamus hominem ad imaginem et similitudinem nostram.'

nothing of our nature except that we possess bodies, and only to realize vaguely that we have souls, because people say so and it is a doctrine of faith. Rarely do we reflect upon what gifts our souls may possess, Who dwells within them, or how extremely precious they are.   Therefore we do little to preserve their beauty; all our care is concentrated on our bodies, which are but the coarse setting of the diamond, or the outer walls of the castle.[6]

4. Let us imagine, as I said, that there are many rooms in this castle, of which some are above, some below, others at the side; in the centre, in the very midst of them all, is the principal chamber in which God and the soul hold their most secret intercourse.[7] Think over this comparison very carefully; God grant it may enlighten you about the different kinds of graces He is pleased to bestow upon the soul. No one can know all about them, much less a person so ignorant as I am. The knowledge that such things are possible will console you greatly should our Lord ever grant you

[6] *Way of Perf.* ch. xxviii. 5.

[7] St. John of the Cross on the words of his stanza: 'In the inner cellar of my Beloved have I drunk.' 'Here the soul speaks of that sovereign grace of God in taking it into the house of His love, which is the union or transformation of love in God ... The cellar is the highest degree of love to which the soul can attain in this life, and is therefore said to be the inner. It follows from this that there are other cellars not so interior ; that is, the degrees of love by which souls reach to this, the last. These cellars are seven in number, and the soul has entered them all when it has in perfection the seven gifts of the Holy Ghost, so far as it is possible for it. . . . Many souls reach and enter the first cellar, each according to the perfection of its love, but the last and inmost cellar is entered by few in this world, because therein is wrought the perfect union with God, the union of the spiritual marriage.' *A Spiritual Canticle*, stanza xxvi. 1-3. Concept. ch. vi. (*Minor Works* of St. Teresa.)

any of these favours; people themselves deprived of them can then at least praise Him for His great goodness in bestowing them on others. The thought of heaven and the happiness of the saints does us no harm, but cheers and urges us to win this joy for ourselves, nor will it injure us to know that during this exile God can communicate Himself to us loathsome worms; it will rather make us love Him for such immense goodness and infinite mercy.

5. I feel sure that vexation at thinking that during our life on earth God can bestow these graces on the souls of others shows a want of humility and charity for one's neighbour, for why should we not feel glad at a brother's receiving divine favours which do not deprive us of our own share? Should we not rather rejoice at His Majesty's thus manifesting His greatness wherever He chooses?[8] Sometimes our Lord acts thus solely for the sake of showing His power, as He declared when the Apostles questioned whether the blind man whom He cured had been suffering for his own or his parents' sins.[9] God does not bestow these favours on certain souls because they are more holy than others who do not receive them, but to manifest His greatness, as in the case of St. Paul and St. Mary Magdalen, and that we may glorify Him in His creatures.

6. People may say such things appear impossible and it is best not to scandalize the weak in faith by

[8] St. Matt. xx. 15: 'Aut non licet mihi quod volo, facere? an oculus tuus nequam est, quia ego bonus sum?'

[9] St. John ix. 2: 'Quis peccavit, hic, aut parentes ejus, ut cæcus nasceretur?'

speaking about them. But it is better that the latter
should disbelieve us, than that we should desist from
enlightening souls which receive these graces, that
they may rejoice and may endeavour to love God
better for His favours, seeing He is so mighty and
so great. There is no danger here of shocking
those for whom I write by treating of such matters,
for they know and believe that God gives even
greater proofs of His love. I am certain that if any
one of you doubts the truth of this, God will
never allow her to learn it by experience, for He
desires that no limits should be set to His work:
therefore, never discredit them because you are
not thus led yourselves.

7. Now let us return to our beautiful and charming
castle and discover how to enter it. This appears
incongruous: if this castle is the soul, clearly no
one can have to enter it, for it is the person himself: one might as well tell some one to go into a
room he is already in! There are, however, very
different ways of being in this castle; many souls
live in the courtyard of the building where the
sentinels stand, neither caring to enter farther, nor
to know who dwells in that most delightful place,
what is in it and what rooms it contains.

8. Certain books on prayer that you have read advise the soul to enter into itself,[10] and this is what
I mean. I was recently told by a great theologian
that souls without prayer are like bodies, palsied
and lame, having hands and feet they cannot use.

[10] *Imitation*, bk. ii. ch. i: 'Regnum Dei intra vos est.' Luke. xvii. 21.
The *Imitation* is one of the books which according to St. Teresa's
Constitutions, (§ 7) every prioress was bound to provide for her convent

Just so, there are souls so infirm and accustomed to think of nothing but earthly matters, that there seems no cure for them. It appears impossible for them to retire into their own hearts; accustomed as they are to be with the reptiles and other creatures which live outside the castle, they have come at last to imitate their habits. Though these souls are by their nature so richly endowed, capable of communion even with God Himself, yet their case seems hopeless. Unless they endeavour to understand and remedy their most miserable plight, their minds will become, as it were, bereft of movement, just as Lot's wife became a pillar of salt for looking backwards in disobedience to God's command." [11]

9. As far as I can understand, the gate by which to enter this castle is prayer and meditation. I do not allude more to mental than to vocal prayer, for if it is prayer at all, the mind must take part in it. If a person neither considers to Whom he is addressing himself, what he asks, nor what he is who ventures to speak to God, although his lips may utter many words, I do not call it prayer." [12] Sometimes, indeed, one may pray devoutly without making all these considerations through having practised them at other times. The custom of speaking to God Almighty as freely as with a slave —caring nothing whether the words are suitable or not, but simply saying the first thing that comes to mind from being learnt by rote by frequent repetition—cannot be called prayer: God grant that

[11] Gen. xix. 26: 'Respiciensque uxor ejus ꝑost se, versa est in statuam salis.'

[12] *Way of Perf.* ch. xxi. 6; xxix. 4.

no Chriatian may address Him in this manner. I
trust His Majesty will prevent any of you, sisters,
from doing so. Our habit in this Order of conver-
sing about spiritual matters is a good preservative
against such evil ways.

10. Let us speak no more of these crippled souls,
who are in a most miserable and dangerous state,
unless our Lord bid them rise, as He did the palsied
man who had waited more than thirty years at the
pool of Bethsaida.[13] We will now think of the
others who at last enter the precincts of the castle;
they are still very worldly, yet have some desire to
do right, and at times, though rarely, commend
themselves to God's care. They think about their
souls every now and then; although very busy, they
pray a few times a month, with minds generally
filled with a thousand other matters, for where their
treasure is, there is their heart also.[14] Still, occasionally they cast aside these cares; it is a great boon
for them to realize to some extent the state of their
souls, and to see that they will never reach the gate
by the road they are following.

11. At length they enter the first rooms in the
basement of the castle, accompanied by numerous
reptiles[15] which disturb their peace, and prevent
their seeing the beauty of the building; still, it is
a great gain that these persons should have found
their way in at all.

[13] St. John v. 5: 'Erat autem quidam homo ibi triginta et octo annos
habens in infirmitate sua.'

[14] St. Matt. vi. 21: 'Ubi enim est thesaurus tuus ibi est et cor tuum.

[15] Many an ancient castle was provided with a bear-garden where
rare animals were kept for the amusement of the inhabitants. This
may have supplied the material for St. Teresa's comparison.

12. You may think, my daughters, that all this does not concern you, because, by God's grace, you are farther advanced; still, you must be patient with me, for I can explain myself on some spiritual matters concerning prayer in no other way. May our Lord enable me to speak to the point; the subject is most difficult to understand without personal experience of such graces. Any one who has received them will know how impossible it is to avoid touching on subjects which, by the mercy of God, will never apply to us.

CHAPTER II.

DESCRIBES THE HIDEOUS APPEARANCE OF A SOUL IN MORTAL SIN AS REVEALED BY GOD TO SOME ONE: OFFERS A FEW RE-MARKS ON SELF-KNOWLEDGE: THIS CHAPTER IS USEFUL AS IT CONTAINS SOME POINTS REQUIRING ATTENTION. AN EXPLAN-ATION OF THE MANSIONS.

1. Effects of mortal sin. 2. It prevents the soul's gaining merit. 3. The soul compared to a tree. 4. Disorder of the soul in mortal sin. 5. Vision of a sinful soul. 6. Profit of realizing these lessons. 7. Prayer. 8. Beauty of the Castle. 9. Self-knowledge 10. Gained by meditating on the divine perfections. 11. Advantages of such meditation. 12. Christ should be our model. 13. The devil entraps beginners. 14. Our strength must come from God. 15. Sin blinds the soul. 16. Worldliness. 17. The world in the cloister. 18. Assaults of the devil. 19. Examples of the devil's arts. 20. Perfection consists in charity. 21. Indiscreet zeal. 22. Danger of detraction.

1. BEFORE going farther, I wish you to consider the state to which mortal sin[1] brings this magnificent and beautiful castle, this pearl of the East, this tree of life, planted beside the living waters of life[2]

---

[1] *Life,* ch. xxxviii. 31; ch. xl. 15.

[2] Ps. i. 3: 'Et erit tamquam lignum quod plantatum est secus decursus aquarum.'

which symbolize God Himself. No night can be so dark, no gloom nor blackness can compare to its obscurity. Suffice it to say that the sun in the centre of the soul, which gave it such splendour and beauty, is totally eclipsed, though the spirit is as fitted to enjoy God's presence as is the crystal to reflect the sun.[3]

2. While the soul is in mortal sin nothing can profit it; none of its good works merit an eternal reward, since they do not proceed from God as their first principle, and by Him alone is our virtue real virtue. The soul separated from Him is no longer pleasing in His eyes, because by committing a mortal sin, instead of seeking to please God, it prefers to gratify the devil, the prince of darkness, and so comes to share his blackness. I knew a person to whom our Lord revealed the result of a mortal sin[4] and who said she thought no one who realized its effects could ever commit it, but would suffer unimaginable torments to avoid it. This vision made her very desirous for all to grasp this truth, therefore I beg you, my daughters, to pray fervently to God for sinners, who live in blindness and do deeds of darkness.

3. In a state of grace the soul is like a well of limpid water, from which flow only streams of clearest crystal. Its works are pleasing both to God and man, rising from the River of Life, beside which it is rooted like a tree. Otherwise it would produce neither leaves nor fruit, for the waters of grace

---

[3] *Way of Perf.* ch. xxviii. 9.
[4] In this as in most other cases when the Saint speaks of 'a person she knows,' she means herself. *Life*, ch. xl. 15.

nourish it, keep it from withering from drought, and cause it to bring forth good fruit. But the soul by sinning withdraws from this stream of life, and growing beside a black and fetid pool, can produce nothing but disgusting and unwholesome fruit. Notice that it is not the fountain and the brilliant sun which lose their splendour and beauty, for they are placed in the very centre of the soul and cannot be deprived of their lustre. The soul is like a crystal in the sunshine over which a thick black cloth has been thrown, so that however brightly the sun may shine the crystal can never reflect it.

4. O souls, redeemed by the Blood of Jesus Christ, take these things to heart; have mercy on yourselves! If you realize your pitiable condition, how can you refrain from trying to remove the darkness from the crystal of your souls? Remember, if death should take you now, you would never again enjoy the light of this Sun. O Jesus! how sad a sight must be a soul deprived of light! What a terrible state the chambers of this castle are in! How disorderly must be the senses—the inhabitants of the castle—the powers of the soul—its magistrates, governors, and stewards—blind and uncontrolled as they are! In short, as the soil in which the tree is now planted is in the devil's domain, how can its fruit be anything but evil? A man of great spiritual insight once told me he was not so much surprised at such a soul's wicked deeds as astonished that it did not commit even worse sins. May God in His mercy keep us from such great evil, for nothing in this life merits the name of evil in comparison with

this, which delivers us over to evil which is eternal.

5. This is what we must dread and pray God to deliver us from, for we are weakness itself, and unless He guards the city, in vain shall we labour to defend it.[5] The person of whom I spoke[6] said that she had learnt two things from the vision granted her. The first was, a great fear of offending God; seeing how terrible were the consequences, she constantly begged Him to preserve her from falling into sin. Secondly, it was a mirror to teach her humility, for she saw that nothing good in us springs from ourselves but comes from the waters of grace near which the soul remains like a tree planted beside a river, and from that Sun which gives life to our works. She realized this so vividly that on seeing any good deed performed by herself or by other people she at once turned to God as to its fountain head—without whose help she knew well we can do nothing—and broke out into songs of praise to Him. Generally she forgot all about herself and only thought of God when she did any meritorious action.

6. The time which has been spent in reading or writing on this subject will not have been lost if it has taught us these two truths; for though learned, clever men know them perfectly, women's wits are dull and need help in every way. Perhaps this is why our Lord has suggested these comparisons to me; may He give us grace to profit by them!

7. So obscure are these spiritual matters that to

[5] cxxvi. 1 : 'Nisi Dominus custodierit civitatem, frustra vigilat qui custodit eam.'
[6] *Life*, ch. xxxviii. 33 ; ch. xl. 15, 16.

explain them an ignorant person like myself must say much that is superfluous, and even alien to the subject, before coming to the point. My readers must be patient with me, as I am with myself while writing what I do not understand; indeed, I often take up the paper like a dunce, not knowing what to say, nor how to begin. Doubtless there is need for me to do my best to explain these spiritual subjects to you, for we often hear how beneficial prayer is for our souls; our Constitutions oblige us to pray so many hours a day, yet tell us nothing of what part we ourselves can take in it and very little of the work God does in the soul by its means.[7] It will be helpful, in setting it before you in various ways, to consider this heavenly edifice within us, so little understood by men, near as they often come to it. Our Lord gave me grace to understand something of such matters when I wrote on them before, yet I think I have more light now, especially on the more difficult questions. Unfortunately I am too ignorant to treat of such subjects without saying much that is already well known.

8. Now let us turn at last to our castle with its many mansions. You must not think of a suite of rooms placed in succession, but fix your eyes on the keep, the court inhabited by the King.[8] Like the kernel of the palmito,[9] from which several rinds

---

[7] *Life*, ch. x. 2 *sqq. Constitut.* 2, 6.

[8] *Way of Perf.* ch. xxviii. 1.

[9] The palmito here referred to is not a palm, but a shrub about four feet high and very dense with leaves, resembling palm leaves. The poorer classes and principally children dig it up by the roots, which they peel of its many layers until a sort of kernel is disclosed, which is

must be removed before coming to the eatable part, this principal chamber is surrounded by many others. However large, magnificent, and spacious you imagine this castle to be, you cannot exaggerate it; the capacity of the soul is beyond all our understanding, and the Sun within this palace enlightens every part of it.

9. A soul which gives itself to prayer, either much or little, should on no account be kept within narrow bounds. Since God has given it such great dignity, permit it to wander at will through the rooms of the castle, from the lowest to the highest. Let it not force itself to remain for very long in the same mansion, even that of self-knowledge. Mark well, however, that self-knowledge is indispensable, even for those whom God takes to dwell in the same mansion with Himself. Nothing else, however elevated, perfects the soul which must never seek to forget its own nothingness. Let humility be always at work, like the bee at the honeycomb, or all will be lost. But, remember, the bee leaves its hive to fly in search of flowers and the soul should sometimes cease thinking of itself to rise in meditation on the grandeur and majesty of its God. It will learn its own baseness better thus than by self-contemplation, and will be freer from the reptiles which enter the first room where self-knowledge is acquired. Although it is a great grace from God to practise self-examination, yet 'too much is as bad as too little,' as they say; believe me, by God's help, we shall advance more by contemplating the

eaten, not without relish, and is somewhat like a filbert in taste. See St. John of the Cross, *Ascent of Mount Carmel*, bk. ii. ch. xiv. 3.

Divinity than by keeping our eyes fixed on our-selves, poor creatures of earth that we are.

10. I do not know whether I have put this clearly; self-knowledge is of such consequence that I would not have you careless of it, though you may be lifted to heaven in prayer, because while on earth nothing is more needful than humility. Therefore, I repeat, not only a *good* way, but the *best* of all ways, is to endeavour to enter first by the room where humility is practised, which is far better than at once rushing on to the others. This is the right road;—if we know how easy and safe it is to walk by it, why ask for wings with which to fly? Let us rather try to learn how to advance quickly. I believe we shall never learn to know ourselves except by endeavouring to know God, for, beholding His greatness we are struck by our own baseness, His purity shows our foulness, and by meditating on His humility we find how very far we are from being humble.

11. Two advantages are gained by this practice. First, it is clear that white looks far whiter when placed near something black, and on the contrary, black never looks so dark as when seen beside something white. Secondly, our understanding and will become more noble and capable of good in every way when we turn from ourselves to God: it is very injurious never to raise our minds above the mire of our own faults. I described how murky and fetid are the streams that spring from the source of a soul in mortal sin.[10] Thus (although the case is

[10] *Supra*, § 3.

not really the same, God forbid! this is only a comparison), while we are continually absorbed in contemplating the weakness of our earthly nature, the springs of our actions will never flow free from the mire of timid, weak, and cowardly thoughts, such as: 'I wonder whether people are noticing me or not! If I follow this course, will harm come to me? Dare I begin this work? Would it not be presumptuous? Is it right for any one as faulty as myself to speak on sublime spiritual subjects?" Will not people think too well of me, if I make myself singular? Extremes are bad, even in virtue; sinful as I am I shall only fall the lower. Perhaps I shall fail and be a source of scandal to good people; such a person as I am has no need of peculiarities.'

12. Alas, my daughters, what loss the devil must have caused to many a soul by such thoughts as these! It thinks such ideas and many others of the same sort I could mention arise from humility. This comes from not understanding our own nature; self-knowledge becomes so warped that, unless we take our thoughts off ourselves, I am not surprised that these and many worse fears should threaten us. Therefore I maintain, my daughters, that we should fix our eyes on Christ our only good, and on His saints; there we shall learn true humility, and our minds will be ennobled, so that self-knowledge will not make us base and cowardly. Although only the first, this mansion contains great riches and such treasures that if the soul only manages to

[11] *Life*, ch. viii. 6, x. 4, xxiii. 3-5. *Way of Perf.* ch. xxxix. 1.

elude the reptiles dwelling here, it cannot fail to advance farther. Terrible are the wiles and stratagems the devil uses to hinder people from realizing their weakness and detecting his snares.

13. From personal experience I could give you much information as to what happens in these first mansions. I will only say that you must not imagine there are only a few, but a number of rooms, for souls enter them by many different ways, and always with a good intention. The devil is so angry at this that he keeps legions of evil spirits hidden in each room to stop the progress of Christians, whom, being ignorant of this, he entraps in a thousand ways. He cannot so easily deceive souls which dwell nearer to the King as he can beginners still absorbed in the world, immersed in its pleasures, and eager for its honours and distinctions. As the vassals of their souls, the senses and powers bestowed on them by God, are weak, such people are easily vanquished, although desirous not to offend God.

14. Those conscious of being in this state must as often as possible have recourse to His Majesty, taking His Blessed Mother and the saints for their advocates to do battle for them, because we creatures possess little strength for self-defence. Indeed in every state of life all our help must come from God; may He in His mercy grant it us, Amen! What a miserable life we lead! As I have spoken more fully in other writings [12] on the ill that results from ignoring the need of humility and self-knowledge, I will treat

[12] *Life* ch. xiii. 23. *Way of Perf.* ch. x. 4. *Castle*, M. iii. ch. ii. 8. *Concep.* ch. ii. 20. *Const.* 21.

no more about it here, my daughters, although it is of the first importance. God grant that what I have said may be useful to you.

15 You must notice that the light which comes from the King's palace hardly shines at all in these first mansions; although not as gloomy and black as the soul in mortal sin, yet they are in semidarkness, and their inhabitants see scarcely anything. I cannot explain myself; I do not mean that this is the fault of the mansions themselves, but that the number of snakes, vipers, and venomous reptiles from outside the castle prevent souls entering them from seeing the light. They resemble a person entering a chamber full of brilliant sunshine, with eyes clogged and half closed with dust. Though the room itself is light, he cannot see because of his self-imposed impediment. In the same way, these fierce and wild beasts blind the eyes of the beginner, so that he sees nothing but them.

16. Such, it appears to me, is the soul which, though not in a state of mortal sin, is so worldly and preoccupied with earthly riches, honours, and affairs, that as I said, even if it sincerely wishes to enter into itself and enjoy the beauties of the castle, it is prevented by these distractions and seems unable to overcome so many obstacles. It is most important to withdraw from all unnecessary cares and business, as far as compatible with the duties of one's state of life, in order to enter the second mansion. This is so essential, that unless done immediately I think it impossible for any one ever to reach the principal room, or even to remain

where he is without great risk of losing what is already gained; otherwise, although he is inside the castle, he will find it impossible to avoid being bitten some time or other by some of the very venomous creatures surrounding him.

17. What then would become of a religious like ourselves, my daughters, if, after having escaped from all these impediments, and having entered much farther into the more secret mansion, she should, by her own fault, return to all this turmoil? Through her sins, many other people on whom God had bestowed great graces would culpably relapse into their wretched state. In our convents we are free from these exterior evils; please God our minds may be as free from them, and may He deliver us from such ills.

18. Do not trouble yourselves, my daughters, with cares which do not concern you. You must notice that the struggle with the demons continues through nearly all the mansions of this castle. True, in some of them, the guards, which, as I explained, are the powers of the soul, have strength for the combat, but we must be keenly on the watch against the devils's arts, lest he deceive us in the form of an angel of light. He creeps in gradually, in numberless ways, and does us much harm, though we do not discover it until too late.[13]

19. As I said elsewhere,[14] he works like a file, secretly and silently wearing its way: I will give you some examples to show how he begins his wiles.

[13] *Life* ch. xxxi. 23.
[14] No doubt the Saint often used this excellent comparison in her verbal instructions, but it occurs nowhere else in her writings.

For instance: a nun has such a longing for penance as to feel no peace unless she is tormenting herself in some way.[15] This is good in itself; but suppose that the Prioress has forbidden her to practise any mortifications without special leave, and the sister thinking that, in such a meritorious cause, she may venture to disobey, secretly leads such a life that she loses her health and cannot even fulfil the requirements of her rule—you see how this show of good ends. Another nun is very zealous about religious perfection; this is very right, but may cause her to think every small fault she sees in her sisters a serious crime, and to watch constantly whether they do anything wrong, that she may run to the Prioress to accuse them of it. At the same time, may be she never notices her own shortcomings because of her great zeal about other people's religious observance, while perhaps her sisters, not seeing her intention but only knowing of the watch she keeps on them, do not take her behaviour in good part.

20. The devil's chief aim here is to cool the charity and lessen the mutual affection of the nuns, which would injure them seriously. Be sure, my daughters, that true perfection consists in the love of God and our neighbour, and the better we keep both these commandments, the more perfect we shall be. The sole object of our Rule and Constitutions is to help us to observe these two laws.

21. Indiscreet zeal about others must not be indulged in; it may do us much harm; let each one look to herself. However, as I have spoken fully

---

[15] *Way of Perf.* ch. x. 5; xxxix. 4; *Rel.* iii. 12.

on this subject elsewhere,[16] I will not enlarge on it here, and will only beg you to remember the necessity of this mutual affection. Our souls may lose their peace and even disturb other people's if we are always criticizing trivial actions which often are not real defects at all, but we construe them wrongly through ignorance of their motives. See how much it costs to attain perfection! Sometimes the devil tempts nuns in this way about the Prioress, which is still more dangerous. Great prudence is then required, for if she disobeys the Rule or Constitutions the matter must not always be overlooked, but should be mentioned to her;[17] if, after this, she does not amend, the Superior of the Order should be informed of it. It is true charity to speak in this case, as it would be if we saw our sisters commit a grave fault; to keep silence for fear that speech would be a temptation against charity, would be that very temptation itself.[18]

22. However, I must warn you seriously not to talk to each other about such things, lest the devil deceive you. He would gain greatly by your doing so, because it would lead to the habit of detraction; rather, as I said, state the matter to those whose duty it is to remedy it. Thank God our custom

[16] The Saint must frequently have spoken on the subject, but she never treated it more fully than in this place. *Way of Perf.* ch. xli. 7. *Life*, ch. xiii. 11, 14 *sqq.* Visitation of convents.

[17] *Way of Perfection*, ch. ii 3. *Visit.* 20-22, 34, 36.

[18] 'It is terrible to think what harm a Prioress can do! For although the Sisters witness things which scandalize them (of which there are plenty here!), yet they think it would be sinning against obedience to see any harm in them.' (Letter to Father Gracian, written at Malagon at the beginning of December, 1579. *Letters*, Vol. III.)

here of keeping almost perpetual silence gives little opportunity for such conversations, still, it is well to stand ever on our guard.

THE SECOND MANSIONS

ONLY CHAPTER

TREATS OF THE GREAT IMPORTANCE OF PERSEVERANCE IN
ORDER TO ENTER THE LAST MANSIONS, AND OF THE FIERCE
WAR THE DEVIL WAGES AGAINST US. HOW ESSENTIAL IT IS TO
TAKE THE RIGHT PATH FROM THE VERY COMMENCEMENT OF
OUR JOURNEY. A METHOD OF ACTION WHICH HAS PROVED
VERY EFFICACIOUS.

*1. Souls in the second mansions. 2. Their state. 3. Their sufferings.
4. They cannot get rid of their imperfections. 5. How God calls
these souls. 6. Perseverance is essential. 7. Temptations of the
devil. 8. Delusion of earthly joys. 9. God alone to be loved.
10. Reasons for continuing the journey. 11. Warfare of the
devil. 12. Importance of choice of friends. 13. Valour required.
14. Presumption of expecting spiritual consolations at first.
15. In the Cross is strength. 16. Our falls should raise us higher.
17. Confidence and perseverance. 18. Recollection. 19. Why we
must practise prayer. 20. Meditation kindles love.*

1. Now let us consider which are the souls that
enter the second mansions, and what they do there:
I do not wish to enlarge on this subject, having
already treated it very fully elsewhere,[1] for I could
not avoid repeating myself, as my memory is very
bad. If I could state my ideas in another form they
would not weary you, for we never tire of reading
books on this subject, numerous as they are.

[1] *Life*, ch. xi-xiii. *Way of Perf.* ch. xx.-xxix.

2. In this part of the castle are found souls which have begun to practise prayer; they realize the importance of their not remaining in the first mansions, yet often lack determination to quit their present condition by avoiding occasions of sin, which is a very perilous state to be in.

3. However, it is a great grace that they should sometimes make good their escape from the vipers and poisonous creatures around them and should understand the need of avoiding them. In some way these souls suffer a great deal more than those in the first mansions, although not in such danger, as they begin to understand their peril and there are great hopes of their entering farther into the castle. I say that they suffer a great deal more, for those in an earlier stage are like deaf-mutes and are not so distressed at being unable to speak, while the others, who can hear but cannot talk, find it much harder. At the same time, it is better not to be deaf, and a decided advantage to hear what is said to us.

4. These souls hear our Lord calling them, for as they approach nearer to where His Majesty dwells He proves a loving Neighbour, though they may still be engaged in the amusements and business, the pleasures and vanities of this world. While in this state we continually fall into sin and rise again, for the creatures amongst whom we dwell are so venomous, so vicious, and so dangerous, that it is almost impossible to avoid being tripped up by them. Yet such are the pity and compassion of this Lord of ours, so desirous is He that we should

seek Him and enjoy His company, that in one way or another He never ceases calling us to Him. So sweet is His voice, that the poor soul is disconsolate at being unable to follow His bidding at once, and therefore, as I said, suffers more than if it could not hear Him.

5. I do not mean that divine communications and inspirations received in this mansion are the same as those I shall describe later on; God here speaks to souls through words uttered by pious people, by sermons or good books, and in many other such ways. Sometimes He calls souls by means of sickness or troubles, or by some truth He teaches them during prayer, for tepid as they may be in seeking Him, yet God holds them very dear.

6. Do not think lightly, sisters, of this first grace, nor be downcast if you have not responded immediately to Our Lord's voice, for His Majesty is willing to wait for us many a day and even many a year, especially when He sees perseverance and good desires in our hearts. Perseverance is the first essential; with this we are sure to profit greatly. However, the devils now fiercely assault the soul in a thousand different ways: it suffers more than ever, because formerly it was mute and deaf, or at least could hear very little, and offered but feeble resistance, like one who has almost lost all hope of victory.

7. Here, however, the understanding being more vigilant and the powers more on the alert, we cannot avoid hearing the fighting and cannonading around us. For now the devils set on us the reptiles, that is to say, thoughts about the world and its joys

which they picture as unending; they remind us of the high esteem men held us in, of our friends and relations; they tell us how the penances which souls in this mansion always begin to wish to perform would injure our health: in fine, the evil spirits place a thousand impediments in the way.

8. O Jesus! What turmoil the devils cause in the poor soul! How unhappy it feels, not knowing whether to go forward or to return to the first mansion! On the other hand, reason shows it the delusion of overrating worldly things, while faith teaches what alone can satisfy its cravings. Memory reminds the soul how all earthly joys end, recalling the death of those who lived at ease; how some died suddenly and were soon forgotten, how others, once so prosperous, are now buried beneath the ground and men pass by the graves where they lie, the prey of worms,[2] while the mind recalls many other such incidents.

9. The will inclines to love Our Lord and longs to make some return to Him Who is so amiable, and Who has given so many proofs of His love, especially by His constant presence with the soul, which this faithful Lover never quits, ever accompanying it and giving it life and being. The under-

---

[2] 'How many, thinking to live long, have been deceived and unexpectedly have been snatched away! How often hast thou heard that such a one was slain by the sword; another drowned; another, falling from on high, broke his neck; this man died at the table; that other came to his death while he was at play. . . . Thus death is the end of all; and man's life passeth suddenly like a shadow' (*Imitation*, bk. 1. ch. xxiii. 7). The edition of the *Imitation* known to St. Teresa under the title of *Contemptus Mundi* was translated by Luis de Granada, printed at Seville in 1536, at Lisbon in 1542, and at Alcalá in 1548. See *Life*, ch. xxxix. 21, note.

standing aids by showing that however many years
life might last, no one could ever wish for a better
friend than God; that the world is full of falsehood,
and that the worldly pleasures pictured by the
devil to the mind were but troubles and cares and
annoyances in disguise.

10. Reason convinces the soul that as outside its
interior castle are found neither peace nor security,
it should cease to seek another home abroad, its
own being full of riches that it can enjoy at will.
Besides, it is not every one who, like itself, possesses
all he needs within his own dwelling, and above
all, such a Host, Who will give it all it can desire,
unless, like the prodigal son, it chooses to go astray
and feed with the swine.[3] Surely these arguments
are strong enough to defeat the devil's wiles! But,
O my God, how the force of worldly habits and
the example of others who practise them ruin
everything! Our faith is so dead that we trust less
to its teaching than to what is visible, though,
indeed, we see that worldly lives bring nothing but
unhappiness. All this results from those venomous
thoughts I described, which, unless we are very
careful, will deform the soul as the sting of a viper
poisons and swells the body.

11. When this happens, great care is evidently
needed to cure it, and only God's signal mercy
prevents its resulting in death. Indeed, the soul
passes through severe trials at this time, especially
when the devil perceives from a person's character
and behaviour that she is likely to make very great

[3] St. Luke xv. 16: 'Et cupiebat implere ventrem suum de siliquis
quas porci manducabant.'

progress, for then all hell will league together to force her to turn back. O my Lord! what need there is here that, by Thy mercy, Thou shouldst prevent the soul from being deluded into forsaking the good begun! Enlighten it to see that its welfare consists in perseverance in the right way, and in the withdrawing from bad company.

12. It is of the utmost importance for the beginner to associate with those who lead a spiritual life,[4] and not only with those in the same mansion as herself, but with others who have travelled farther into the castle, who will aid her greatly and draw her to join them. The soul should firmly resolve never to submit to defeat, for if the devil sees it staunchly determined to lose life and comfort and all that he can offer, rather than return to the first mansion, he will the sooner leave it alone.

13. Let the Christian be valiant; let him not be like those who lay down to drink from the brook when they went to battle (I do not remember when).[5] Let him resolve to go forth to combat with the host of demons, and be convinced that there is no better weapon than the cross. I have already said,[6] yet it is of such importance that I repeat it here: let no one think on starting of the reward to be reaped: this would be a very ignoble way of commencing such a large and stately building. If built on sand it would soon fall down.[7] Souls

---

[4] *Life*, ch. vii. 33-37 ; xvi. 12 ; xxx. 6. *Way of Perfection*, ch. vi. 1; vii. 4.

[5] With Gedeon. Jud. vii. 5: ' Qui lingua lambuerint aquas, sicut solent canes lambere, separabis eos seorsum.'

[6] *Life*, ch. xi 16.

[7] St. Matt. vii. 26, 27: 'Qui ædificavit domum suam super arenam ...

who acted thus would continually suffer from discouragement and temptations, for in these mansions no manna rains;[8] farther on, the soul is pleased with all that comes, because it desires nothing but what God wills.

14. What a farce it is! Here are we, with a thousand obstacles, drawbacks, and imperfections within ourselves, our virtues so newly born that they have scarcely the strength to act (and God grant that they exist at all!) yet we are not ashamed to expect sweetness in prayer and to complain of feeling dryness.[9]

15. Do not act thus, sisters; embrace the cross your Spouse bore on His shoulders; know that your motto should be: 'Most happy she who suffers most if it be for Christ!'[10] All else should be looked upon as secondary: if our Lord give it you, render Him grateful thanks. You may imagine you would be resolute in enduring external trials if God gave you interior consolations: His Majesty knows best what is good for us; it is not for us to advise Him how to treat us, for He has the right to tell us that we know not what we ask.[11] Remember, it is of the greatest importance—the sole aim of one beginning to practise prayer should be to endure trials, and to resolve and strive to the utmost of her power to conform her own will to the will of

et fuit ruina illius magna.'
[8] Ps. lxxvii. 24: 'Pluit illis manna ad manducandum.' *Way of Perf.* ch. x. 4.
[9] *Life*, ch. xii. 5.
[10] *Way of Perf.* ch. xvii. 6; xxiii. 1.
[11] St. Matt. xx. 22: 'Nescitis quid petatis.'

God.[12] Be certain that in this consists all the greatest perfection to be attained in the spiritual life, as I will explain later. She who practises this most perfectly will receive from God the highest reward and is the farthest advanced on the right road. Do not imagine that we have need of a cabalistic formula or any other occult or mysterious thing to attain it—our whole welfare consists in doing the will of God. If we start with the false principle of wishing God to follow our will and to lead us in the way we think best, upon what firm foundation can this spiritual edifice rest?

16. Let us endeavour to do our best: beware of the poisonous reptiles—that is to say, the bad thoughts and aridities which are often permitted by God to assail and torment us so that we cannot repel them. Indeed, perchance we feel their sting! He allows this to teach us to be more on our guard in the future and to see whether we grieve much at offending Him. Therefore if you occasionally lapse into sin, do not lose heart and cease trying to advance, for God will draw good even out of our falls, like the merchant who sells theriac, who first takes poison, then the theriac, to prove the power of his elixir.[13] This combat would suffice to teach us to amend our habits if we realized our failings in no other way, and would show us the injury we receive from a life of dissipation. Can any evil be greater than that we find at home? What peace can we hope to find elsewhere, if we have none

[12] *Way of Perf.* ch. xvi. 2. *Found.* ch. v. 2, 3. *Life,* ch. iv. 11; xi. 20.
[13] A drug greatly in vogue until recent times. It was composed of all the essences supposed to contain life-giving and life-preserving qualities of animals and plants.

within us? What friends or kindred can be so close and intimate as the powers of our soul, which, whether we will or no, must ever bear us company? These seem to wage war on us as if they knew the harm our vices had wrought them. 'Peace, peace be unto you,' my sisters, as our Lord said, and many a time proclaimed to His Apostles.[14] Believe me, if we neither possess nor strive to obtain this peace at home, we shall never find it abroad.

17. By the blood which our Lord shed for us, I implore those who have not yet begun to enter into themselves, to stop this warfare: I beg those already started in the right path, not to let the combat turn them back from it. Let them reflect that a relapse is worse than a fall, and see what ruin it would bring. They should confide in God's mercy, trusting nothing in themselves; then they will see how His Majesty will lead them from one mansion to another, and will set them in a place where these wild beasts can no more touch or annoy them, but will be entirely at their mercy and merely objects of ridicule. Then, even in this life, they will enjoy a far greater happiness than they are able even to desire.

18. As I said at the beginning of this work, I have explained elsewhere[15] how you should behave when the devil thus disturbs you. I also told you that the habit of recollection is not to be gained by force of arms, but with calmness, which will enable you to practise it for a longer space of time.[16]

[14] St. Luke xxiv. 36. St. John xx. 19.
[15] *Life*, ch. xi. and xix. 8. *Way of Perfection*, ch. xxiii. 3.
[16] *Way of Perf.* ch. xix. 3.

I will say no more now, except that I think it very helpful for those of you who are beginners to consult persons experienced in such matters, lest you imagine that you are injuring yourselves by leaving your prayer to perform any necessary duties. This is not the case; our Lord will direct such things to our profit, although we may have no one to counsel us.[17] The only remedy for having given up a habit of recollection is to recommence it, otherwise the soul will continue to lose it more and more every day, and God grant it may realize its danger.

19. You may think, that if it is so very injurious to desist, it would have been better never to have begun, and to have remained outside the castle. But, as I began by saying, and as God Himself declares: 'He that loves danger shall perish by it,'[18] and the door by which we must enter this castle is prayer. Remember, we *must* get to heaven, and it would be madness to think we could do so without sometimes retiring into our souls so as to know ourselves, or thinking of our failings and of what we owe to God, or frequently imploring His mercy. Our Lord also says, 'No man cometh to the Father but by Me'[19] (I am not sure whether this quotation is correct, but I think so), and, 'He that seeth Me seeth the Father also.'[20]

20. If we never look up at Him and reflect on what we owe Him for having died for us, I do not understand how we can know Him, or perform

[17] *Way of Perf.* ch. xxiii. 3.
[18] Ecclus. iii. 27 : 'Qui amat periculum, in illo peribit.'
[19] St. John xiv. 6 : 'Nemo venit ad Patrem, nisi per Me.'
[20] St. John xiv. 9. 'Qui videt me, videt et Patrem.'

good deeds in His service. What value is there in faith without works? and what are they worth if they are not united to the merits of Jesus Christ, our only good? What would incite us to love our Lord unless we thought of Him? May He give us grace to understand how much we cost Him; that 'the servant is not above his lord'[21]; that we must toil for Him if we would enjoy His glory; and prayer is a necessity to prevent us from constantly falling into temptation.[22]

[21] St. Matt. x. 24: 'Nec servus super dominum suum.'
[22] St. Matt. xxvi. 41: 'Orate ut non intretis in tentationem.'

THE THIRD MANSIONS

CHAPTER I.

TREATS OF THE INSECURITY OF LIFE IN THIS EXILE, HOWEVER
HIGH WE MAY BE RAISED, AND OF HOW WE MUST ALWAYS
WALK IN FEAR. CONTAINS SOME GOOD POINTS.

*1. Souls in the Third Mansions. 2. Insecurity of this life. 3. Our
danger of falling from grace. 4. The Saint bewails her past life.
5. Our Lady's patronage. 6. Fear necessary even for religious.
7. St. Teresa's contrition. 8. Characteristics of those in the Third
Mansions. 9. The rich young man in the Gospel. 10. Reason
of aridities in prayer. 11. Humility. 12. Tepidity. 13. We must
give all to God. 14. Our debt. 15. Consolations and aridities.*

1. As for those who, by the mercy of God, have
vanquished in these combats and persevered until
they reached the third mansions, what can we say to
them but 'Blessed is the man that feareth the Lord'?[1]
It is no small favour from God that I should be
able to translate this verse into Spanish so as to
explain its meaning, considering how dense I usually am in such matters. We may well call these
souls blessed, for, as far as we can tell, unless they
turn back in their course they are on the safe road
to salvation. Now, my sisters, you see how important it is for them to conquer in their former
struggles, for I am convinced that our Lord will

[1] Ps. cxi: 1. 'Beatus vir qui timet Dominum.'

henceforth never cease to keep them in security of conscience, which is no small boon.

2. I am wrong in saying 'security,' for there is no security in this life; understand that in such cases I always imply: 'If they do not cease to continue as they have begun.' What misery to live in this world! We are like men whose enemies are at the door, who must not lay aside their arms, even while sleeping or eating, and are always in dread lest the foe should enter the fortress by some breach in the walls. O my Lord and my all! How canst Thou wish us to prize such a wretched existence? We could not desist from longing and begging Thee to take us from it, were it not for the hope of losing it for Thy sake or devoting it entirely to Thy service—and above all. because we know it is Thy will that we should live. Since it is so, 'Let us die with Thee!'[2] as St. Thomas said, for to be away from Thee is but to die again and again, haunted as we are by the dread of losing Thee for ever !

3. This is why I say, daughters, that we ought to ask our Lord as our boon to grant us one day to dwell in safety with the Saints, for with such fears, what pleasure can she enjoy whose only pleasure is to please God? Remember, many Saints have felt this as we do, and were even far more fervent, yet fell into grave sin, and we cannot be sure that God would stretch forth His hand to raise us from sin again to do such penance as they performed. This applies to extraordinary grace.[3] Truly, my

[2] St. John xi. 16: 'Eamus et nos ut moriamur cum eo.'

[3] These last words, in the margin, but in the handwriting of the Saint, were scored through by one of the censors, but Fr. Luis de Leon wrote

daughters, I feel such terror as I tell you this, that I know not how to write it, nor even how to go on living, when I reflect upon it as I very often do. Beg of His Majesty, my daughters, to abide within me, for otherwise, what security could I feel, after a life so badly spent as mine has been?

4. Do not grieve at knowing this. I have often seen you troubled when I spoke about it, for you wish that my past had been a very holy one, in which you are right—indeed, I wish the same myself. But what can be done, now that I have wasted it entirely through my own fault? I have no right to complain that God withheld the aid I needed to fulfil your wishes. It is impossible for me to write this without tears and great shame, when I see that I am explaining these matters to those capable of teaching me. What a hard task has obedience laid upon me! God grant that, as I do it for Him, it may be of some service to you; therefore beg Him to pardon me for my miserable presumption.

5. His Majesty knows that I have nothing to rely upon but His mercy; as I cannot cancel the past, I have no other remedy but to flee to Him, and to confide in the merits of His Son and of His Virgin Mother, whose habit, unworthy as I am, I wear as you do also. Praise Him, then, my daughters, for making you truly daughters of our Lady, so that you need not blush for my wickedness as you have such a good Mother. Imitate her; think how great she must be and what a blessing it is for you to have her for a patroness, since my sins and evil

underneath, (as he did in other cases) 'Nothing to be crossed out.'

character have brought no tarnish on the lustre of our holy Order.

6. Still I must give you one warning: be not too confident because you are nuns and the daughters of such a Mother. David was very holy, yet you know what Solomon became.[4] Therefore do not rely on your enclosure, on your penitential life, nor on your continual exercise of prayer and constant communion with God, nor trust in having left the world or in the idea that you hold its ways in horror. All this is good, but is not enough, as I have already said, to remove all fear; therefore meditate on this text and often recall it: 'Blessed is the man that feareth the Lord.'[5]

7. I do not recollect what I was saying, and have digressed very much: for when I think of myself my mind cannot soar to higher things but is like a bird with broken wings; so I will leave this subject for the present.

8. To return to what I began to explain about the souls which have entered the third mansions. God has shown them no small favour, but a very great one, in enabling them to pass through the first difficulties. Thanks to His mercy I believe there are many such people in the world: they are very desirous not to offend His Majesty even by venial sins, they love penance and spend hours in meditation, they employ their time well, exercise themselves in works of charity to their neighbours, are well-ordered in their conversation and dress,

[4] St. Teresa wrote 'Solomon'; Father Gracian corrected 'Absalom,' and Fr. Luis de Leon restored the original text.
[5] Ps. cxi. 1.

and those who own a household govern it well. This is certainly to be desired, and there appears no reason to forbid their entrance to the last mansions; nor will our Lord deny it them if they desire it, for this is the right disposition for receiving all His favours.

9. O Jesus! can any one declare that he does not desire this great blessing, especially after he has passed through the chief difficulties? No; no one can! We all say we desire it, but there is need of more than that for the Lord to possess entire dominion over the soul. It is not enough to say so, any more than it was enough for the young man when our Lord told him what he must do if he desired to be perfect.[6] Since I began to speak of these dwelling-rooms I have him constantly before my mind, for we are exactly like him; this very frequently produces the great dryness we feel in prayer, though sometimes it proceeds from other causes as well. I am not speaking of certain interior sufferings which give intolerable pain to many devout souls through no fault of their own; from these trials, however, our Lord always delivers them with much profit to themselves. I also except people who suffer from melancholy and other infirmities. But in these cases, as in all others, we must leave aside the judgments of God.

10. I hold that these effects usually result from the first cause I mentioned; such souls know that nothing would induce them to commit a sin (many of them would not even commit a venial sin

[6] Matt. xix. 21.

advertently), and that they employ their life and riches well. They cannot, therefore, patiently endure to be excluded from the presence of our King, Whose vassals they consider themselves, as indeed they are. An earthly king may have many subjects yet all do not enter his court. Enter then, enter, my daughters, into your interior; pass beyond the thought of your own petty works, which are no more, nor even as much, as Christians are bound to perform: let it suffice that you are God's servants, do not pursue so much as to catch nothing.[7] Think of the saints, who have entered the Divine Presence, and you will see the difference between them and ourselves.

11. Do not ask for what you do not deserve, nor should we ever think, however much we may have done for God, that we merit the reward of the saints, for we have offended Him. Oh, humility, humility! I know not why, but I am always tempted to think that persons who complain so much of aridities must be a little wanting in this virtue. However, I am not speaking of severe interior sufferings, which are far worse than a want of devotion.

12. Let us try ourselves, my sisters, or let our Lord try us; He knows well how to do so (although we often pretend to misunderstand Him). We will now speak of these well-ordered souls. Let us consider what they do for God and we shall see at once what little right we have to murmur against His Majesty. If we turn our backs on Him and go away sorrowfully like the youth in the Gospel[8]

[7] Proverbially, like 'having too many irons in the fire.'
[8] St. Mark. x. 22.   *Way of Perf.* ch. xvii. 5.

when He tells us what to do to be perfect, what
can God do? for He must proportion the reward
to our love for Him. This love, my daughters,
must not be the fabric of our imagination; we must
prove it by our works. Yet do not suppose that our
Lord has need of any works of ours; He only
expects us to manifest our goodwill.[9]

13. It seems to us we have done everything by
taking the religious habit of our own will, and
renouncing worldly things and all our possessions
for God (although they may have been but the nets
of St. Peter,[10] yet they seemed much to us, for they
were our all). This is an excellent disposition: if
we continue in it and do not return, even in desire,
to the company of the reptiles of the first rooms,
doubtless, by persevering in this poverty and detachment of soul, we shall obtain all for which we
strive. But, mark this—it must be on one condition
—that we 'hold ourselves for unprofitable servants,'[11]
as we are told either by St. Paul or by Christ, and
that we do not consider that our Lord is bound to
grant us any favours, but that, as we have received
more from Him, we are the deeper in His debt.

14. How little is all we can do for so generous a
God, Who died for us, Who created us, Who gives
us being, that we should not think ourselves happy
to be able to acquit ourselves of part of the debt
we owe Him for having served us, without asking
Him for fresh mercies and favours? I am loth to

---

[9] *Rel.* ix. 15.

[10] St. Matt. iv. 20: 'Relictis retibus secuti sunt eum.'

[11] St. Luke xvii. 10: 'Servi inutiles sumus: quod debuimus facere
fecimus.'

use this expression, yet so it is, for He did nothing else during the whole time He lived in this world but serve us.

15. Think well my daughters, over some of the points I have treated, although confusedly, for I do not know how to explain them better. Our Lord will make you understand them, that you may reap humility from your dryness, instead of the disquietude the devil strives to cause by it. I believe that where true humility exists, although God should never bestow consolations, yet He gives a peace and resignation which make the soul happier than are others with sensible devotion. These consolations, as you have read, are often given by the Divine Majesty to the weakest souls who, I suppose would not exchange them for the fortitude of Christians serving God in aridities: we love consolations better than the cross! Do Thou, O Lord, Who knowest all truth, so prove us that we may know ourselves.

CHAPTER II.

CONTINUES THE SAME SUBJECT AND SPEAKS OF ARIDITIES IN PRAYER AND THEIR RESULTS: OF THE NECESSITY OF TRYING OURSELVES AND HOW OUR LORD PROVES THOSE WHO ARE IN THESE MANSIONS.

1. Imperfections of dwellers in the first three mansions. 2. Our trials show us our weakness. 3. Humility learnt by our faults. 4. Love of money. 5. Liberty of spirit. 6. On bearing contempt. 7. Detachment proved by trials. 8. Virtue and humility are the essentials. 9. Perfection requires detachment. 10. We should try to make rapid progress. 11. Leave our cares in God's hands. 12. Humility more necessary than corporal penances. 13. Consolations rarely received until the fourth mansions. 14. Advantages of hearing of them. 15. Perfection consists in love, not in reward. 16. St. Teresa's joy at seeing other souls favoured. 17. These graces should be striven for. 18. Obedience and direction. 19. Misguided zeal for others.

1. I HAVE known some, in fact, I may say numerous souls, who have reached this state, and for many years lived, apparently, a regular and well-ordered life, both of body and mind. It would seem that they must have gained the mastery over this world, or at least be extremely detached from it, yet if His Majesty sends very moderate trials they become so disturbed and disheartened as not only to astonish but to make me anxious about them. Advice is useless; having practised virtue for so long they

78

think themselves capable of teaching it, and believe that they have abundant reason to feel miserable.

2. The only way to help them is to compassionate their troubles;[1] indeed, one cannot but feel sorry at seeing people in such an unhappy state. They must not be argued with, for they are convinced they suffer only for God's sake, and cannot be made to understand they are acting imperfectly, which is a further error in persons so far advanced. No wonder that they should feel these trials for a time, but I think they ought speedily to overcome their concern about such matters. God, wishing His elect to realize their own misery, often temporarily withdraws His favours: no more is needed to prove to us in a very short time what we really are.[2]

3. Souls soon learn in this way; they perceive their faults very clearly, and sometimes the discovery of how quickly they are overcome by but slight earthly trials is more painful than the subtraction of God's sensible favours. I consider that God thus shows them great mercy, for though their behaviour may be faulty, yet they gain greatly in humility. Not so with the people of whom I first spoke; they believe their conduct is saintly, and wish others to agree with them. I will give you some examples which will help us to understand and to try ourselves, without waiting for God to try us, since it would be far better to have prepared and examined ourselves beforehand.

4. A rich man, without son or heir, loses part of

[1] See letter concerning Francisco de Salcedo. Nov. 1576. Vol. II.
[2] *Way of Perf.* ch. xxxviii. 7.

his property,[3] but still has more than enough to keep himself and his household. If this misfortune grieves and disquiets him as though he were left to beg his bread, how can our Lord ask him to give up all things for His sake? This man will tell you he regrets losing his money because he wished to bestow it on the poor.

5. I believe His Majesty would prefer me to conform to His will, and keep peace of soul while attending to my interests, to such charity as this. If this person cannot resign himself because God has not raised him so high in virtue, well and good: let him know that he is wanting in liberty of spirit; let him beg our Lord to grant it him, and be rightly disposed to receive it. Another person has more than sufficient means to live on, when an opportunity occurs for acquiring more property: if it is offered him, by all means let him accept it; but if he must go out of his way to obtain it and then continues working to gain more and more— however good his intention may be (and it must be good, for I am speaking of people who lead prayerful and good lives), he cannot possibly enter the mansions near the King.

6. Something of the same sort happens if such people meet with contempt or want of due respect. God often gives them grace to bear it well, as He loves to see virtue upheld in public, and will not have it condemned in those who practise it, or else because these persons have served Him faithfully, and He, our supreme Good, is exceedingly good to us all; nevertheless, these persons are disturbed, and

[3] *Way of Perf.* ch. xxxviii. 10. *Concep.* ch. ii. 11, 12. *Life*, xi. 3.

cannot overcome or get rid of the feeling for some time[4] Alas! have they not long meditated on the pains our Lord endured and how well it is for us to suffer, and have even longed to do so? They wish every one were as virtuous as they are; and God grant they do not consider other people to blame for their troubles and attribute merit to themselves!

7. You may think, my daughters, that I have wandered from the subject, for all this does not concern you: nothing of the sort occurs to us here, where we neither own nor wish for any property, nor endeavour to gain it, and no one does us any wrong. The instances I have mentioned do not coincide exactly, yet conclusions applicable to us may be drawn from them, which it would be neither well nor necessary to state. These will teach you whether you are really detached from all you have left; trifling occasions often occur, although perhaps not quite of the same kind, by which you can prove to yourselves whether you have obtained the mastery over your passions.

8. Believe me, the question is not whether we wear the religious habit or not, but whether we practise the virtues and submit our will in all things to the will of God. The object of our life must be to do what He requires of us: let us not ask that *our* will may be done, but *His.* If we have not yet attained to this, let us be humble, as I said above. Humility is the ointment for our wounds; if we have it, although perhaps He may defer His coming for a time, God, Who is our Physician, will come and heal us.

4 *Way of Perf.* ch. xxxviii. 12.

9. The penances performed by the persons I spoke
of are as well regulated as their life, which they
value very highly because they wish to serve our
Lord with it—in which there is nothing to blame
—so they are very discreet in their mortifications
lest they should injure their health. Never fear
they will kill themselves: they are far too sensible!
Their love is not strong enough to overcome their
reason; I wish it were—that they might not be
content to creep on their way to God: a pace that
will never bring them to their journey's end!

10. We seem to ourselves to be making progress,
yet we become weary, for, believe me, we are walk-
ing through a mist; it will be fortunate if we do
not lose ourselves. Do you think, my daughters, if
we could travel from one country to another in
eight days, that it would be well to spend a year on
the journey, through wind, snow, and inundations
and over bad roads?⁵ Would it not be better to get
it over at once, for it is full of dangers and serpents?
Oh, how many striking instances could I give you
of this! God grant that I have passed beyond this
state myself: often I think that I have not.

11. All things obstruct us while prudence rules our
actions; we are afraid of everything and therefore
fear to make progress—as if we could reach the inner chambers while others make the journey for us!
As this is impossible, sisters, for the love of God
let us exert ourselves, and leave our reason and

⁵ St. Teresa very probably had in her mind her journey to make a
foundation at Seville, when the boat, which was crossing the Guadal-
quivir, narrowly escaped being carried down the river by the current.
Found. ch. xxiv. 6

our fears in His hands, paying no attention to the weaknesses of nature which might retard us. Let our Superiors, to whom the charge belongs, look after our bodies; let our only care be to hasten to our Lord's presence—for though there are few or no indulgences to be obtained here, yet regard for health might mislead us and it would be none the better for our care, as I know well.

12. I know, too, that our bodies are not the chief factors in the work we have before us; they are accessory: extreme humility is the principal point. It is the want of this, I believe, that stops people's progress. It may seem that we have made but little way: we should believe that is the case, and that our sisters are advancing much more rapidly than we are. Not only should we wish others to consider us the worst of all; we should endeavour to make them think so. If we act in this manner, our soul will do well; otherwise we shall make no progress and shall always remain the prey to a thousand troubles and miseries. The way will be difficult and wearisome without self-renunciation, weighed down as we are by the burden and frailties of human nature, which are no longer felt in the more interior mansions.

13. In these third mansions the Lord never fails to repay our services, both as a just and even as a merciful God, Who always bestows on us far more than we deserve, giving us greater happiness than could be obtained from any earthly pleasures and amusements. I think He grants few consolations here, except, perhaps, occasionally to entice us to

prepare ourselves to enter the last mansions by showing us their contents. There may *appear* to you to be no difference except in name between sensible devotion, and consolations and you may ask why I distinguish them. I think there *is* a very great difference, but I may be mistaken.

14. This will be best explained while writing of the fourth mansion, which comes next, when I must speak of the consolations received there from our Lord. The subject may appear futile, yet may prove useful by urging souls who know what each mansion contains to strive to enter the best. It will solace those whom God has advanced so far; others, who thought they had reached the summit, will be abashed, yet if they are humble they will be led to thank God.

15. Those who do not receive these consolations may feel a despondency that is uncalled for, since perfection does not consist in consolation but in greater love; our reward will be in proportion to this, and to the justice and sincerity of our actions. Perhaps you wonder, then, why I treat of these interior favours and their nature. I do not know; ask him who bade me write this. I must obey Superiors, not argue with them, which I have no right to do.

16. I assure you that when I had neither received these favours,[6] nor understood them by experience, or ever expected to (and rightly so, for I should have felt reassured if I had known or even conjectured that I was pleasing to God in any way),

6 *Life*, ch. xii. 2. *Rel.* vii. 3.

yet when I read of the mercies and consolations that our Lord grants to His servants, I was delighted and praised Him fervently. If such as myself acted thus, how much more would the humble and good glorify Him! I think it is worth while to explain these subjects and show what consolations and delights we lose through our own fault, if only for the sake of moving a single soul to praise God once.

17. When these joys are from God they come laden with love and strength, which aid the soul on its way and increase its good works and virtues. Do not imagine that it is unimportant whether you try to obtain these graces or no; if you are not to blame, the Lord is just: what He refuses in one way, His Majesty will give you in another, as He knows how; His secret ways are very mysterious, and doubtless He will do what is best for you.

18. Souls who by God's mercy are brought so far (which, as I said, is no small mercy, for they are likely to ascend still higher) will be greatly benefited by practising prompt obedience. Even if they are not in the religious state, it would be well if they, like certain other people, were to take a director,[7] so as never to follow their own will, which is the cause of most of our ills. They should not choose one of their own turn of mind[8] (as the saying goes), who is over prudent in his actions, but should select one thoroughly detached from worldly things; it is very helpful to consult a person who has learnt and can teach this. It is encouraging to see that trials which seemed to us impossible to

---

[7] *Life*, ch. xiii. 29.   [8] *Rel.* vii. 18.

submit to are possible to others, and that they bear them sweetly. Their flight makes us try to soar, like nestlings taught by the elder birds, who, though they cannot fly far at first, little by little imitate their parents: I know the great benefit of this. However determined such persons may be not to offend our Lord, they must not expose themselves to temptation: they are still near the first mansions to which they might easily return. Their strength is not yet established on a solid foundation like that of souls exercised in sufferings, who know how little cause there is to fear the tempests of this world and care nothing for its pleasures: beginners might succumb before any severe trial. Some great persecution, such as the devil knows how to raise to injure us, might make beginners turn back; while zealously trying to withdraw others from sin they might succumb to the attacks made upon them.

19. Let us look at our own faults, and not at other persons'. People who are extremely correct themselves are often shocked at everything they see[9]; however, we might often learn a great deal that is essential from the very persons whom we censure. Our exterior comportment and manners may be better—this is well enough, but not of the first importance. We ought not to insist on every one following in our footsteps, nor to take upon ourselves to give instructions in spirituality when, perhaps, we do not even know what it is. Zeal for the good of souls, though given us by God, may

[9] *Way of Perf.* ch. vii. 6. *Castle*, M. I. ch. ii. 20, 21.

often lead us astray, sisters; it is best to keep our rule, which bids us ever to live in silence and in hope.[10] Our Lord will care for the souls belonging to Him; and if we beg His Majesty to do so, by His grace we shall be able to aid them greatly. May He be for ever blessed!

[10] Isa. xxx. 15: 'In silentio et in spe erit fortitudo vestra.' *Rule* § 13.

THE FOURTH MANSIONS

CHAPTER I.

HOW SWEETNESS AND TENDERNESS IN PRAYER DIFFER FROM
CONSOLATIONS. EXPLAINS HOW ADVANTAGEOUS IT WAS FOR
ST. TERESA TO COMPREHEND THAT THE IMAGINATION AND THE
UNDERSTANDING ARE NOT THE SAME THING. THIS CHAPTER IS
USEFUL FOR THOSE WHOSE THOUGHTS WANDER MUCH DURING
PRAYER.

1. Graces received in this mansion. 2. Mystic favours. 3. Temptations bring humility and merit. 4. Sensible devotion and natural joys. 5. Sweetness in devotion. 6. St. Teresa's experience of it. 7. Love of God, and how to foster it. 8. Distractions. 9. They do not destroy divine union. 10. St. Teresa's physical distractions. 11. How to treat distractions. 12. They should be disregarded. 13. Self-knowledge necessary.

1. Now that I commence writing about the fourth mansions, it is requisite, as I said,[1] to commend myself to the Holy Ghost and to beg Him henceforth to speak for me, that I may be enabled to treat these matters intelligibly. Henceforth they begin to be supernatural and it will be most difficult to speak clearly about them,[2] unless His Majesty

[1] First Mansions, ch. i. 1.

[2] There are two kinds of contemplation: acquired or natural, and infused or supernatural. In their widest sense, including many remarkable phenomena of Natural religion, and, of course, the most wonderful manifestations recorded in the Old Testament, they form the sys-

undertakes it for me, as He did when I explained the subject (as far as I understood it) somewhat about fourteen years ago.[3] I believe I now possess more light about the favours God grants some souls, but that is different from being able to elucidate them.[4] May His Majesty enable me to do so if it would be useful, but not otherwise.

2. As these mansions are nearer the King's dwelling they are very beautiful, and so subtle are the things seen and heard in them, that, as those tell us who have tried to do so, the mind cannot give a lucid idea of them to those inexperienced in the matter. People who have enjoyed these favours, especially if it was to any great extent, will easily comprehend me.

3. Apparently a person must have dwelt for a long time in the former mansions before entering these; although in ordinary cases the soul must have been in the last one spoken of, yet, as you must often have heard, there is no fixed rule, for God gives when,

tem called Mysticism and are the proper object of Mystical theology. Natural or acquired contemplation is based upon an idealistic turn of mind which enables the soul to gaze upon the Godhead (simple gaze, as St. Teresa calls it) without approaching Him by the laborious process of reasoning, and in so doing embraces Him with its affective powers; like a person who, devoid of technical skill, takes in and is enamoured by, the beauty of a painting. Infused contemplation is the highest act of the Gifts of the Holy Ghost of Knowledge and Wisdom. It is often impossible, nor is it always essential, to determine where acquired contemplation ends and infused contemplation begins. But it should be borne in mind that both the one and the other are operations and not merely a passive state or mere fruition. Even the highest form of contemplation, the Beatific Vision, is a supernatural act of the soul, an operation of unending duration. A ship moved by a gentle breeze is rightly said to be actually sailing though the rowers are at rest.

[3] *Life*, ch. xii. 11. [4] *Life*, ch. xvii. 7.

how, and to whom He wills[5]—the goods are His own, and His choice wrongs no one.[6] The poisonous reptiles rarely come into these rooms, and, if they enter, do more good than harm. I think it is far better for them to get in and make war on the soul in this state of prayer; were it not tempted, the devil might sometimes deceive it about divine consolations, thus injuring it far more. Besides, the soul would benefit less, because all occasions of gaining merit would be withdrawn, were it left continually absorbed in God. I am not confident that this absorption is genuine when it always remains in the same state, nor does it appear to me possible for the Holy Ghost to dwell constantly within us, to the same extent, during our earthly exile.

4. I will now describe, as I promised, the difference between sweetness in prayer and spiritual consolations. It appears to me that what we acquire for ourselves in meditation and petitions to our Lord may be termed 'sweetness in devotion.'[7] It is natural, although ultimately aided by the grace of God. I must be understood to imply this in all I say, for we can do nothing without Him. This

[5] Philippus a SS. Trinitate, *Summa Theologiæ Mysticæ*, pars iii. tract. i. disc. iii. art. 2. *Life*, ch. xv. 11, xxii. 22, 23. *Way of Perf.* ch. xvi 4, xli. 2. *Concep.* ch. v. 3.

[6] S. Matt. xx. 15: 'Aut non licet mihi quod volo facere?'

[7] *Way of Perf.*, ch. xix. 8. *Castle*, M. iv. ch. ii. 4. The first three mansions of the Interior Castle correspond with the 'first water,' or the prayer of Meditation, explained in ch. xi-xiii. of the *Life*; the fourth mansion, or the prayer of Quiet, with the 'second water,' *Life*, ch. xiv. and xv.; the fifth mansion, or the prayer of Union, with the 'third water,' *Life*, ch. xvi. and xvii.; and the sixth mansion, ecstasy, etc., with the 'fourth water,' *Life*, ch. xviii.-xxi.

sweetness arises principally from the good work we perform, and appears to result from our labours: well may we feel happy at having thus spent our time. We shall find, on consideration, that many temporal matters give us the same pleasure—such as unexpectedly coming into a large fortune, suddenly meeting with a dearly-loved friend, or succeeding in any important or influential affair which makes a sensation in the world. Again, it would be felt by one who had been told her husband, brother, or son was dead, and who saw him return to her alive. I have seen people weep from such happiness, as I have done myself. I consider both these joys and those we feel in religious matters to be natural ones. Although there is nothing wrong about the former, yet those produced by devotion spring from a more noble source—in short, they begin in ourselves and end in God. Spiritual consolations, on the contrary, arise from God, and our nature feels them and rejoices as keenly in them, and indeed far more keenly, than in the others I described.

5. O Jesus! how I wish I could elucidate this point! It seems to me that I can perfectly distinguish the difference between the two joys, yet I have not the skill to make myself understood; may God give it me! I remember a verse we say at Prime at the end of the final Psalm; the last words are: 'Cum dilatasti cor meum'—'When Thou didst dilate my heart.'[8] To those with much experience, this suffices to show the difference between sweetness in prayer and spiritual consolations; other people will

[8] Ps. cxviii. 32. *Way of Perf.* ch. xxviii. 11.

require more explanation. The sensible devotion
I mentioned does not dilate the heart, but generally appears to narrow it slightly; although joyful
at seeing herself work for God, yet such a person
sheds tears of sorrow which seem partly produced
by the passions. I know little about the passions
of the soul, or I could write of them more clearly
and could better define what comes from the sensitive disposition and what is natural, having passed
through this state myself, but I am very stupid.
Knowledge and learning are a great advantage to
every one.

6. My own experience of this delight and sweetness in meditation was that when I began to weep
over the Passion I could not stop until I had a severe
headache;[9] the same thing occurred when I grieved
over my sins: this was a great grace from our Lord.
I do not intend to inquire now which of these states
of prayer is the better, but I wish I knew how to
explain the difference between the two. In that of
which I speak, the tears and good desires are often
partly caused by the natural disposition, but although this may be the case, yet, as I said, these feelings terminate in God. Sensible devotion is very
desirable if the soul is humble enough to understand that it is not more holy on account of these
sentiments, which cannot always with certainty be
ascribed to charity, and even then are still the gift
of God.

7. These feelings of devotion are most common
with souls in the first three mansions, who are
nearly always using their understanding and reason

[9] *Life*, ch. iii. 1.

in making meditations. This is good for them, for they have not been given grace for more; they should, however, try occasionally to elicit some acts such as praising God, rejoicing in His goodness and that He is what He is: let them desire that He may be honoured and glorified. They must do this as best they can, for it greatly inflames the will. Let them be very careful, when God gives these sentiments, not to set them aside in order to finish their accustomed meditation. But, having spoken fully on this subject elsewhere,[10] I will say no more now. I only wish to warn you that to make rapid progress and to reach the mansions we wish to enter, it is not so essential to *think* much as to *love* much: therefore you must practise whatever most excites you to this. Perhaps we do not know what love is, nor does this greatly surprise me. Love does not consist in great sweetness of devotion, but in a fervent determination to strive to please God in all things, in avoiding, as far as possible, all that would offend Him, and in praying for the increase of the glory and honour of His Son and for the growth of the Catholic Church. These are the signs of love; do not imagine that it consists in never thinking of anything but God, and that if your thoughts wander a little all is lost.[11]

8. I, myself, have sometimes been troubled by this turmoil of thoughts. I learnt by experience, but little more than four years ago, that our thoughts, or it is clearer to call it our imagination, are not

[10] *Life*, ch. xii. 2-4.
[11] *Found.* ch. v. 2. *Way of Perf.* ch. xxxi. 6, 12. *Life*, ch. xv. 10, ch. xxx. 19.

the same thing as the understanding. I questioned a theologian on the subject; he told me it was the fact, which consoled me not a little. As the understanding is one of the powers of the soul, it puzzled me to see it so sluggish at times, while, as a rule, the imagination takes flight at once, so that God alone can control it by so uniting us to Himself[12] that we seem, in a manner, detached from our bodies. It puzzled me to see that while to all appearance the powers of the soul were occupied with God and recollected in Him, the imagination was wandering elsewhere.

9. Do Thou, O Lord, take into account all that we suffer in this way through our ignorance. We err in thinking that we need only know that we must keep our thoughts fixed on Thee. We do not understand that we should consult those better instructed than ourselves, nor are we aware that there is anything for us to learn. We pass through terrible trials, on account of not understanding our own nature and take what is not merely harmless, but good, for a grave fault. This causes the sufferings felt by many people, particularly by the unlearned, who practise prayer. They complain of interior trials, become melancholy, lose their health, and even give up prayer altogether for want of recognizing that we have within ourselves as it were, an interior world. We cannot stop the revolution of the heavens as they rush with velocity upon their course, neither can we control our imagination. When this wanders we at once imagine that all the powers of the soul follow it; we think everything

[12] *Life.* ch. xv. 9, 10.

is lost, and that the time spent in God's presence is wasted. Meanwhile, the soul is perhaps entirely united to Him in the innermost mansions, while the imagination is in the precincts of the castle, struggling with a thousand wild and venomous creatures and gaining merit by its warfare. Therefore we need not let ourselves be disturbed, nor give up prayer, as the devil is striving to persuade us. As a rule, all our anxieties and troubles come from misunderstanding our own nature.

10. Whilst writing this I am thinking of the loud noise in my head which I mentioned in the Introduction, and which has made it almost impossible to obey the command given me to write this. It sounds as if there were a number of rushing waterfalls within my brain, while in other parts, drowned by the sound of the waters, are the voices of birds singing and whistling. This tumult is not in my ears, but in the upper part of my head, where, they say, is placed the superior part of the soul. I have long thought that this must be so because the flight of the spirit seems to take place from this part with great velocity.[13] Please God I may recollect to explain the cause when writing of the latter mansions, this not being the proper place for it. It may be that God has sent this suffering in my head to help me to understand the matter, for all this tumult in my brain does not interfere with my prayer, nor with my speaking to you, but the great calm and love and desires in my soul remain undisturbed and my mind is clear.

11. How, then, can the superior part of the soul

[13] Second Relation addressed to Fr. Rodrigo Alvarez.

remain undisturbed if it resides in the upper part of the brain? I cannot account for it, but am sure that I am speaking the truth. This noise disturbs my prayer when unaccompanied with ecstasy, but when it is ecstatic I do not feel any pain, however great. I should suffer keenly were I forced to cease praying on account of these infirmities. We should not be distressed by reason of our thoughts, nor allow ourselves to be worried by them: if they come from the devil, he will let us alone if we take no notice of them; and if they are, as often happens, one of the many frailties entailed by Adam's sin, let us be patient and suffer them for the love of God. Likewise, since we must eat and sleep without being able to avoid it, much to our grief, let us acknowledge that we are human, and long to be where no one may despise us.[14] Sometimes I recall these words, spoken by the Spouse in the Canticle;[15] truly never in our lives have we better reason to say them, for I think no earthly scorn or suffering can try us so severely as these struggles within our souls. All uneasiness or conflict can be borne while we have peace in ourselves, as I said; but if, while seeking for rest amidst the thousand trials of the world—knowing that God has prepared this rest for us—the obstacle is found in ourselves, the trial must needs prove painful and almost insufferable.

12. Take us therefore, O Lord, to where these miseries can no longer cause us to be despised, for

[14] *Way of Perf.* ch. xxxiii. 8. *Life*, ch. xxi. 8. *Rel.* ii. 12.

[15] According to Fr. Gracian the Saint here refers to Cant. viii. 1 : 'Et jam me nemo despiciat.'

sometimes it seems as if they mocked our souls. Even in this life God delivers us from them when we reach the last mansion, as by His grace I will show you. Everybody is not so violently distressed and assaulted by these weaknesses as I have been for many years,[16] on account of my wickedness, so that it seems as if I strove to take vengeance on myself.[17] Since I suffer so much in this way, perhaps you may do the same, so I shall continue to explain the subject to you in different ways, in order to find some means of making it clear. The thing is inevitable, therefore do not let it disturb or grieve you, but let the mill clack on while we grind our wheat; that is, let us continue to work with our will and intellect.

13. These troubles annoy us more or less according to the state of our health or in different circumstances. The poor soul suffers; although not now to blame, it has sinned at other times, and must be patient. We are so ignorant that what we have read and been told has not sufficed to teach us to disregard wandering thoughts, therefore I shall not be wasting time in instructing and consoling you about these trials. However, this will help you but little until God chooses to enlighten you, and additional measures are needed: His Majesty wishes us to learn by ordinary means to understand ourselves and to recognize the share taken in these troubles by our wandering imagination, our nature, and the devil's temptations, instead of laying all the blame on our souls.

[16] *Way of Perf.* ch. xvii. 2.
[17] *Way of Perf.* ch. xxxi. 9.

CHAPTER II.

1. GOD help me! how I have wandered from my subject! I forget what I was speaking about, for my occupations and ill-health often force me to cease writing until some more suitable time. The sense will be very disconnected; as my memory is extremely bad and I have no time to read over what is written, even what I really understand is expressed very vaguely, at least so I fear. I think I said that spiritual consolations are occasionally connected with the passions. These feelings of devotion produce fits of sobbing; I have even heard that sometimes they cause a compression of the chest, and uncontrollable exterior motions violent enough to cause bleeding at the nose and other painful effects.[1]

2. I can say nothing about this, never having experienced anything of the kind myself; but there appears some cause for comfort in it, because, as I said, all ends in the desire to please God and to

[1] 'A clear description of an attack of hysteria with the significant remark that she herself had never experienced anything of the kind'. (Dr. Goix, quoted by P. Grégoire, *La prétendue hystérie de Sainte Thérèse*, Lyon, Vitte, 1895, p. 53.)

98

enjoy His presence. What I call divine consolations, or have termed elsewhere the 'prayer of quiet,' is a very different thing, as those will understand who, by the mercy of God, have experienced them.

3. To make the matter clearer, let us imagine we see two fountains with basins which fill with water. I can find no simile more appropriate than water by which to explain spiritual things, as I am very ignorant and have poor wits to help me.[2] Besides, I love this element so much that I have studied it more attentively than other things. God, Who is so great, so wise, has doubtless hidden secrets in all things He created, which we should greatly benefit by knowing, as those say who understand such matters. Indeed, I believe that in each smallest creature He has made, though it be but a tiny ant, there are more wonders than can be comprehended. These two basins are filled in different ways; the one with water from a distance flowing into it through many pipes and waterworks, while the other basin is built near the source of the spring itself and fills quite noiselessly. If the fountain is plentiful, like the one we speak of, after the basin is full the water overflows in a great stream which flows continually. No machinery is needed here, nor does the water run through aqueducts.

4. Such is the difference between the two kinds of prayer. The water running through the aqueducts resembles sensible devotion, which is obtained by meditation. We gain it by our thoughts, by meditating on created things, and by the labour of

---

[2] *Way of Perf.* ch. xix.5 ; also St. John of the Cross, *Ascent of Mount Carmel*, bk. ii. ch. xiv. 2, and xxi. 3.

our minds; in short, it is the result of our endeavours, and so makes the commotion I spoke of, while profiting the soul.[3] The other fountain, like divine consolations, receives the water from the source itself, which signifies God: as usual, when His Majesty wills to bestow on us any supernatural favours, we experience the greatest peace, calm, and sweetness in the inmost depths of our being; I know neither where nor how.

5. This joy is not, like earthly happiness, at once felt by the heart; after gradually filling it to the brim, the delight overflows throughout all the mansions and faculties, until at last it reaches the body. Therefore, I say it arises from God and ends in ourselves, for whoever experiences it will find that the whole physical part of our nature shares in this delight and sweetness. While writing this I have been thinking that the verse 'Dilatasti cor meum,' 'Thou hast dilated my heart,'[4] declares that the heart is dilated. This joy does not appear to me to originate in the heart, but in some more interior part and, as it were, in the depths of our being. I think this must be the centre of the soul, as I have since learnt and will explain later on. I discover secrets within us which often fill me with astonishment: how many more must there be unknown to me! O my Lord and my God! how stupendous is Thy grandeur! We are like so many foolish peasant lads: we think we know something of Thee, yet it must be comparatively nothing, for there are profound secrets even in ourselves of

[3] *Life*, ch. x. 2.
[4] Ps. cxviii. 32. *Life*, ch. xvii. 14.

which we know naught. I say 'comparatively no-thing' in proportion with all the secrets hidden within Thee, yet how great are Thy mysteries that we are acquainted with and can learn even by the study of such of Thy works as we see![5]

6. To return to the verse I quoted, which may help to explain the dilation begun by the celestial waters in the depths of our being. They appear to dilate and enlarge us internally, and benefit us in an inexplicable manner, nor does even the soul itself understand what it receives. It is conscious of what may be described as a certain fragrance, as if within its inmost depths were a brazier sprinkled with sweet perfumes. Although the spirit neither sees the flame nor knows where it is, yet it is penetrated by the warmth, and scented fumes, which are even sometimes perceived by the body. Understand me, the soul does not feel any real heat or scent, but something far more subtle, which I use this metaphor to explain. Let those who have never experienced it believe that it really occurs to others: the soul is conscious of it and feels it more distinctly than can be expressed. It is not a thing we can fancy or gain by anything we can do; clearly it does not arise from the base coin of human nature, but from the most pure gold of Divine Wisdom. I believe that in this case the powers of the soul are not united to God, but are absorbed and astounded at the marvel before them. I may possibly be contradicting what I wrote elsewhere;[6] nor would

---

[5] *Life*, ch. xiv. 9 *Way of Perf.* ch. xxviii. 11.

[6] *Life*, ch. xiv. 3: 'The faculties are not lost, neither are they asleep; the will alone is occupied in such a way that without knowing how it has become a captive it gives a simple consent to become the prisoner

this be surprising, for it was done about fifteen years ago, and perhaps God has given me since then a clearer insight into the matter. I may be entirely mistaken on the subject, both then and now, but never do I wilfully say what is untrue. No; by the mercy of God, I would rather die a thousand times than tell a falsehood: I speak of the matter as I understand it. I believe that in this case the will must in some way be united with that of God. The after effects on the soul, and the subsequent behaviour of the person, show whether this prayer was genuine or no: this is the best crucible by which to test it.

7. Our Lord bestows a signal grace on the soul if it realizes how great is this favour, and another greater still if it does not turn back on the right road. You are longing, my daughters, to enter into this state of prayer at once, and you are right, for, as I said, the soul cannot understand the value of the graces there bestowed by God upon it, nor the love which draws Him ever closer to it: we should certainly desire to learn how to obtain this favour. I will tell you what I know about it, setting aside certain cases in which God bestows these graces for no other reason than His own choice, into which we have no right to enquire.

8. Practise what I advised in the preceding mansions, then—humility, humility! for God lets Himself be vanquished by this and grants us all we ask.[7]

of God.' *Ibid.* § 4: 'The other two faculties help the will that it may render itself capable of the fruition of so great a good; nevertheless, it occasionally happens even when the will is in union that they hinder it very much.' See also *Way of Perf.* ch. xxxi. 8.

[7] *Way of Perf.* ch. xvi. 1. *Life*, ch. xxii. 16.

The first proof[8] that you possess humility is that
you neither think you now deserve these graces and
consolations from God, nor that you ever will as
long as you live. You ask me: 'How shall we receive them, if we do not try to gain them?' I answer, that there is no surer way to obtain them than
the one I have told you, therefore make no efforts
to acquire them, for the following reasons. The
first is, that the chief means of obtaining them is
to love God without self-interest. The second, that
it is a slight lack of humility to think that our
wretched services can win so great a reward The
third, that the real preparation for them is to desire to suffer and imitate our Lord, rather than to
receive consolations, for indeed we have all offended
Him. The fourth reason is, that His Majesty has
not promised to give us these favours in the same
way as He has bound Himself to bestow eternal
glory on us if we keep His commandments. We
can be saved without these special graces; He sees
better than we do what is best for us and which of
us love Him sincerely. I know for a certain truth,
being acquainted with some who walk by the way
of love (and therefore only seek to serve Jesus Christ
crucified), that not only they neither ask for nor
desire consolation, but they even beg Him not to
give it them during this life: this is a fact. Fifthly,
we should but labour in vain: this water does not
flow through aqueducts, like that we first spoke of,
and if the spring does not afford it, in vain shall we
toil to obtain it. I mean, that though we may
meditate and try our hardest, and though we shed

[8] Philippus a SS. Trinitate, *l.c.* art. 3.

tears to gain it, we cannot make this water flow. God alone gives it to whom He chooses, and often when the soul is least thinking of it. We are His, sisters, let Him do what He will with us, and lead us where He will. If we are really humble and annihilate ourselves, not only in our imagination (which often deceives us), but if we truly detach ourselves from all things, our Lord will not only grant us these favours but many others that we do not know even how to desire. May He be for ever praised and blessed! Amen.

CHAPTER III.

OF THE PRAYER OF RECOLLECTION WHICH GOD GENERALLY GIVES THE SOUL BEFORE GRANTING IT THAT LAST DESCRIBED. ITS EFFECTS: ALSO THOSE OF THE PRAYER OF DIVINE CONSO-LATIONS DESCRIBED IN THE LAST CHAPTER.

1. The prayer of recollection compared to the inhabitants of the castle. 2. The Shepherd recalls His flock into the castle. 3. This recollection supernatural. 4. It prepares us for higher favours. 5. The mind must act until God calls it to recollection by love. 6. The soul should here abandon itself into God's hands. 7. The prayer of recollection, and distractions in prayer. 8. Liberty of spirit gained by consolations. 9. The soul must be watchful. 10. The devil specially tempts such souls. 11. False trances and raptures. 12. How to treat those deluded in this way. 13. Risks of delusion in this mansion.

1. THE effects of divine consolations are very numerous: before describing them, I will speak of another kind of prayer which usually precedes them. I need not say much on this subject, having written about it elsewhere.[1] This is a kind of recollection which, I believe, is supernatural. There is

[1] *Life*, ch. xiv. 2. The Saint says in the second chapter of this mansion, §5, and also in letters dated Dec. 7, 1577 (Vol. II) and Jan. 14, 1580, that when writing the *Interior Castle* she had more experience in

no occasion to retire nor to shut the eyes, nor does it depend on anything exterior; involuntarily the eyes suddenly close and solitude is found. Without any labour of one's own, the temple of which I spoke is reared for the soul in which to pray: the senses and exterior surroundings appear to lose their hold, while the spirit gradually regains its lost sovereignty. Some say the soul enters into itself; others, that it rises above itself.[2] I can say nothing about these terms, but had better speak of the subject as I understand it. You will probably grasp my

spiritual things than when she composed her former works. This is fully borne out by the present chapter. In the corresponding part of her *Life* she practically confounded the prayer of recollection with the prayer of quiet (the second state of the soul). Likewise, in the *Way of Perfection*, ch. xxviii., she speaks of but one kind of prayer of recollection and then passes on to the prayer of quiet. Here, however, she mentions a second form of the prayer of recollection. See Philippus a SS. Trinitate, pars iii. tract. 1, disc. iii. art. 1, 'De oratione recollectionis' (page 81 of the third vol. of the edition of 1874); 'de secundo modo recollectionis' (*ibid.* p. 82.); and art. 2: 'De oratione quietis' (*ibid.* p. 84.) Antonius a Spiritu Sancto, *Direct. Mystic.* tract. iv. n. 78: 'Duo sunt hujus recollectionis modi, primus quidem activus [reference to the *Way of Perfection*, *l. c.*], secundus autem passivus, [reference to this chapter of the Fourth Mansion].' The former is not supernatural, in the sense that with special grace from above it can be acquired; the second is altogether supernatural and more like gratuitous grace (*ibid.* no. 80 and 81). On the meaning of 'Solitude,' 'Silence,' etc., see Anton. a Sp. S. *l. c.*, tract. 1, n. 78-82.

[2] The edition of Burgos (vol. iv, P. 59) refers appropriately to the following passage in the *Tercer Abecedario* (See *Life*, ch. iv, 8) by the Franciscan friar Francisco de Osuna, a work which exercised a profound influence on St. Teresa: 'Entering within oneself, and rising above oneself, are the two principal points in this exercise, those which, above all others, one ought to strive after, and which give the highest satisfaction to the soul. There is less labour in entering within oneself than in rising above oneself and therefore it appears to me that when the soul is ready and fit for either, you ought to do the former, because the other will follow without any effort, and will be all the more pure and spiritual; however, follow what course your soul prefers as this will bring you more grace and benefit.' (Tr. ix. ch. viii).

meaning, although, perhaps, I may be the only person who understands it. Let us imagine that the senses and powers of the soul (which I compared in my allegory to the inhabitants of the castle) have fled and joined the enemy outside. After long days and years of absence, perceiving how great has been their loss, they return to the neighbourhood of the castle, but cannot manage to re-enter it, for their evil habits are hard to break off; still, they are no longer traitors, and they wander about outside.

2. The King, Who holds His court within it, sees their good will, and out of His great mercy desires them to return to Him. Like a good Shepherd, He plays so sweetly on His pipe, that although scarcely hearing it they recognize His call and no longer wander, but return, like lost sheep, to the mansions. So strong is this Pastor's power over His flock, that they abandon the worldly cares which misled them and re-enter the castle.

3. I think I never put this matter so clearly before. To seek God within ourselves avails us far more than to look for Him amongst creatures; Saint Augustine tells us how he found the Almighty within his own soul, after having long sought for Him elsewhere.[3] This recollection helps us greatly

[3] Some editors of the *Interior Castle* think that St. Teresa refers to the following passage taken from the *Confessions* of St. Augustine: 'Too late have I loved Thee, O Beauty, ever ancient yet ever new! too late have I loved Thee! And behold, Thou wert within me and I abroad, and there I searched for Thee, and, deformed as I was, I pursued the beauties that Thou hast made. Thou wert with me, but I was not with Thee. Those things kept me far from Thee, which, unless they were in Thee, could have had no being' (*St. Augustine's Confessions,* bk. x. ch. xxvii.). The *Confessions of St. Augustine* were first translated

when God bestows it upon us. But do not fancy you can gain it by thinking of God dwelling within you, or by imagining Him as present in your soul: this is a good practice and an excellent kind of meditation, for it is founded on the fact that God resides within us;[4] it is not, however, the prayer of recollection, for by the divine assistance every one can practise it, but what I mean is quite a different thing. Sometimes, before they have begun to think of God, the powers of the soul find themselves within the castle. I know not by what means they entered, nor how they heard the Shepherd's pipe; the ears perceived no sound but the soul is keenly conscious of a delicious sense of recollection experienced by those who enjoy this favour, which I cannot describe more clearly.

4. I think I read somewhere[5] that the soul is then like a tortoise or sea-urchin, which retreats into it-

into Spanish by Sebastian Toscano, a Portuguese Augustinian. This edition, which was published at Salamanca in 1554, was the one used by St. Teresa. However, it is more probable that here and elsewhere (*Life*, ch. xli. 10; *Way of Perf.* ch. xxviii. 2) St. Teresa quotes a passage which occurs in a pious book entitled *Soliloquia*, and erroneously attributed to St. Augustine: 'I have gone about the streets and the broad ways of the city of this world seeking Thee, but have not found Thee for I was wrong in seeking without for what was within.' (ch. xxxi.) This treatise which is also quoted by St. John of the Cross, *Spiritual Canticle*, stanza i. 7, *Ascent of Mount Carmel*, bk. i. ch. v. 1, appeared in a Spanish translation at Valladolid in 1515, at Medina del Campo in 1553, and at Toledo in 1565.

[4] *Life*, ch. xiv. 7, 8; xviii. 20.

[5] St. Teresa read this in the *Tercer Abecedario* of Francisco de Osuna (tr. VI, ch, IV): 'This exercise concentrates the senses of man in the interior of the heart where dwells 'the daughter of the king'; that is, the Catholic soul; thus recollected, man may well be compared to the tortoise or sea-urchin which rolls itself up and withdraws within itself, disregarding everything outside.'

self. Those who said this no doubt understood what they were talking about; but these creatures can withdraw into themselves at will, while here it is not in our power to retire into ourselves, unless God gives us the grace. In my opinion, His Majesty only bestows this favour on those who have renounced the world, in *desire* at least, if their state of life does not permit their doing so in *fact*. He thus specially calls them to devote themselves to spiritual things; if they allow Him power to act freely He will bestow still greater graces on those whom He thus begins calling to a higher life. Those who enjoy this recollection should thank God fervently: it is of the highest importance for them to realize the value of this favour, gratitude for which would prepare them to receive still more signal graces. Some books advise that as a preparation for hearing what our Lord may say to us we should keep our minds at rest, waiting to see what He will work in our souls.[6] But unless His Majesty has begun to suspend our faculties, I cannot understand how we are to stop thinking, without doing ourselves more harm than good. This point has been much debated by those learned in spiritual matters; I confess my want of humility in having been unable to yield to their opinion.[7]

5. Some one told me of a certain book written on the subject by the saintly Friar Peter of Alcantara (as I think I may justly call him); I should have submitted to his decision, knowing that he was competent to judge, but on reading it I found he

⁶ *Life*, ch. xii. 8.   ⁷ *Life*, ch. xiv. 10.

agreed with me that the mind must act until called
to recollection by love, although he stated it in
other words.⁸ Possibly I may be mistaken, but I rely
on these reasons. Firstly, he who reasons less and
tries to do least, does most in spiritual matters. We

⁸ A Golden Treatise of Mental Prayer by St. Peter of Alcantara,
translated by Rev. G. F. Bullock M.A. and edited by Rev. George
Seymour Hollings S.S.J.E. London, Mowbray, 1905, p. 117.
    Eighth Counsel.   Let the last and chiefest counsel be that in this
holy exercise we should endeavour to unite Meditation with Contemplation making of the one a ladder for attaining to the other. For
this we must know that (p. 118) the very office of Meditation is to
consider Divine things with studiousness and attention passing from one
to another, to move our hearts to some affection and deep feeling for
them, which is as though one should strike a flint to draw from it the
spark.
    For Contemplation is to have drawn forth this spark: I mean to
have now found this affection and feeling which were sought for, and
to be in peace and silence enjoying them; not with many discursive
and intellectual speculations but with simple gaze upon the truth.
    Wherefore, says a holy teacher, Meditation goes its way and brings
forth fruit, with labour, but Contemplation bears fruit without labour.
The one seeketh, the other findeth; the one consumeth the food, the
other enjoys it; the one discourseth, and maketh reflections, the other
is contented with a simple gaze upon the things, for it hath in possession their love and joy.   Lastly, the one is as the means, the other as
the end; the one as the road and journeying along it, the other as the
end of the road and of the journeying.
    From this is to be inferred a very common thing, which all masters
of the spiritual life teach, although it is little (p. 119) understood
of those who learn it; which is this, that, as the means cease when the
end has been attained, as the voyaging is over when the port has been
touched, so when, through the working out of our Meditation, we
have come to the repose and sweet savour of Contemplation, we ought
then to cease from that pious and laborious searching; and being
satisfied with the simple gaze upon, and thought of, God—as though
we had Him there present before us—we should rest in the enjoyment
of that affection then given, whether it be of love, or of admiration,
or joy, or other like sentiment.
    The reason why this counsel is given is this, that as the aim of this
devotion is love and the affections of the will rather than the speculations of the understanding, when the will has been caught and taken

sh'ould make our petitions like beggars before a
powerful and rich Emperor; then, with downcast
eyes, humbly wait. When He secretly shows us He
hears our prayers, it is well to be silent, as He has
drawn us into His presence; there would then be
no harm in trying to keep our minds at rest (that
is to say, if we can). If, however, the King makes
no sign of listening or of seeing us, there is no need
to stand inert, like a dolt, which the soul would

by this affection, we should put away all those discursive and intellectual speculations, so far as we can, in order that our soul with all its
forces may be fastened upon this affection without being diverted by
the action of other influences. A learned teacher, therefore, counsels
us that as soon as anyone feels himself fired by the love of God, he
should first put aside (p. 120.) all these considerations and thoughts—
however exalted they may seem—not because they are really not good
in themselves, but because they are then hindrances to what is better.
and more important. For this is nothing else than that, having come
to the end and purpose of our work, we should stay therein, and leave
Meditation for the love of Contemplation. This may especially be done
at the end of any exercise, that is, after the petition for the Divine love
of which we have spoken, for one reason, because then it is supposed
that the labour of the exercise we have just gone through has produced
some divine devotion and feeling, since, saith the wise man, 'Better
is the end of prayer than the beginning': and for another reason, that,
after the work of Prayer and Meditation, it is well that one should
give his mind a little rest, and allow it to repose in the arms of Contemplation. At this point, then, we should put away all other thoughts
that may present themselves, and, quieting the mind and stilling the
memory, fix all upon our Lord; and remembering that we are then in
His presence, no longer dwell upon the details of divine things.
Ibidem p. 121. And not only at the end of the exercise but in the
midst of it, and at whatever part of it, this spiritual swoon should
come upon us, when the intellect is laid to sleep, we should make this
pause, and enjoy the blessing bestowed; and then, when we have
finished the digestion of it, turn to the matter we have in hand, as
the gardener does, when he waters his garden-bed; who, after giving
it (p. 122) a sufficiency of water, holds back the stream, and lets it
soak and spread itself through the depths of the earth; and then when
this hath somewhat dried up, he turns down upon it again the flow
of water that it may receive still more, and be well irrigated.'

resemble if it continued inactive. In this case its dryness would greatly increase, and the imagination would be made more restless than before by its very effort to think of nothing. Our Lord wishes us at such a time to offer Him our petitions and to place ourselves in His presence; He knows what is best for us.

6. I believe that human efforts avail nothing in these matters, which His Majesty appears to reserve to Himself, setting this limit to our powers. In many other things, such as penances, good works, and prayers, with His aid we can help ourselves as far as human weakness will allow. The second reason is, that these interior operations being sweet and peaceful,[9] any painful effort does us more harm than good. By 'painful effort' I mean any forcible restraint we place on ourselves, such as holding our breath.[10] We should rather abandon our souls into the hands of God, leaving Him to do as He chooses with us, as far as possible forgetting all self-interest and resigning ourselves entirely to His will. The third reason is, that the very effort to think of nothing excites our imagination the more. The fourth is, because we render God the most true and acceptable service by caring only for His honour and glory and forgetting ourselves, our advantages, comfort and happiness. How can we be self-oblivious, while keeping ourselves under such strict control that we are afraid to move, or even to think, or to leave our minds enough liberty to desire God's greater glory and to rejoice in the

[9] *Sap.* viii. 1 : 'Disponit omnia suaviter.'
[10] *Life*, ch. xv. 1.

glory which He possesses? When His Majesty
wishes the mind to rest from working He employs
it in another manner, giving it a light and knowledge far above any obtainable by its own efforts and
absorbing it entirely into Himself. Then, though
it knows not how, it is filled with wisdom such as
it could never gain for itself by striving to suspend
the thoughts. God gave us faculties for our use;
each of them will receive its proper reward. Then
do not let us try to charm them to sleep, but permit them to do their work until divinely called to
something higher."

7. In my opinion, when God chooses to place the
soul in this mansion it is best for it to do as I advised, and then endeavour, without force or disturbance, to keep free from wandering thoughts. No
effort, however, should be made to suspend the
imagination entirely from acting, for it is well to
remember God's presence and to consider Who He
is. If transported out of itself by its feelings, well
and good; but let it not try to understand what is
passing within it, for this favour is bestowed on
the will which should be left to enjoy it in peace,

[11] 'The whole of the time in which our Lord communicates the
simple, loving general attention of which I made mention before, or
when the soul, assisted by grace, is established in that state, we must
contrive to keep the understanding in repose, undisturbed by the in-
trusion of forms, figures, or particular knowledge, unless it were slightly
and for an instant, and that with sweetness of love, to enkindle our
souls the more. At other times, however, in all our acts of devotion
and good works, we must make use of good recollections and meditations, so that we may feel an increase of profit and devotion; most
especially applying ourselves to the life, passion, and death of Jesus
Christ, our Lord, that our life and conduct may be an imitation of
His.' (St. John of the Cross, *Ascent of Mount Carmel*, bk. ii. ch. xxxii. 7.)

only making loving aspirations occasionally. Although, in this kind of prayer, the soul makes no effort towards it, yet often, for a very short time, the mind ceases to think at all. I explained elsewhere why this occurs during this spiritual state.[12] On first speaking of the fourth mansions, I told you I had mentioned divine consolations before the prayer of recollection. The latter should have come first, as it is far inferior to consolations, of which it is the commencement. Recollection does not require us to give up meditation, nor to cease using our intellect. In the prayer of quiet, when the water flows from the spring itself and not through conduits, the mind ceases to act; it is forced to do so, although it does not understand what is happening, and so wanders hither and thither in bewilderment, finding no place for rest. Meanwhile the will, entirely united to God, is much disturbed by the tumult of the thoughts: no notice, however, should be taken of them, or they would cause the loss of a great part of the favour the soul is enjoying. Let the spirit ignore these distractions and abandon itself in the arms of divine love: His Majesty will teach it how best to act, which chiefly consists in its recognizing its unworthiness of so great a good and occupying itself in thanking Him for it.

8. In order to treat of the prayer of recollection, I passed over in silence the effects and symptoms to be found in souls thus favoured by God. Divine consolations evidently cause a dilation or enlargement of the soul that may be compared to water

[12] *Life*, ch. xv. 2.

flowing from a spring into a basin which has no
outlet, but is so constructed as to increase in size
and proportion to the quantity poured into it. God
seems to work the same effect by this prayer, besides
giving many other marvellous graces, so preparing
and disposing the soul to contain all He intends to
give it. After interior sweetness and dilation the
soul is not so restrained as formerly in God's service,
but possesses much more liberty of spirit. It is no
longer distressed by the terror of hell, for though
more anxious than ever not to offend God, it has
lost servile fear and feels sure that one day it will
possess its Lord. It does not dread the loss of health
by austerities;[13] believing that there is nothing it
could not do by His grace, it is more desirous than
before of doing penance. Greater indifference is
felt for sufferings because faith being stronger, it
trusts that if borne for God He will give the grace
to endure them patiently. Indeed, such a one at
times even longs for trials, having a most ardent
desire to do something for His sake. As the soul
better understands the Divine Majesty, it realizes
more vividly its own baseness. Divine consolation
shows it how vile are earthly pleasures; by gradually withdrawing from them, it gains greater self-
mastery. In short, its virtues are increased and it
will not cease to advance in perfection, unless it turns
back and offends God. Should it act thus, it would
lose everything, however high the state it may
have reached.

9. It is not to be supposed that all these effects
are produced merely by God's having shown these

favours once or twice. They must be received continually, for it is on their frequent reception that
the whole welfare of the soul depends. I strongly
urge those who have reached this state to avoid
most carefully all occasions of offending God.[14]
The soul is not yet fully established in virtue, but
is like a new-born babe first feeding at its mother's
breast:[15] if it leaves her, what can it do but die?
I greatly fear that when a soul to whom God has
granted this favour discontinues prayer, except
under urgent necessity, it will, unless it returns to
the practice at once, go from bad to worse.

10. I realize the danger of such a case, having
had the grief of witnessing the fall of persons I
knew through their withdrawal from Him Who
sought, with so much love, to make Himself their
friend, as He proved by His treatment of them. I
urgently warn such persons not to run the risk of
sinning, for the devil would rather gain one of
these souls than many to whom our Lord does not
grant such graces,[16] as the former may cause him
severe loss by leading others to follow their example,
and may even render great service to the Church
of God. Were there no other reason except that
he saw the special love His Majesty bears these
people, it would suffice to make Satan frantic to
destroy God's work in them, so that they might
be lost eternally. Therefore they suffer grievous
temptations, and if they fall, they fall lower than
others.

[14] *Way of Perf.* ch. xvi. 5. *Castle*, M. v. ch. i, 2, 3; ii. 4, 5; iii.
2, 6, 12.　　　[15] *Way of Perf.* ch. xxxi. 7. *Concept.* ch. iv. 6.
[16] *Way of Perf.* ch. xl. 3.

11. You, my sisters, are free from such dangers, as far as we can tell: God keep you from pride and vainglory! The devil sometimes offers counterfeits of the graces I have mentioned: this can easily be detected—the effects being exactly contrary to those of the genuine ones.[17] Although I have spoken of it elsewhere,[18] I wish to warn you here of a special danger to which those who practise prayer are subject, particularly women, whose weakness of constitution makes them more liable to such mistakes. On account of their penances, prayers, and vigils, or even merely because of debility of health, some persons cannot receive spiritual consolation without being overcome by it. On feeling any interior joy, their bodies being languid and weak, they fall into a slumber—they call it spiritual sleep —which is a more advanced stage of what I have described; they think the soul shares in it as well as the body, and abandon themselves to a sort of intoxication. The more they lose self-control, the more do their feelings get possession of them, because the frame becomes more feeble. They fancy this is a trance and call it one, but I call it nonsense; it does nothing but waste their time and injure their health.

12. This state lasted with a certain person for eight hours, during which time she was neither insensible, nor had she any thought of God.[19] She was cured by being made to eat and sleep well and to leave off some of her penances. Her recovery

[17] *Life*, ch. xx. 31.
[18] *Found.* ch. vi.
[19] *Found.* ch. vi. 15.

was owing to some one who understood her case; hitherto she had unintentionally deceived both her confessor and other people, as well as herself. I feel quite sure the devil had been at work here to serve his own ends and he was beginning to gain a great deal from it. It should be known that when God bestows such favours on the soul, although there may be languor both of mind and body, it is not shared by the soul, which feels great delight at seeing itself so near God, nor does this state ever continue for more than a very short time.[20] Although the soul may become absorbed again, yet, as I said, unless already feeble, the body suffers neither exhaustion nor pain. I advise any of you who experience the latter to tell the Prioress, and to divert your thoughts as much as possible from such matters. The Superior should prevent such a nun from spending more than a very few hours in prayer, and should make her eat and sleep well until her usual strength is restored, if she has lost it in this way.[21] If the nun's constitution is so delicate that this does not suffice, let her believe me when I tell her that God only calls her to the active life. There must be such people in monasteries: employ her in the various offices and be careful that she is never left very long alone, otherwise she will entirely lose her health. This treatment will be a great mortification to her: our Lord tests her love for Him by the way in which she bears His absence. He may be pleased, after a time, to restore her strength; if not, she will make as

[20] *Life* ch. xviii. 16, 17.
[21] *Letter* of Oct. 23, 1576. Vol. II.

much progress, and earn as great a reward by vocal prayer and obedience as she would have done by contemplation, and perhaps more.

13. There are people, some of whom I have known, whose minds and imaginations are so active as to fancy they see whatever they think about, which is very dangerous.[22] Perhaps I may treat of this later on, but cannot do so now. I have dwelt at length on this mansion, as I believe it to be the one most souls enter. As the natural is combined with the supernatural, the devil can do more harm here than later on, when God does not leave him so many opportunities. May God be for ever praised ! Amen.

[22] *Found.* ch. viii. 7-8.

THE FIFTH MANSIONS

CHAPTER I.

TREAT OF THE UNION OF THE SOUL WITH GOD IN
HOW TO BE SURE THAT WE ARE NOT DECEIVED IN
THIS MATTER.

*s of the fifth mansions. 2. Contemplation to be striven
3. Physical effects of the prayer of union. 4. Amazement
he intellect. 5. The prayer of union and of quiet contrasted.
Divine and earthly union. 7. Competent directors in these
matters. 8. Proof of union. 9. Assurance left in the soul. 10.
Divine union beyond our power to obtain.*

1. Oh, my sisters, how shall I describe the riches, treasures, and joys contained in the fifth mansions ! Would it not be better to say nothing about them ? They are impossible to depict, nor can the mind conceive, nor any comparisons portray them, all earthly things being too vile to serve the purpose. Send me, O my Lord, light from heaven that I may give some to these Thy servants, some of whom by Thy good will often enjoy these delights, lest the devil in the guise of an angel of light should deceive those whose only desire is to please Thee.

2. I said 'some,' but in reality there are very *few*[1] who never enter this mansion: some more and some less, but most of them may be said at least

[1] *Found.* ch. iv. 8.

to gain admittance into these rooms. I think that certain graces I am about to describe are bestowed on only a few of the nuns, but if the rest only arrive at the portal they receive a great boon from God, for 'many are called, but few are chosen.'[2] All we who wear the holy habit of the Carmelites are called to prayer and contemplation. This was the object of our Order,[3] to this lineage we belong. Our holy Fathers of Mount Carmel sought in perfect solitude and utter contempt of the world for this treasure, this precious pearl,[4] of which we speak, and we are their descendants. How little do most of us care to prepare our souls, that our Lord may reveal this jewel to us! Outwardly we may appear to practise the requisite virtues, but we have far more to do than this before it is possible to attain to contemplation, to gain which we should neglect no means, either small or great. Rouse yourselves, my sisters, and since some foretaste of heaven may be had on earth, beg our Lord to give us grace not to miss it through our own fault. Ask Him to show us where to find it—ask Him to give us strength of soul to dig until we find this hidden treasure, which lies buried within our hearts, as I wish to show you if it please God to enable me. I said 'strength of soul,' that you might understand that strength of body is not indispensable when our Lord God chooses to withhold it. He makes it impossible for no one to gain these riches,

[2] St. Matt. xx. 16: 'Multi enim sunt vocati, pauci vero electi.'
[3] Maneant singuli in cellulis suis, vel juxta eas, die ac nocte in lege Domini meditantes et in orationibus vigilantes.' (*Carmelite Rule*).
[4] St. Matt. xiii. 46.

but is content that each should do his best. Blessed be so just a God!

3. But, daughters, if you would purchase this treasure of which we are speaking, God would have you keep back nothing from Him, little or great. He will have it all;[5] in proportion to what you know you have given will your reward be great or small. There is no more certain sign whether or not we have reached the prayer of union. Do not imagine that this state of prayer is, like the one preceding it, a sort of drowsiness (I call it 'drowsiness' because the soul seems to slumber, being neither quite asleep nor wholly awake). In the prayer of union the soul is asleep, fast asleep, as regards the world and itself: in fact, during the short time this state lasts it is deprived of all feeling whatever, being unable to think on any subject, even if it wished. No effort is needed here to suspend the thoughts: if the soul can love—it knows not how, nor whom it loves, nor what it desires. In fact, it has died entirely to this world, to live more truly than ever in God. This is a delicious death, for the soul is deprived of the faculties it exercised while in the body:[6] delicious because, (although not really the case), it seems to have left its mortal covering to abide more entirely in God. So completely does this take place, that I know not whether the body retains sufficient life to continue breathing; on

---

[5] 'The reason why there are so few contemplatives is that there are so few persons who wholly withdraw themselves from transitory and created things' (*Imitation*, bk. iii. ch. xxxi. 1). See also *Way of Perf.* ch, xvi. 5. *Life*, ch. xi. 2-4; xxii. 18, 19.

[6] *Way of Perf.* ch. xxv. 1. *Life*, ch. xvi. *Rel.* I. i; viii. 7.

consideration, I believe it does not; at any rate, if it still breathes, it does so unconsciously.

4. The mind entirely concentrates itself on trying to understand what is happening, which is beyond its power; it is so astounded that, if consciousness is not completely lost, at least no movement is possible: the person may be compared to one who falls into a dead faint with dismay.[7]

5. Oh, mighty secrets of God! Never should I weary of trying to explain them if I thought it possible to succeed! I would write a thousand foolish things that one might be to the point, if only it might make us praise God more. I said this prayer produced no drowsiness in the mind; on the other hand, in the prayer (of quiet) described in the last mansion, until the soul has gained much experience it doubts what really happened to it. 'Was it nothing but fancy, or was it a sleep? Did it come from God or from the devil, disguised as an angel of light?' The mind feels a thousand misgivings, and well for it that it should, because, at I said, nature may sometimes deceive us in this case. Although there is little chance of the poisonous reptiles entering here, yet agile little lizards will try to slip in, though they can do no harm, especially if they remain unnoticed. These, as I said, are trivial fancies of the imagination, which are often very troublesome. However active these small lizards may be, they cannot enter the fifth mansion, for neither the imagination, the understanding, nor the memory has power to hinder the graces bestowed on it.

[7] *Life*, ch. xvii. 2.

6. I dare venture to assert that, if this is genuine union with God, the devil cannot interfere nor do any harm, for His Majesty is so joined and united with the essence of the soul, that the evil one dare not approach, nor can he even understand this mystery. This is certain, for it is said that the devil does not know our thoughts, much less can he penetrate a secret so profound that God does not reveal it even to us.[8] Oh, blessed state, in which this cursed one cannot injure us! What riches we receive while God so works in us that neither we ourselves nor any one else can impede Him! What will He not bestow, Who is so eager to give, and Who can give us all He desires! You may perhaps have been puzzled at my saying 'if this is genuine union with God,' as if there might be other unions. There are indeed—not with God, but with vanities —when the devil transports the soul passionately addicted to them, but the union differs from that which is divine and the mind misses the delight and satisfaction, peace and happiness of divine union. These heavenly consolations are above all earthly joys, pleasure, and satisfaction. As great a difference exists between their origin and that of worldly pleasures as between their opposite effects, as you know by experience.

7. I said somewhere[9] that the one seems only to touch the surface of the body, while the other penetrates to the very marrow: I believe this is

---

[8] According to St. Thomas, angels—whether good or bad—do not know the thoughts of man unless they become manifest by some exterior sign. S. Theol. I. q. lvii. art. 4. See also St. John of the Cross, *Dark Night*, bk. II, ch. xxiii. 2, 5.

[9] Mansion iv. ch. i. 5.

corre&, and I cannot express myself better. I fancy
that you are not yet satisfied on this question, but
are afraid of deception, for spiritual matters are
very hard to explain. Enough, however, has been
said for those who have received this grace, as the
difference between divine union and any other is
very striking. However, I will give you a clear
proof which cannot mislead you, nor leave any
doubt whether the favour comes from God or no.
His Majesty brought it back to my memory this
very day; it appears to me to be an unmistakable
sign. In difficult questions, although I think I understand them and am speaking the truth, I always
say 'it appears to me'; for, in case my opinion is
wrong, I am most willing to submit to the judgment of theologians. Although they may not have
had personal experience in such matters, yet in
some way I do not understand, God Who sets
them to give light to His Church enables them to
recognize the truth when it is put before them.
If they are not thoughtless and indevout, but
servants of God, they are never dismayed at His
mighty works, knowing perfectly well that it is in
His power to perform far greater wonders. If some
of the marvels told are new to them, yet they
have read of others of the same kind, showing the
former to be possible. I have had great experience
as to this and have also met with timid, half-in-
structed people whose ignorance has cost me very
dear.[10] I am convinced that those who refuse to
believe that God can do far more than this, and
that He is pleased now, as in the past, to commu-

[10] *Life*, ch. viii. 15.

nicate Himself to His creatures, shut fast their hearts against receiving such favours themselves. Do not imitate them, sisters: be convinced that it is possible for God to perform still greater wonders. Do not concern yourselves as to whether those who receive these graces are good or wicked; as I said, He knows best and it is no business of yours: you should serve Him with a single heart and with humility, and should praise Him for His works and wonders."

8. Let us now speak of the sign which proves the prayer of union to have been genuine. As you have seen, God then deprives the soul of all its senses that He may the better imprint in it true wisdom: it neither sees, hears, nor understands anything while this state lasts, which is never more than a very brief time;" it appears to the soul to be much shorter than it really is. God visits the soul in a manner which prevents its doubting, on returning to itself, that it dwelt in Him and that He was within it, and so firmly is it convinced of this truth that, although years may pass before this favour recurs, the soul can never forget it nor doubt the fact," setting aside the effects left by this prayer, to which I will refer later on. The conviction felt by the soul is the main point.

9. But, you may ask, how can a person who is incapable of sight and hearing see " or know these

---

[11] *Life*, ch. xviii. 16.

[12] *Life*, ch. xx. 13, 24.

[13] Philippus a SS. Trinitate, *l.c.*, pars iii. tr. i. disc. iv. art, 2, where he adds some further signs. Anton. a Sp. S., *l.c.*, tract. i. nn. 116 and 117.

[14] 'The soul does not see the good Master who teaches it, although

things? I do not say that she saw it at the time, but that she perceives it clearly afterwards, not by any vision but by a certitude which remains in the heart which God alone could give. I know of some one who was unaware of God's being in all things by presence, power and essence, yet was firmly convinced of it by a divine favour of this sort.[15] She asked an ill-instructed priest of the kind I mentioned to tell her in what way God dwelt within us: he was as ignorant on the subject as she had been before our Lord revealed to her the truth, and answered that the Almighty was only present in us by grace.[16] Yet so strong was her

clearly conscious of His presence.' (*Concept.* ch. iv. 3.)

[15] 'There are three ways in which God is present in the soul. The first is His presence in essence, not in holy souls only, but in wretched and sinful souls as well, and also in all created things; for it is by this presence that He gives life and being, and were it withdrawn at once all things would return to nothing. This presence never fails in the soul. The second is His presence by grace, whereby He dwells in the soul, pleased and satisfied with it. This presence is not in all souls; for those who fall into mortal sin lose it, and no soul can know in a natural way whether it has it or not. The third is His presence by spiritual affection. God is wont to show His presence in many devout souls in divers ways, in refreshment, joy and gladness.' (St. John of the Cross, *Spiritual Canticle*, stanza xi. 2.)

'In every soul, even that of the greatest sinner in the world, God dwells and is substantially present. This way of union or presence of God, in the order of nature, subsists between Him and all His creatures; by this He preserves them in being, and if He withdraws it they immediately perish and cease to be. And so, when I speak of the union of the soul with God, I do not mean this substantial presence which is in every creature, but that union and transformation of the soul in God by love which is only then accomplished when there subsists the likeness which love begets.' (St. John of the Cross, *Ascent*, bk. ii. ch. v. 3.)

Fr. Gracian, *Peregrinación de Anastasio* (Burgos, 1905), p. 171.

[16] *Life*, ch. xviii. 20. *Rel.* ix. 17; xi. 8. St. Teresa was so deeply impressed by the ignorance of this priest that she very frequently referred to it.

conviction of the truth learnt during her prayer that she did not believe him and questioned other spiritual persons on the subject, who confirmed her in the true doctrine, much to her joy. Do not mistake and imagine that this certainty of God's having visited the soul concerns any corporal presence such as that of our Lord Jesus Christ Who dwells in the Blessed Sacrament, although we do not see Him: it relates solely to the Divinity. If we did not see it, how can we feel so sure of it? That I do not know: it is the work of the Almighty and I am certain that what I say is the fact. I maintain that a soul which does not feel this assurance has not been united to God entirely, but only by one of its powers, or has received one of the many other favours God is accustomed to bestow on men. In all such matters we must not seek to know how things happened: our understanding could not grasp them, therefore why trouble ourselves on the subject? It is enough to know that it is He, the all-powerful God, Who has performed the work. We can do nothing on our own part to gain this favour; it comes from God alone; therefore let us not strive to understand it.

10. Concerning my words: 'We can do nothing on our own part,' I was struck by the words of the Bride in the Canticles, which you will remember to have heard: 'The King brought me into the cellar of wine,'[17] (or 'placed me' I think she says): she does not say she went of her own accord,

---

[17] *Cant.* i. 3 : 'Introduxit me rex in cellaria sua.' *Castle*, M. v. ch. ii. 11. *Way of Perf.* ch. xviii. 1. *Concep.* ch. iv. 4-8 ; v. 5 ; vi. 7 ; vii. 2-5. *Life*, ch. xviii. 17.

although telling us how she wandered up and down seeking her Beloved.[18] I think the prayer of union is the 'cellar' in which our Lord places us when and how He chooses, but we cannot enter it through any effort of our own. His Majesty alone can bring us there and come into the centre of our souls. In order to declare His wondrous works more clearly, He will leave us no share in them except complete conformity of our wills to His and abandonment of all things: He does not require the faculties or senses to open the door to Him; they are all asleep. He enters the innermost depths of our souls without a door, as He entered the room where the disciples sat, saying 'Pax vobis,'[19] and as He emerged from the sepulchre without removing the stone that closed the entrance. You will see farther on, in the seventh mansion, far better than here, how God makes the soul enjoy His presence in its very centre. O daughters, what wonders shall we see, if we keep ever before our eyes our own baseness and frailty and recognize how unworthy we are to be the handmaids of so great a Lord, Whose marvels are beyond our comprehension! May He be for ever praised! Amen.

[18] *Cant.* iii. 2: 'Per vicos et plateas quæram quem diligit anima mea.'
[19] St. John, xx. 19.

CHAPTER II.

1. You may imagine that there is no more left to
be described of the contents of this mansion, but a
great deal remains to be told, for as I said, it contains
favours of various degrees. I think there is nothing
to add about the prayer of union, but when the
soul on which God bestows this grace disposes
itself for their reception, I could tell you much
about the marvels our Lord works in it. I will describe some of them in my own way, also the state
in which they leave the soul, and will use a suitable
comparison to elucidate the matter, explaining that
though we can take no active part in this work of
God within us,[1] yet we may do much to prepare
ourselves to receive this grace. You have heard
how wonderfully silk is made—in a way such as
God alone could plan—how it all comes from an
egg resembling a tiny pepper-corn. Not having
seen it myself, I only know of it by hearsay, so if the
facts are inaccurate the fault will not be mine.
When, in the warm weather, the mulberry trees

[1] *Way of Perf.* ch. **xxv.** 3.

129

come into leaf, the little egg which was lifeless before its food was ready, begins to live. The caterpillar nourishes itself upon the mulberry leaves until, when it has grown large, people place near it small twigs upon which, of its own accord, it spins silk from its tiny mouth until it has made a narrow little cocoon in which it buries itself. Then this large and ugly worm leaves the cocoon as a lovely little white butterfly.

2. If we had not seen this but had only heard of it as an old legend, who could believe it? Could we persuade ourselves that insects so utterly without the use of reason as a silkworm or a bee would work with such industry and skill in our service that the poor little silkworm loses its life over the task? This would suffice for a short meditation, sisters, without my adding more, for you may learn from it the wonders and the wisdom of God. How if we knew the properties of all things? It is most profitable to ponder over the grandeurs of creation and to exult in being the brides of such a wise and mighty King.

3. Let us return to our subject. The silkworm symbolizes the soul which begins to live when, kindled by the Holy Spirit, it commences using the ordinary aids given by God to all, and applies the remedies left by Him in His Church, such as regular confession, religious books, and sermons; these are the cure for a soul dead in its negligence and sins and liable to fall into temptation. Then it comes to life and continues nourishing itself on this food and on devout meditation until it has attained full vigour, which is the essential point,

for I attach no importance to the rest. When the silkworm is full-grown as I told you in the first part of this chapter, it begins to spin silk and to build the house wherein it must die. By this house, when speaking of the soul, I mean Christ. I think I read or heard somewhere, either that our life is hid in Christ, or in God (which means the same thing) or that Christ is our life.[2] It makes little difference to my meaning which of these quotations is correct.

4. This shows, my daughters, how much, by God's grace, we can do, by preparing this home for ourselves, towards making Him our dwelling-place as He is in the prayer of union. You will suppose that I mean we can take away from or add something to God when I say that He is our home, and that we can make this home and dwell in it by our own power. Indeed we can: though we can neither deprive God of anything nor add aught to Him, yet we can take away from and add to ourselves, like the silkworms. The little we can do will hardly have been accomplished when this insignificant work of ours, which amounts to nothing at all, will be united by God to His greatness and thus enhanced with such immense value that our Lord Himself will be the reward of our toil. Although He has had the greatest share in it, He will join our trifling pains to the bitter sufferings He endured for us and make them one.

5. Forward then, my daughters! hasten over your work and build the little cocoon. Let us renounce

[2] Col. iii. 3: 'Vita vestra est abscondita cum Christo in Deo.' Gal. ii. 20: 'Vivo autem, jam non ego; vivit vero in me Christus.'

self-love and self-will,[3] care for nothing earthly, do penance, pray, mortify ourselves, be obedient, and perform all the other good works of which you know. Act up to your light; you have been taught your duties. Die! die as the silkworm does when it has fulfilled the office of its creation, and you will see God and be immersed in His greatness, as the little silkworm is enveloped in its cocoon. Understand that when I say 'you will see God,' I mean in the manner described, in which He manifests Himself in this kind of union.

6. Now let us see what becomes of the 'silkworm,' for all I have been saying leads to this. As soon as, by means of this prayer, the soul has become entirely dead to the world, it comes forth like a lovely little white butterfly![4] Oh, how great God is! How beautiful is the soul after having been immersed in God's grandeur and united closely to Him for but a short time! Indeed, I do not think it is ever as long as half an hour.[5] Truly, the spirit does not recognize itself, being as different from what it was as is the white butterfly from the repulsive caterpillar. It does not know how it can have merited so great a good, or rather, whence this grace came[6] which it well knows it merits not. The soul desires to praise our Lord God and longs to sacrifice itself and die a thousand deaths for Him. It feels an unconquerable desire for great

[3] *Way of Perf.* ch. xxxi. 11.

[4] St. Teresa must have been thinking of this simile when she chose 'butterflies' as the pseudonym for her nuns in her letters at the time when she was obliged to be cautious on account of the troubles of the Reform.

[5] *Life*, ch. xviii. 16.   [6] *Life*, ch. xviii. 5-7.

crosses and would like to perform the most severe penances; it sighs for solitude and would have all men know God, while it is bitterly grieved at seeing them offend Him. These matters will be described more fully in the next mansion; there they are of the same nature, yet in a more advanced state the effects are far stronger, because, as I told you, if, after the soul has received these favours, it strives to make still farther progress, it will experience great things. Oh, to see the restlessness of this charming little butterfly, although never in its life has it been more tranquil and at peace! May God be praised! It knows not where to stay nor take its rest; everything on earth disgusts it after what it has experienced, particularly when God has often given it this wine which leaves fresh graces behind it at every draught.

7. It despises the work it did while yet a caterpillar —the slow weaving of its cocoon thread by thread —its wings have grown and it can fly; could it be content to crawl? All that it can do for God seems nothing to the soul compared with its desire. It no longer wonders at what the saints bore for Him, knowing by experience how our Lord aids and transforms the soul until it no longer seems the same in character and appearance. Formerly it feared penance, now it is strong: it wanted courage to forsake relations, friends, or possessions: neither its actions, its resolutions, nor separation from those it loved could detach the soul, but rather seemed to increase its fondness. Now it finds even their rightful claims a burden,[7] fearing contact with

7 *Rel.* ix. 11.

them lest it should offend God. It wearies of everything, realizing that no true rest can be found in
creatures.

8. I seem to have enlarged on this subject, yet far
more might be said about it; those who have
received this favour will think I have treated it too
briefly. No wonder this pretty butterfly, estrang-
ed from earthly things, seeks repose elsewhere.
Where can the poor little creature go? It cannot
return to whence it came, for as I told you, that is
not in the soul's power, do what it will, but depends
upon God's pleasure. Alas, what fresh trials begin
to afflict the mind! Who would expect this after
such a sublime grace?[8] In fact in one way or another
we must carry the cross all our lives. If people
told me that ever since attaining to the prayer of
union they had enjoyed constant peace and consolation, I should reply that they could never have
reached that state, but that, at the most, if they had
arrived as far as the last mansion, their emotion
must have been some spiritual satisfaction joined to
physical debility. It might even have been a false
sweetness caused by the devil, who gives peace for
a time only to wage far fiercer war later on. I do
not mean that those who reach this stage possess
no peace; they do so in a very high degree, for their
sorrows, though extremely severe, are so beneficial
and proceed from so good a source as to procure
both peace and happiness.

9. Discontent with this world gives such a painful
longing to quit it that, if the heart finds comfort,

[8] *Way of Perf.* ch. xviii. 1-4. *Castle*, M. vi ch. i. 3, *sqq.* M. vii. ch.
iv. 7.

it is solely from the thought that God wishes it to remain here in banishment. Even this is not enough to reconcile it to fate, for after all the gifts received, it is not yet so entirely surrendered to the will of God as it afterwards becomes. Here, although conformed to His will, the soul feels an unconquerable reluctance to submit, for our Lord has not given it higher grace. During prayer this grief breaks forth in floods of tears, probably from the great pain felt at seeing God offended and at thinking how many souls, both heretics and heathens, are lost eternally, and keenest grief of all, Christians also! The soul realizes the greatness of God's mercy and knows that however wicked men are, they may still repent and be saved; yet it fears that many precipitate themselves into hell.

10. Oh, infinite greatness of God! A few years ago—indeed, perhaps but a few days—this soul thought of nothing but itself. Who has made it feel such tormenting cares? If we tried for many years to obtain such sorrow by means of meditation, we could not succeed.

11. God help me! If for long days and years I considered how great a wrong it is that God should be offended, and that lost souls are His children and my brethren; if I pondered over the dangers of this world and how blessed it would be to leave this wretched life, would not that suffice? No, daughters, the pain would not be the same. For this, by the help of God, we can obtain by such meditation; but it does not seem to penetrate the very depths of our being like the other which

appears to cut the soul to pieces and grind it to powder through no action—even sometimes with no wish—of its own. What is this sorrow, then? Whence does it come? I will tell you. Have you not heard (I quoted the words to you just now, but did not apply to them this meaning)⁹ how the Bride says that God 'brought her into the cellar of wine and set in order charity in her'?¹⁰ This is what happens here. The soul has so entirely yielded itself into His hands and is so subdued by love for Him that it knows or cares for nothing but that God should dispose of it according to His will. I believe that He only bestows this grace on those He takes entirely for His own. He desires that, without knowing how, the spirit should come forth stamped with His seal for indeed it does no more than does the wax when impressed with the signet. It does not mould itself but need only be in a fit condition—soft and pliable; even then it does not soften itself but must merely remain still and submit to the impression.

12. How good Thou art, O God! All is done for us by Thee, Who dost but ask us to give our wills to Thee that we may be plastic as wax in Thy hands. You see, sisters, what God does to this soul so that it may know that it is His. He gives it something of His own—that which His Son possessed when living on earth—He could bestow on greater gift on us. Who could ever have longed more eagerly to leave this life than did Christ?

⁹ Fifth Mansions, ch. i. 10.

¹⁰ *Cant.* ii. 4. 'Introduxit me in cellam vinariam, ordinavit in me caritatem.'

As He said at the Last Supper: 'With desire have I desired'[11] this. O Lord! does not that bitter death Thou art to undergo present itself before Thine eyes in all its pain and horror? 'No, for My ardent love and My desire to save souls are immeasurably stronger than the torments. This deeper sorrow I have suffered and still suffer while living here on earth, makes other pain seem as nothing in comparison.'

13. I have often meditated on this and I know that the torture a friend of mine[12] has felt, and still feels, at seeing our Lord sinned against is so unbearable that she would far rather die than continue in such anguish. Then I thought that if a soul whose charity is so weak compared to that of Christ —indeed, in comparison with His this charity might be said not to exist—experiences this insufferable grief, what must have been the feelings of our Lord Jesus Christ and what must His life have been? for all things were present before His eyes and He was the constant witness of the great offences committed against His Father. I believe without doubt that this pained Him far more than His most sacred Passion. There, at least, He found the end of all His trials, while His agony was allayed by the consolation of gaining our salvation through His death and of proving how He loved His Father by suffering for Him. Thus, people who, urged by fervent love, perform great penances

---

[11] St. Luke xxii. 15: 'Desiderio desideravi hoc pascha manducare vobiscum, antequam patiar.'

[12] This friend is, of course, St. Teresa herself. See *Life*, ch. xiii. 14; xxxii. 9. *Way of Perf.* ch. i. 3. *Castle*, M. vii. ch. i. 5, 6. *Excl.* x. 9.

hardly feel them but want to do still more and count even that as little. What, then, must His Majesty have felt at thus publicly manifesting His perfect obedience to His Father and His love for His brethren? What joy to suffer in doing God's will! Yet I think the constant sight of the many sins committed against God and of the numberless souls on their way to hell must have caused Him such anguish that, had He not been more than man, one day of such torment would have destroyed not only His life but many more lives, had they been His.

CHAPTER III.

THIS CHAPTER CONTINUES THE SAME SUBJECT AND SPEAKS OF ANOTHER KIND OF UNION WHICH THE SOUL CAN OBTAIN WITH THE HELP OF GOD. THE IMPORTANCE OF LOVE OF OUR NEIGHBOUR IN THIS MATTER. THIS IS VERY USEFUL TO READ.

1. Zeal for souls left by divine union. 2. The soul may fall from such a state. 3. How divine union may always be obtained. 4. Union with the will of God the basis of all supernatural union. 5. Advantage of union gained by self-mortification. 6. Defects which hinder this union. 7. Divine union obtained by perfect love of God and our neighbour. 8. Love for God and our neighbour are proportionate. 9. Real and imaginary virtues. 10. Illusionary good resolutions. 11. Works, not feelings, procure union. 12. Fraternal charity will certainly gain this union.

1. LET us now return to our little dove and see what graces God gives it in this state. This implies that the soul endeavours to advance in the service of our Lord and in self-knowledge. If it receives the grace of union and then does no more, thinking itself safe, and so leads a careless life, wandering off the road to heaven (that is, the keeping of the

commandments) it will share the fate of the butterfly that comes from the silkworm, which lays some
eggs that produce more of its kind and then dies
for ever. I say it leaves some eggs, for I believe
God will not allow so great a favour to be lost but
that if the recipient does not profit by it, others
will. For while it keeps to the right path, this soul,
with its ardent desires and great virtues, helps others
and kindles their fervour with its own. Yet even
after having lost this it may still long to benefit
others and delight to make known the mercies
shown by God to those who love and serve Him.[1]

2. I knew a person to whom this happened. Although greatly erring, she longed that others should
profit by the favours God had bestowed on her and
taught the way of prayer to people ignorant of it,
thus helping them immensely. God afterwards
bestowed fresh light upon her; indeed the prayer
of union had not hitherto produced the above effects
in her. How many people there must be to whom
our Lord communicates Himself, who, like Judas,
are called to the Apostleship and made kings by
Him, as was Saul, yet who afterwards lose everything by their own fault! We should learn from
this, sisters, that if we would merit fresh favours
and avoid losing those we already possess, our only
safety lies in obedience and in following the law of
God. This I say, both to those who have received
these graces and to those who have not.

3. In spite of all I have written, there still seems
some difficulty in understanding this mansion. The

---

[1] *Life*, ch. vii. 18. *Way of Perf.* xli. 8.
[2] *Life.* ch. vii. 21.

advantage of entering is so great, that it is well that
none should despair of doing so because God does
not give them the supernatural gifts described
above. With the help of divine grace true union
can always be attained by forcing ourselves to renounce our own will and by following the will of
God in all things.[3]

4. Oh, how many of us affirm that we do this, and
believe we seek nothing else—indeed we would
die for the truth of what we say! If this be the case
I can only declare, as I fancy I did before, and I
shall again and again, that we have already obtained
this grace from God. Therefore we need not wish
for that other delightful union described above, for
its chief value lies in the resignation of our will to
that of God without which it could not be reached.[4]
Oh, how desirable is this union! The happy soul
which has attained it will live in this world and
in the next without care of any sort. No earthly
events can trouble it, unless it should see itself in
danger of losing God or should witness any offence
offered Him. Neither sickness, poverty, nor the loss
of any one by death affect it, except that of persons
useful to the Church of God, for the soul realizes
thoroughly that God's disposal is wiser than its
own desires.

5. You must know that there are different kinds

[3] *Found.* ch. v. 10.   'These shall not attain to the true liberty of a
pure heart, nor to the grace of a delightful familiarity with Me, unless
they first resign themselves and offer themselves a daily sacrifice to Me:
for without this, divine union neither is nor will be obtained.' (*Imitation*,
book iii. ch. xxxvii. 4.)

[4] Philippus a SS. Trinitate, *l.c.*, p. iii. tr. 1. disc. ii. art. 4.

of sorrow: there are both griefs and joys rising
from an impulse of nature or from a charity which
makes us pity our neighbour, like that felt by our
Saviour when He raised Lazarus from the dead.[5]
These feelings do not destroy union with the will
of God nor do they disturb the soul by a restless,
turbulent, and lasting passion. They soon pass away,
for as I said of sweetness in prayer,[6] they do not
affect the depths of the soul but only its senses and
faculties. They are found in the former mansions,
but do not enter the last of all. Is it necessary, in
order to attain to this kind of divine union, for the
powers of the soul to be suspended? No; God has
many ways of enriching the soul and bringing it
to these mansions besides what might be called a
'short cut.' But, be sure of this, my daughters: in
any case the silkworm must die and it will cost
you more in this way. In the former manner this
death is facilitated by finding ourselves introduced
into a new life; here, on the contrary, we must
give ourselves the death-blow. I own that the
work will be much harder, but then it will be of
higher value so that your reward will be greater
if you come forth victorious;[7] yet there is no doubt
it is possible for you to attain this true union with
the will of God.

6. This is the union I have longed for all my life
and that I beg our Lord to grant me; it is the most
certain and the safest. But alas, how few of us ever

---

[5] St. John xi. 35, 36: 'Et lacrymatus est Jesus. Dixerunt ergo Judæi:
Ecce quomodo amabat eum.'

[6] Fourth Mansions, ch. i. 5.   Fifth Mansions, ch. i. 7.

[7] *Way of Perf.* ch. xvii. 2.

obtain it ! Those who are careful not to offend God, and who enter the religious state, think there is nothing more to do. How many maggots remain in hiding until, like the worm which gnawed at Jonas's ivy,[8] they have destroyed our virtues. These pests are such evils as self-love, self-esteem, rash judgment of others even in small matters, and a want of charity in not loving our neighbour quite as much as ourselves. Although perforce we satisfy our obligations sufficiently to avoid sin, yet we fall far short of what must be done in order to obtain perfect union with the will of God.

7. What do you think, daughters, is His will? That we may become quite perfect and so be made one with Him and with His Father as He prayed we might be.[9] Observe, then, what is wanting in us to obtain this. I assure you it is most painful for me to write on this subject, for I see how far I am, through my own fault, from having attained perfection. There is no need for us to receive special consolations from God in order to arrive at conformity with His will; He has done enough in giving us His Son to teach the way. This does not mean that we must so submit to the will of God as not to sorrow at such troubles as the death of a father or brother, or that we must bear crosses

---

[8] Jonas iv. 6, 7: 'And the Lord God prepared an ivy, and it came up over the head of Jonas, to be a shadow over his head, and to cover him, for he was fatigued; and Jonas was exceeding glad of the ivy. But God prepared a worm, when the morning arose on the following day: and it struck the ivy and it withered.'

[9] St. John xvii. 22, 23: 'Ut sint unum, sicut et nos unum sumus. Ego in eis, et tu in me: ut sint consummati in unum.' *Way of Perf.* ch. xxxii. 6.

and sickness with joy.[10] This is well, but it sometimes comes from common sense which, as we cannot help ourselves, makes a virtue of necessity. How
often the great wisdom of the heathen philosophers
led them to act thus in trials of this kind! Our
Lord asks but two things of us: love for Him and
for our neighbour: these are what we must strive
to obtain. If we practise both these virtues perfectly we shall be doing His will and so shall be
united to Him. But, as I said, we are very far from
obeying and serving our great Master perfectly in
these two matters: may His Majesty give us the
grace to merit union with Him; it is in our power
to gain it if we will.

8. I think the most certain sign that we keep these
two commandments is that we have a genuine love
for others. We cannot know whether we love God
although there may be strong reasons for thinking
so, but there can be no doubt about whether we
love our neighbour or no.[11] Be sure that in proportion as you advance in fraternal charity, you are
increasing in your love of God,[12] for His Majesty
bears so tender an affection for us that I cannot
doubt He will repay our love for others by aug-
menting, in a thousand different ways, that which
we bear for Him. We should watch most carefully
over ourselves in this matter, for if we are faultless
on this point we have done all. I believe human
nature is so evil that we could not feel a perfect

[10] *Way of Perf.* ch. ix. 1, 2.

[11] 1 St. John iv. 20: 'Qui enim non diligit fratrem suum quem
videt, Deum quem non videt quomodo potest diligere?'

[12] *Way of Perf.* ch. xviii. 5.

charity for our neighbour unless it were rooted in
the love of God.

9. In this most important matter, sisters, we should
be most vigilant in little things, taking no notice
of the great works we plan during prayer which
we imagine that we would perform for other people,
even perhaps for the sake of saving a single soul. If
our actions afterwards belie these grand schemes,
there is no reason to imagine that we should do
anything of the sort. I say the same of humility and
the other virtues. The devil's wiles are many; he
would turn hell upside down a thousand times to
make us think ourselves better than we are. He
has good reason for it, for such fancies are most
injurious; sham virtues springing from this root
are always accompanied by a vainglory never found
in those of divine origin, which are free from pride.

10. It is amusing to see souls who, while they are
at prayer, fancy they are willing to be despised
and publicly insulted for the love of God, yet
afterwards do all they can to hide their small defects;
if any one unjustly accuses them of a fault, God
deliver us from their outcries! Let those who cannot bear such things take no notice of the splendid
plans they made when alone, which could have
been no genuine determination of the will but only
some trick of the imagination, or the results would
have been very different. The devil assaults and
deceives people in this way, often doing great harm
to women and others too ignorant to understand
the difference between the powers of the soul and
the imagination, and a thousand other matters of

the sort. O sisters! how easy it is to know which of you have attained to a sincere love of your neighbour, and which of you are far from it. If you knew the importance of this virtue, your only care would be to gain it.

11. When I see people very anxious to know what sort of prayer they practise, covering their faces and afraid to move or think lest they should lose any slight tenderness and devotion they feel, I know how little they understand how to attain union with God since they think it consists in such things as these. No, sisters, no; our Lord expects *works* from us. If you see a sick sister whom you can relieve,[13] never fear losing your devotion; compassionate her; if she is in pain, feel for it as if it were your own and, when there is need, fast so that she may eat, not so much for her sake as because you know your Lord asks it of you. This is the true union of our will with the will of God. If some one else is well spoken of, be more pleased than if it were yourself; this is easy enough, for if you were really humble it would vex you to be praised. It is a great good to rejoice at your sister's virtues being known and to feel as sorry for the fault you see in her as if it were yours, hiding it from the sight of others.

12. I have often spoken on this subject elsewhere,[14] because, my sisters, if we fail in this I know that all is lost: please God this may never be our case. If you possess fraternal charity, I assure you that you will certainly obtain the union I have described.

[13] *Way of Perf.* ch. vii. 4.
[14] *Way of Perf.* ch. iv. 3; vii. 4.

If you are conscious that you are wanting in this charity, although you may feel devotion and sweetness and a short absorption in the prayer of quiet (which makes you think you have attained to union with God), believe me you have not yet reached it. Beg our Lord to grant you perfect love for your neighbour, and leave the rest to Him. He will give you more than you know how to desire if you constrain yourselves and strive with all your power to gain it, forcing your will as far as possible to comply in all things with your sisters' wishes although you may sometimes forfeit your own rights by so doing. Forget your self-interests for theirs, however much nature may rebel; when opportunity occurs take some burden upon yourself to ease your neighbour of it. Do not fancy it will cost you nothing and that you will find it all done for you: think what the love He bore for us cost our Spouse, Who to free us from death, Himself suffered the most painful death of all—the death of the Cross.

CHAPTER IV.

1. You appear anxious to know what has become of the little dove and where she obtains rest, since obviously she can find it neither in spiritual consolations nor in earthly pleasures but takes a higher flight. I cannot tell you until we come to the last mansion: God grant I may remember or have leisure to write it. It is nearly five months since I began this work, and as my head is too weak to read it again, no doubt it will be very disconnected and full of repetitions: however, as it is only for my sisters, that will matter little. Yet I should like to express myself more fully about the prayer of union and will make use, to the best of my scanty wits, of a comparison. Later on we will speak of the little butterfly, which is never still, for it can find no true repose, yet always fertile, doing good both to itself and others.[1] You have often heard that God spiritually espouses souls: may He be

---

[1] Compare: 'habebit fructum in respectione animarum sanctarum' (*Breviar. Rom. Ant. ad Laudes de Com. Virg.*); 'quasi apis argumentosa Domino deservisti' (*Ibid.* Feast of St. Cæcilia.)

praised for His mercy in thus humbling Himself
so utterly. Though but a homely comparison, yet
I can find nothing better to express my meaning
than the Sacrament of Matrimony although the
two things are very different. In divine union
everything is spiritual and far removed from anything corporal, all the joys our Lord gives and the
mutual delight felt in it being celestial and very
unlike human marriage, which it excels a thousand
times. Here all is love united to love; its operations
are more pure, refined, and sweet than can be described, though our Lord knows how to make the
soul sensible of them.

2. I think this union does not attain as far as the
spiritual espousals but resembles the preliminaries
that take place when two people are contemplating
a betrothal. Their suitability and willingness for
the alliance are first discussed; then they may be
allowed to see one another sometimes so as to come
to a decision. Thus it is in the spiritual espousals:
when the preliminary agreement has been made
and the soul thoroughly understands what great
advantages she will gain, having resolved to fulfil
the will of her Spouse in all things and to do all she
can to please Him, His Majesty Who knows well
whether this is so in reality, wishes in return to
gratify His bride. He therefore bestows this favour
upon her, visits her and draws her into His presence,
as He wishes her to know Him better. We might
compare the prayer of union to a visit, for it lasts
but a very little while.[2] There is no longer any

[2] *Life*, ch. xviii. 16.

question of deliberation, but the soul in a secret manner sees to what a Bridegroom it is betrothed; the senses and faculties could not, in a thousand years, gain the knowledge thus imparted in a very short time. The Spouse, being Who He is, leaves the soul far more deserving of completing the espousals, as we may call them; the enamoured soul in its love for Him makes every effort to prevent their being frustrated. Should it grow neglectful and set its affections on anything except our Lord, it will forfeit everything: this loss is as great as are the favours the soul has continually received, which are precious beyond description.[3]

3. O Christian souls! you whom God has brought thus far! I implore you for His dear sake not to grow careless, but to avoid all occasions of sin; you are not strong enough yet to undergo temptation, as you will be after the espousals which take place in the next mansion. Here the betrothed are, as they say, only acquainted by sight,[4] and the devil will spare no pains to oppose and prevent their nuptials. Afterwards, when he sees the Bride is wholly given to her Bridegroom, he is afraid to interfere, having learnt by experience that if he molests her, while he loses much, she will gain greatly in merit.

4. I can assure you, my daughters,[5] that I have known people far advanced in the spiritual life who had reached this state of prayer yet whom the devil reclaimed by his subtlety and wiles: as I

[3] *Way of Perf.* ch. xxxi. 10.

[4] Phil. a SS. Trinit. *l.c.* p. iii. tract. i. disc. ii. art. 2.

[5] Contrast with this paragraph what the Saint says in her *Life*, ch. xix. § 8.

have often said, all hell leagues together against such souls because the loss of one of them entails the perdition of many more, as Satan is well aware. If we considered how many men God draws to Himself by means of one, we should praise Him fervently. Think of the multitudes converted by the martyrs or by one young maiden like St. Ursula! Again, of how many victims the evil one was deprived by St. Dominic, St. Francis, and other founders of religious orders. How many more he loses, even now, through Father Ignatius [Loyola], who founded the Company [of Jesus]! As we read their lives, we learn that they received such graces from God. How was this great good done except by their efforts not to forfeit, through any fault of theirs, these divine espousals? Oh, my daughters, how willing our Lord is to grant us the same graces! In fact, there is even more urgent need now for persons to prepare for such favours, since there are fewer who care for His honour. We love ourselves too much and are too prudent to give up any of our rights. What a deception! May God in His mercy give us light, lest we sink into such darkness.

5. You may question or be in doubt on two points. Firstly: if the soul is entirely united with the will of God, as I have stated, how can it be deceived, since it ever seeks to follow His pleasure? Secondly, how can the devil enter and work such havoc as to destroy your soul while you are so utterly withdrawn from the world and constantly frequent the Sacraments?[6] At the same time you enjoy the society

[6] *Life*, ch. xxxvi. 26 ; xxxix. 14.   *Found.* ch. i. 1-4.

of angels (as we might call them) and by the mercy of God you desire nothing but to serve and please Him in all things?[7] It is not surprising that people in the world should run such risks. I admit you have the right to say this, for God has shown us signal mercy; but, as I said above, knowing as I do that Judas was amongst the Apostles and that he held constant intercourse with God Himself, to Whose words he listened, I learn that the state of religion does not make us safe.

6. To your first question I reply that doubtless if such a soul is always faithful to the will of God, it cannot be lost; the evil one, however, comes with his keen subtlety and, under the pretext of good, leads it astray in some trivial matter and causes it to commit small defects which he makes it believe are harmless. Thus, little by little, the reason is obscured and the will is weakened while the devil fosters his victim's self-love, until, by degrees, he succeeds in withdrawing it from union with the will of God and makes it follow its own will.

7. The answer to your first inquiry will serve for the second. No enclosure can be too strict for Satan to enter nor any desert too remote for him to visit. Besides, God may permit him to tempt the soul to prove its virtue; for as He intends it to enlighten others, it is better for it to fail in the beginning than when it might do them great harm.

8. We must beg God constantly in our prayers to uphold us by His hand; we should keep ever in our minds the truth that if He leaves us, most

[7] *Way of Perf.* ch. i. 2 ; xiii. 5.   *Found.* ch. i. 3.

certainly we shall fall at once into the abyss, for
we must never be so foolish as to trust in ourselves.
After this I think the greatest safeguard is to be very
careful and to watch how we advance in virtue; we
must notice whether we are making progress or
falling back in it, especially as regards the love of
our neighbour, the desire to be thought the least
of all and how we perform our ordinary, everyday
duties. If we attend to this and beg Our Lord to
enlighten us, we shall at once perceive our gain
or loss.

9. Do not suppose that after advancing the soul
to such a state God abandons it so easily that it is
light work for the devil to regain it. When His
Majesty sees it leaving Him, He feels the loss so
keenly that He gives it in many a way a thousand
secret warnings which reveal to it the hidden
danger.[8]

10. In conclusion, let us strive to make constant
progress: we ought to feel great alarm if we do
not find ourselves advancing, for without doubt
the evil one must be planning to injure us in some
way; it is impossible for a soul that has come to
this state not to go still farther, for love is never
idle. Therefore it is a very bad sign when one
comes to a stand-still in virtue. She who aspires
to become the spouse of God Himself, and has
treated with His Majesty and come to such an
understanding with Him, must not leave off and
go to sleep.[9]

11. To show you, my daughters, how Christ treats
the souls He takes for His brides, I will now speak

of the sixth mansions. You will then see how little in comparison is all that we can do or suffer in His service to prepare ourselves for the reception of such immense favours. Perhaps our Lord decreed that I should write this in order that the knowledge of the great reward to come, and of His infinite mercy in seeking to give and to manifest Himself to such worms as we are, might make us forget our wretched, petty, earthly pleasures and run on our way with eyes fixed on His grandeur, inflamed with love for Him.

12. May He enable me to explain some of these difficult matters; if our Lord and the Holy Ghost do not guide my pen, I know the task will prove impossible. I beg Him to prevent my saying anything unless it will profit you. His Majesty knows that, as far as I can judge, I have no other wish but that His Name may be glorified and that we may strive to serve a Lord Who thus recompenses our efforts even in this world. What, then, will be our joy in heaven where it will be continuous, without the interruptions, labours, and dangers of this tempestuous sea of life? Were it not for the fear of losing or offending Him, we should wish to live until the end of the world [10] in order to work for so great a God—our Lord and our Spouse. May His Majesty enable us to render Him some service free from the many faults we always commit, even in good works! Amen.

[10] *Rel.* ix. 19.

THE SIXTH MANSIONS

CHAPTER I.

THIS CHAPTER SHOWS HOW, WHEN GOD BESTOWS GREATER FAVOURS ON THE SOUL, IT SUFFERS MORE SEVERE AFFLICTIONS. SOME OF THE LATTER ARE DESCRIBED AND DIRECTIONS HOW TO BEAR THEM GIVEN TO THE DWELLERS IN THIS MANSION. THIS CHAPTER IS USEFUL FOR THOSE SUFFERING INTERIOR TRIALS.

1. Love kindled by divine favours. 2. Our Lord excites the soul's longings. 3. Courage needed to reach the last mansions. 4. Trials accompanying divine favours. 5. Outcry raised against souls striving for perfection. 6. St. Teresa's personal experience of this. 7. Praise distasteful to an enlightened soul. 8. This changes to indifference. 9. Humility of such souls. 10. Their zeal for God's glory. 11. Perfect and final indifference to praise or blame. 12. Love of enemies. 13. Bodily sufferings. 14. St. Teresa's physical ills. 15. A timorous confessor. 16. Anxiety on account of past sins. 17. Fears and aridity. 18. Scruples and fears raised by the devil. 19. Bewilderment of the soul. 20. God alone relieves these troubles. 21. Human weakness. 22. Earthly consolations are of no avail. 23. Prayer gives no comfort at such a time. 24. Remedies for these interior trials. 25. Trials caused by the devil. 26. Other afflictions. 27. Preparatory to entering the seventh mansions.

1. By the aid of the Holy Ghost I am now about to treat of the sixth mansions, where the soul, wounded with love for its Spouse, sighs more than ever for solitude, withdrawing as far as the duties of its state permit from all that can interrupt it.

The sight it has enjoyed of Him is so deeply imprinted on the spirit that its only desire is to behold Him again. I have already said that,[1] even by the imagination, nothing is seen in this prayer that can be called sight. I speak of it as 'sight' because of the comparison I used.

2. The soul is now determined to take no other Bridegroom than our Lord, but He disregards its desires for its speedy espousals, wishing that these longings should become still more vehement and that this good, which far excels all other benefits, should be purchased at some cost to itself. And although for so great a gain all that we must endure is but a poor price to pay, I assure you, daughters, that this pledge of what is in store for us is needed to inspire us with courage to bear our crosses.

3. O my God, how many troubles both interior and exterior must one suffer before entering the seventh mansions ! Sometimes, while pondering over this I fear that, were they known beforehand, human infirmity could scarcely bear the thought nor resolve to encounter them, however great might appear the gain. If, however, the soul has already reached the seventh mansions, it fears nothing: boldly undertaking to suffer all things for God,[2] it gathers strength from its almost uninterrupted union with Him.

4. I think it would be well to tell you of some of the trials certain to occur in this state. Possibly all souls may not be led in this way, but I think that those who sometimes enjoy such truly heavenly

[1] *Castle*, M. v. ch. i. 9. *Life*, ch. xxviii. 5.
[2] *Life*, ch. xl. 28. *sqq.*

favours cannot be altogether free from some sort of earthly troubles. Therefore, although at first I did not intend to speak on this subject, yet afterwards I thought that it might greatly comfort a soul in this condition if it knew what usually happens to those on whom God bestows graces of this kind, for at the time they really seem to have lost everything.

5. I shall not enumerate these trials in their proper order, but will describe them as they come to my memory, beginning with the least severe. This is an outcry raised against such a person by those amongst whom she lives, and even from others she has nothing to do with but who fancy that at some time in her life they recollect having seen her. They say she wants to pass for a saint, that she goes to extremes in piety to deceive the world and to depreciate people who are better Christians than herself without making such a parade of it. But notice that she does nothing except endeavour to carry out the duties of her state more perfectly. Persons she thought were her friends desert her, making the most bitter remarks of all. They take it much to heart that her soul is ruined—she is manifestly deluded—it is all the devil's work—she will share the fate of so-and-so who was lost through him, and she is leading virtue astray. They cry out that she is deceiving her confessors, and tell them so, citing examples of others who came to ruin in the same way and make a thousand scoffing remarks of the same sort.[3]

[3] The Saint went through all this herself; every detail is taken from her own experience. See *Life*, ch. xxv. 20; xxviii. 20-24; xxx. 6; xxxiii. 2. Anton. a Sp. S. *l.c.* tract. ii. n. 268.

6. I know some one who feared she would be unable to find any priest who would hear her confession, to such a pass did things come; but as it is a long story, I will not stop to tell it now. The worst of it is, these troubles do not blow over but last all her life, for one person warns the other to have nothing to do with people of her kind. You will say that, on the other hand, some speak in her favour. O my daughters, how few think well of her in comparison with the many who hate her!

7. Besides this, praise pains such a soul more than blame because it recognizes clearly that any good it possesses is the gift of God and in no wise its own, seeing that but a short time ago it was weak in virtue and involved in grave sins.⁴ Therefore commendation causes it intolerable suffering, at least at first, although later on, for many reasons, the soul is comparatively indifferent to either.

8. The first is that experience has shown the mind that men are as ready to speak well as ill of others, so it attaches no more importance to the one than to the other. Secondly, our Lord having granted it greater light, it perceives that no good thing in it is its own but is His gift, and becomes oblivious of self, praising God for His graces as if they were found in a third person.

9. The third reason is that, realizing the benefit reaped by others from witnessing graces given it by God, such a one thinks that it is for their profit He causes them to discover in her virtues that do not exist.

⁴ *Life*, ch. xxviii. 19.

10. Fourthly, souls seeking God's honour and glory more than their own are cured of the temptation (which usually besets beginners) of thinking that human praise will cause them the injury they have seen it do to others. Nor do these souls care much for men's contempt if only, by their means, any one should praise God at least once—come what may afterwards.

11. These and other reasons to a certain extent allay the great distress formerly given by human praise which, however, still causes some discomfort unless the soul has become utterly regardless of men's tongues. It is infinitely more grieved at being undeservedly esteemed by the world than by any calumny; and when at last it becomes almost indifferent to praise, it cares still less for censure, which even pleases it and sounds like harmonious music to the ears.

12. This is perfectly true; the soul is rather strengthened than depressed by its trials, experience having taught it the great advantages derived from them. It does not think men offend God by persecuting it, but that He permits them to do so for its greater gain.[5] So strong is this belief that such a person bears a special affection for these people, holding them as truer friends and greater benefactors than those who speak well of her.[6]

13. Our Lord now usually sends severe bodily infirmity. This is a far heavier cross, especially if acute pain is felt: if this is violent, I think it is the

[5] *Rel.* ii. 4.
[6] Anton. a Sp. S. *l.c.* ii. n. 272. *Way of Perf.* ch. xv. 1; xvii. 4. *Found.* ch. xxvii. 19, 20. *Life*, ch. xix. 12; xxxi. 13-17, 25.

hardest of earthly trials. I speak of exterior trials; but corporal pains if of the worst kind enter the interior of our being also, affecting both spirit and body, so that the soul in its anguish knows not what to do with itself and would far rather meet death at once by some quick martyrdom than suffer thus. However, these paroxysms do not last long, for God never sends us more than we can bear and always gives us patience first.

14. Now to speak of other trials and illnesses of many kinds which generally occur to people in this state. I knew some one who, from the time when, forty years ago,[7] our Lord began to bestow on her the favour described, could not affirm with any truth that she had been a single day without pain and other kinds of suffering: I am speaking of physical infirmities besides heavy crosses sent her.[8] True, she had led a wicked life and therefore held these troubles very light in comparison with the hell she had deserved.[9] Our Lord leads those who have offended Him less by some other way, but I should always choose the way of suffering, if only for the sake of imitating our Lord Jesus Christ; though, in fact, it profits us in many other manners. Yet, oh! the rest would seem trifling in comparison could I relate the interior torments met with here, but they are impossible to describe.

15. Let us first speak of the trial of meeting with so timorous and inexperienced a confessor that

---

[7] 'Forty years ago.' The Saint seems to refer to her first experience in the mystical life, which took place during her illness in the winter of 1537-38. See *Life*, ch. iv. 9.

[8] *Life*, ch. iv. 6; v; vi; vii. 18; xi. 23; xxx. 9.

[9] *Ibid.* ch. iii. 6, 7.

nothing seems safe to him; he dreads and suspects everything but the commonplace, especially in a soul in which he detects any imperfection, for he thinks people on whom God bestows such favours must be angels, which is impossible while we live in our bodies.[10]. He at once ascribes everything to the devil or melancholy. As to the latter, I am not surprised; there is so much of it in the world and the evil one works such harm in this way that confessors have the strongest reasons for anxiety and watchfulness about it.

16. The poor soul, beset by the same fears, seeks its confessor as judge, and feels a torture and dismay at his condemnation that can only be realized by those who have experienced it themselves.[11] For one of the severe trials of these souls, especially if they have lived wicked lives, is their belief that God permits them to be deceived in punishment for their sins. While actually receiving these graces they feel secure and cannot but suppose that these favours proceed from the Spirit of God; but this state lasts a very short time, while the remembrance of their misdeeds is ever before them, so that when, as is sure to happen, they discover any faults in themselves, these torturing thoughts return.[12]

17. The soul is quieted for a time when the confessor reassures it although it returns later on to its former apprehensions, but when he augments its fears they become almost unbearable. Especially is this the case when such spiritual dryness ensues

[10] *Life*, ch. xiii. 21-27. *Way of Perf.* ch. v. 1, 2.
[11] *Ibid*, ch. xxx. 15.
[12] *Ibid*, ch. xxxviii. 21. *Rel.* ii. 15.

that the mind feels as if it never had thought of
God nor ever will be able to do so. When men
speak of Him, they seem to be talking of some
person heard of long ago.

18. All this is nothing without the further pain
of thinking we cannot make our confessors understand the case and are deceiving them.[13] Although
such a person may examine her conscience with
the greatest care, and may know that she reveals
even the first movement of her mind to her director,
it does not help her. Her understanding being too
obscure to discern the truth, she believes all that
the imagination, which now has the upper hand,
puts before her mind, besides crediting the falsehoods suggested to her by the devil, whom doubtless our Lord gives leave to tempt her. The evil
spirit even tries to make her think God has rejected
her. Many are the trials which assault this soul,
causing an internal anguish so painful and so intolerable that I can compare it to nothing save that
suffered by the lost in hell, for no comfort can be
found in this tempest of trouble.[14]

19. If the soul seeks for consolation from its confessor, all the demons appear to help him to torment
it more. A confessor who dealt with a person
suffering in this manner thought that her state
must be very dangerous as so many things were
troubling her; therefore, after she had recovered
from her trials, he bade her tell him whenever they

---

[13] *Life*, ch. xxviii. 20 *sqq.*

[14] Anton. a Sp. S. *l.c.* tr. ii. n. 313. On this subject which is commonly called the passive purgation of the intellect, it would be
advisable to consult some good author such as Philippus a SS. Trinitate,
l. c. part. i. tr. iii. disc. iii.-v., especially disc. iv. art. 5, 6.

recurred: however, he found this made matters worse than ever. She lost all control over herself: although she had learnt to read, yet she could no more understand a book in the vulgar tongue than if she had not known the alphabet, for her mind was incapable of acting.[15]

20. In short, there is no other remedy in such a tempest except to wait for the mercy of God Who, unexpectedly, by some casual word or unforeseen circumstance, suddenly dispels all these sorrows; then every cloud of trouble disappears and the mind is left full of light and far happier than before.[16] It praises our Lord God like one who has come out victorious from a dangerous battle, for it was He Who won the victory. The soul is fully conscious that the conquest was not its own as all weapons of self-defence appeared to be in the enemies' hands. Thus it realizes its weakness and how little man can help himself if God forsake him.

21. This truth now needs no demonstration, for past experience has taught the soul its utter incapacity; it realizes the nothingness of human nature and what miserable creatures we are. Although in a state of grace from which it has not fallen—for, in spite of these torments, it has not offended God, nor would it do so for any earthly thing[17]—yet so hidden is this grace, that the sufferer believes that neither now, nor in the past, has she ever possessed the faintest spark of love for God.[18] If at any time she has done good, or if His Majesty ever bestowed

[15] *Life*, ch. xxv. 21.　　　　[16] *Ibid.* ch. xxv. 23.
[17] *Ibid.* ch. xxiv. 3. *Way of Perf.* ch. xli. 5. *Castle*, M. vii. ch. iv. 1.
[18] *Excl.* xvi. 4.

any favours on her, they seem to have been but a dream or a fancy, while her sins stand clearly before her.

22. O Jesus! how sad it is to see a soul thus forsaken, and how little, as I said, can any earthly comfort avail! Do not imagine, sisters, if you are ever brought to such a state, that rich and independent people have more resources than yourselves in these troubles. No, no! to offer such consolations would be like setting all the joys of the world before people condemned to death: far from mitigating, it would increase their torture. So with the souls I spoke of: their comfort must come from above—nothing earthly can help them. This great God wishes us to acknowledge His sovereignty and our own misery—an important point for those who are to advance still farther.

23. What can the poor soul do if such a trial lasts for many days? Prayer makes no difference as far as comforting the heart, which no consolation can enter, nor can the mind even grasp the meaning of the words of vocal prayer: mental prayer is out of the question at such a time, since the faculties are unequal to it. Solitude harms the soul, yet society or conversation is a fresh torment. Strive as the sufferer may to hide it, she is so wearied and out of sorts with all around that she cannot but manifest her condition.

24. How can the soul possibly tell what ails it? Its pains are indescribable; it is wrung with nameless anguish and spiritual suffering. The best remedy for these crosses (I do not mean for gaining deliver-

ance from them, for I know of nothing that will do that, but for enabling one to bear them) is to perform external works of charity and to trust in the mercy of God, which never fails those who hope in Him.'⁹ May He be for ever blessed ! Amen

25. The devils also bring about exterior trials which being more unusual need not be mentioned. They are far less painful, for whatever the demons may do, I believe they never succeed in paralysing the faculties or disturbing the soul in the former manner. In fact, the reason is able to discern that the evil spirits can do no more harm than God permits; and while the mind has not lost its powers, all sufferings are comparatively insignificant.

26. I shall treat of other internal afflictions met with in this mansion when describing the different kinds of prayer and favours bestowed here by our Lord. Although some of these latter pains are harder to endure, as appears by their bodily effects, yet they do not deserve the name of crosses, nor have we the right to call them so. Indeed, they are great graces from God as the soul recognizes amidst its pangs, realizing how far it is from meriting such graces.

27. This severe torture felt by souls just at the entrance of the seventh mansion is accompanied by many other sufferings, some of which I will mention: to speak of them all would be impossible, nor could I portray them because they come from another and far higher source than the rest. If I have succeeded so ill in writing of trials of a lower kind, much less could I treat of the others. May

---

¹⁹ *Life*, ch. xxxi. 27.

God assist me in all things, through the merits of His Son! Amen.

CHAPTER II.

TREATS OF SEVERAL WAYS WHEREBY OUR LORD QUICKENS THE SOUL; THERE APPEARS NO CAUSE FOR ALARM IN THEM ALTHOUGH THEY ARE SIGNAL FAVOURS OF A VERY EXALTED NATURE.

1. Our Lord excites the love of His spouse. 2. The wound of love. 3. The pain it causes. 4. The call of the Bridegroom. 5. Effect on the soul. 6. A spark of the fire of love. 7. The spark dies out. 8. This grace evidently divine. 9. One such wound repays many trials. 10. First reason of immunity from deception. 11. Second and third reasons. 12. The imagination not concerned in it. 13. St. Teresa never alarmed at this prayer. 14. 'The odour of Thine ointment.' 15. No reason to fear deception here.

1. IT seems as if we had deserted the little dove for a long time, but this is not the case, for these past trials cause her to take a far higher flight. I will now describe the way in which the Spouse treats her before uniting her entirely to Himself. He increases her longing for Him by devices so delicate that the soul itself cannot discern them; nor do I think I could explain them except to people who have personally experienced them. These desires are delicate and subtle impulses springing from the inmost depths of the soul; I know of nothing to which they can be compared.

2. These graces differ entirely from anything we ourselves can gain, and even from the spiritual consolation before described.[1] In the present case, even when the mind is not recollected or even thinking of God, although no sound is heard, His

[1] Mansion iv. ch. i. *Life*, ch. xxix. 10-15. *Rel.* ch. viii. 15.

Majesty arouses it suddenly as if by a swiftly flashing comet or by a clap of thunder.[2] Yet the soul thus called by God hears Him well enough—so well, indeed, that sometimes, especially at first, it trembles and even cries out, although it feels no pain. It is conscious of having received a delicious wound but cannot discover how, nor who gave it, yet recognizes it as a most precious grace and hopes the hurt will never heal.

3. The soul makes amorous complaints to its Bridegroom, even uttering them aloud; nor can it control itself, knowing that though He is present He will not manifest Himself so that it may enjoy Him. This causes a pain, keen although sweet and delicious from which the soul could not escape even if it wished; but this it never desires.[3] This favour is more delightful than the pleasing absorption of the faculties in the prayer of quiet which is unaccompanied by suffering.[4]

4. I am at my wits' end, sisters, as to how to make you understand this operation of love: I know not how to do so. It seems contradictory to say that the Beloved clearly shows He dwells in the soul and calls by so unmistakable a sign and a summons so penetrating, that the spirit cannot choose but hear it, while He appears to reside in the seventh mansion. He speaks in this manner, which is not a set form of speech, and the inhabitants of the other

[2] The saint first wrote 'relampago,' flash of lightning, but afterwards altered it to 'trueno,' clap of thunder.

[3] *Rel.* viii. 16. St. John of the Cross, *Spiritual Cant.* st. i. 22 *sqq.* *Poems* 7, 8.

[4] *Life*, ch. xxix. 18.

mansions, the senses, the imagination and the faculties, dare not stir.[5]

5. O Almighty God! how profound are Thy secrets and how different are spiritual matters from anything that can be seen or heard in this world! I can find nothing to which to liken these graces, insignificant as they are compared with many others Thou dost bestow on souls. This favour acts so strongly upon the spirit that it is consumed by desires yet knows not what to ask, for it realizes clearly that its God is with it. You may inquire, if it realizes this so clearly, what more does it desire and why is it pained? What greater good can it seek? I cannot tell: I know that this suffering seems to pierce the very heart, and when He Who wounded it draws out the dart He seems to draw the heart out too, so deep is the love it feels.[6]

6. I have been thinking that God might be likened to a burning furnace[7] from which a small spark flies into the soul that feels the heat of this great fire, which, however, is insufficient to consume it. The sensation is so delightful that the spirit lingers in the pain produced by its contact. This seems to me the best comparison I can find, for the pain is delicious and is not really pain at all, nor does it always continue in the same degree; sometimes it lasts for a long time; on other occasions it passes quickly. This is as God chooses, for no human means can obtain it; and though felt at times for a long while, yet it is intermittent.

[5] *Life*, ch. xv. 1.
[6] *Ibid.* ch. xxix. 17, 18.
[7] *Ibid.* ch. xv. 6; xviii. 4; xxi. 9.

7. In fact it is never permanent and therefore does not wholly inflame the spirit; but when the soul is ready to take fire, the little spark suddenly dies out, leaving the heart longing to suffer anew its loving pangs. No grounds exist for thinking this comes from any natural cause or from melancholy, or that it is an illusion of the devil or the imagination. Undoubtedly this movement of the heart comes from God Who is unchangeable; nor do its effects resemble those of other devotions in which the strong absorption of delight makes us doubt their reality.

8. There is no suspension here of the senses or other faculties: they wonder at what is happening, without impeding it. Nor do I think that they can either increase or dispel this delightful pain. Any one who has received this favour from our Lord will understand my meaning on reading this: let her thank Him fervently: there is no need to fear deception but far more fear of not being sufficiently grateful for so signal a grace. Let her endeavour to serve Him and to amend her life in every respect; then she will see what will follow and how she will obtain still higher and higher gifts.

9. A person on whom this grace was bestowed passed several years without receiving any other favour, yet was perfectly satisfied, for even had she served God for very many years in the midst of severe trials, she would have felt abundantly repaid. May He be for ever blessed! Amen.

10. Perhaps you wonder why we may feel more secure against deception concerning this favour

than in other cases. I think it is for these reasons. Firstly, because the devil cannot give such delicious pain: he may cause pleasure or delight which appears spiritual but is unable to add suffering, especially suffering of so keen a sort, united to peace and joy of soul. His power is limited to what is external; suffering produced by him is never accompanied with peace, but with anxieties and struggles.

11. Secondly, because this welcome storm comes from no region over which Satan has control. Thirdly, because of the great benefits left in the soul which, as a rule, is resolute to suffer for God and longs to bear many crosses. It is also far more determined than before to withdraw from worldly pleasures and intercourse and other things of the same sort.

12. It is very clear that this is no fiction: the imagination may counterfeit some favours but not this, which is too manifest to leave room for doubt. Should any one still remain uncertain, let her know that hers were not genuine impulses;[8] that is, if she is dubious as to whether or no she experienced them, for they are as certainly perceived by the soul as is a loud voice by the ears. It is impossible for these experiences to proceed from melancholy whose whims arise and exist only in the imagination, whereas this emotion comes from the interior of the soul.

13. I may be mistaken, but I shall not change my opinion until I hear reasons to the contrary from

[8] *Life*, ch. xv. 15, 16.

those who understand these matters. I know some
one who has always greatly dreaded such deceptions,
yet could never bring herself to feel any alarm
about this state of prayer.[9]

14. Our Lord also uses other means of rousing
the soul; for instance—when reciting vocal prayer
without seeking to penetrate the sense, a person
may be seized with a delightful fervour[10] as if
suddenly encompassed with a fragrance powerful
enough to diffuse itself through all the senses. I
do not assert that there really is any perfume but
use this comparison because it somewhat resembles
the manner by which the Spouse makes His presence understood, moving the soul to a delicious
desire of enjoying Him and thus disposing it to
heroic acts, and causing it to render Him fervent
praise.

15. This favour springs from the same source as
the former, but causes no suffering here, nor are
the soul's longings to enjoy God painful: this is
what is more usually experienced by the soul.
For the reasons already given there appears no cause
here for fear, but rather for receiving it with
thanksgiving.

[9] *Life*, ch. xxix. 6-10.
[10] *Ibid.* ch. xv. 12.   On the matter treated by St. Teresa in this
chapter, compare St. John of the Cross, *Spiritual Canticle*, stanza i.
(*circa finem*), stanza ix.; *The Living Flame of Love*, stanza ii.

INTRODUCTORY NOTE TO CHAPTER III.

BY THE EDITOR

THE readers, especially those not well acquainted with Scholastic philosophy, will, perhaps, be glad to find here a short explanation of the various kinds of Vision and Locution, Corporal, Imaginary, and Intellectual. The senses of Taste, Touch, and Smell are not so often affected by mystical phenomena, but what we are about to say in respect of Sight and Hearing applies, *mutatis mutandis*, to these also.

I. A CORPORAL VISION is when one sees a bodily object. A Corporal Locution is when one hears words uttered by a human tongue. In both cases the respective senses are exercising their normal function, and the phenomenon differs from ordinary seeing or hearing merely by the fact that in the latter the object seen is a real body, the words perceived come from a real tongue, whereas in the Vision or Locution the object is either only apparent or at any rate is not such as it seems to be. Thus, when young Tobias set out on a journey, his companion, Azarias, was not a real human being, but an archangel in human form. Tobias did really see and hear him, and felt the grip of his hand; Sara and her parents, as well as Tobias's parents, saw and heard him too, but all the time the archangel made himself visible and audible by means of an assumed body, or perhaps of an apparent body. It would be more correct to describe such a phenomenon as an APPARITION than as a Vision, and in fact the apparitions of our Risen Lord to the holy women and the apostles belong to this category. For, though His was a real body, it was glorified and therefore no longer subject to the same laws which govern purely human things. (St. Thomas, *Summa theol. III.*, qu. 54, art. 1-3).

St. Teresa tells us more than once that she never

beheld a Corporal Vision, nor heard a Corporal Locution.

II. An IMAGINARY VISION OR LOCUTION is one where nothing is seen or heard by the senses of seeing or hearing, but where the same impression is received that would be produced upon the imagination by the senses if some real object were perceived by them. For, according to the Scholastics, the Imagination stands half-way between the senses and the intellect, receiving impressions from the former and transmitting them to the latter. This is the reason why imaginary Visions and Locutions are so dangerous that, according to St. Teresa, St. John of the Cross, and other spiritual writers, they should not only never be sought for, but as much as possible shunned and under all circumstances discountenanced. For the Imagination is closely connected with the Memory, so that it is frequently impossible to ascertain whether a Vision, etc., is not perhaps a semi-conscious or unconscious reproduction of scenes witnessed. It is here also that deception, wilful or unwilful, self-deception or deception by a higher agency, is to be feared. Hence the general rule that such Visions or Locutions should only be trusted upon the strongest grounds. According to St. Thomas Aquinas, (*Summa theol. IIa IIæ*, gu. 175, art. 3 ad 4) the visions of Isaias, St. John in the Apocalypse etc., were Imaginary.

As an example of Imaginary Visions we may mention St. Stephen, who saw 'the heavens opened, and the Son of Man standing on the right hand of God'; or St. Peter, who saw 'the heaven opened, and a certain vessel descending, as it were a great linen sheet, let down by the four corners from heaven to the earth . . . and there came a voice to him : Arise, Peter, kill and eat.' (Acts, vii. 55 ; x. 11-13).

These Visions, Locutions, etc., are not hallucinations. The latter are due to physical disorder which affects the memory and causes it to represent impressions formerly received by it, in a disorderly and often grotesque manner. The Imaginary Vision takes place independently of a morbid state, is caused by an extraneous power, good or evil, and has for its object things of which the memory neither has nor ever has had cognizance.

III. An Intellectual Vision or Locution is one where nothing is seen or heard by the eyes and ears, and where no sensation is received by the imagination. But the impression which would be delivered by the imagination to the intellect, had it come through the senses and been handed on to the imagination, is directly imprinted upon the intellect. To understand this it is necessary to bear in mind that the impressions we receive through the senses must undergo a transformation—must be spiritualized—before they reach the intellect. This is one of the most difficult problems of psychology; none of the solutions offered by various schools of philosophy seem to render it entirely free from obscurity. According to St. Thomas Aquinas, the impression received by the eye (*Species sensibilis*) is spiritualized by a faculty called *Intellectus agens* by means of abstraction (*Species impressa*), and is treasured up in the memory, like lantern slides, available at demand. The mind, identifying itself with the *Species impressa*, produces the 'Word of the mind' (*Verbum mentis*), wherein consists the act of Understanding or Mental Conception. In the Intellectual Vision or Locution, God, without co-operation on the part of the senses, the imagination, or the memory, produces directly on the mind the *Species impressa*. As this is supernatural with regard to its origin, and often also with respect to its object, it stands to reason that it is too exalted for the memory to receive it, so that such Visions and Locutions are frequently only imperfectly remembered and sometimes altogether forgotten, as St. Teresa tells us. On the other hand they are far less dangerous than Corporal or Imaginary Visions and Locutions, because the senses and imagination have nothing to do with them, whilst evil spirits are unable to act directly upon the mind, and self-deception is altogether excluded for the reasons stated by St. Teresa.

An instance of such a vision is mentioned by St. Paul: 'I know a man in Christ above fourteen years ago (whether in the body I know not, or out of the body I know not: God knoweth), such an one rapt even to the third heaven. And I know such a man (whether in the body or out of the body, I know not: God knoweth): that he was caught up into paradise, and heard secret words, which it is not granted to man to utter' (2 Cor. xii 2-4).

CHAPTER III.

TREATS OF THE SAME SUBJECT AND OF THE WAY GOD IS SOMETIMES PLEASED TO SPEAK TO THE SOUL. HOW WE SHOULD BEHAVE IN SUCH A CASE, IN WHICH WE MUST NOT FOLLOW OUR OWN OPINION. GIVES SIGNS TO SHOW HOW TO DISCOVER WHETHER THIS FAVOUR IS A DECEPTION OR NOT: THIS IS VERY NOTEWORTHY.

1. Locutions. 2. Sometimes caused by melancholia. 3. Caution needed at first. 4. Locutions frequently occur during prayer. 5. Resist those containing false doctrine. 6. First sign of genuine locutions. 7. Effect of the words: 'Be not troubled.' 8. 'It is I, be not afraid.' 9. 'Be at peace.' 10. Second sign. 11. Third sign. 12. The devil suggests doubts about true locutions. 13. Confidence of the soul rewarded. 14. Its joy at seeing God's words verified. 15. Its zeal for God's honour. 16. Locutions coming from the fancy. 17. Imaginary answers given to prayer. 18. A confessor should be consulted about locutions. 19. Interior locutions. 20. First sign of genuine interior locutions. 21. Second sign. 22. Third sign. 23. Fourth sign. 24. Fifth sign. 25. Results of true locutions. 26. They should remove alarm. 27. Answer to an objection.

1. God arouses the soul in another manner which, though in some ways apparently a greater favour than the above mentioned, yet may prove more dangerous, therefore I will give some particulars about it. He does this by means of words addressed to the soul in many different ways; sometimes they appear to come from without; at other times

from the inner depths of the soul; or again, from its superior part; while other speeches are so exterior as to be heard by the ears like a real voice.

2. At times, indeed very often, this may be only a fancy; especially with persons of a lively imagination or who are afflicted with melancholy to any marked extent. I think that no attention should be paid to either class of people when they say they see, hear, or learn anything supernaturally. Do not disturb them by saying that it comes from the devil,[1] but listen to them as if they were sick persons. Let the prioress or confessor to whom they tell their story bid them think no more of it as such matters are not essential in the service of God: the devil has deceived many Christians thus, although perhaps it is not so in their case; therefore they need not trouble themselves about it. Thus we must accomodate ourselves to their humour: if we tell them their fancies proceed from melancholia, there will be no end to the matter, for they will persist in maintaining they have seen and heard these things, for so it seems to them.

3. The truth is, care should be taken to keep such people from too much prayer and to persuade them, as far as possible, to take no notice of their fancies: the devil makes use of these weak souls to injure others, even if they themselves escape unhurt. There is need for caution both with feeble and strong souls at first, until it is certain from what spirit these things proceed. I maintain that, in the beginning, it is always wiser to resist these

---

[1] *Life*, ch. xxiii. ¡14.

communications; if they come from God this is
the best way to receive more, for they increase
when discouraged. At the same time the soul
should not be too strictly controlled or disquieted,
for it cannot help itself in the matter.

4. To return to discuss the words addressed to
the soul: any kind I mentioned may come either
from God, the devil, or the imagination. By the
help of God I will endeavour to describe the signs
distinguishing the one from the other, and when
these locutions are dangerous, for they occur to
many persons who practise prayer. I do not wish
you to think, sisters, that there is any harm either
in believing or in disregarding them. When they
only console you, or warn you of your faults, it
matters not whence they come or whether they
are only fancies.

5. I caution you on one point—although they may
come from God, you must not esteem yourself
more highly, for He often spoke to the Pharisees[2]
—all the good consists in profiting by His words.
Take no more notice of any speeches you hear
which disagree with the Holy Scriptures than if
you heard them from Satan himself. Though they
may only rise from your vivid imagination, look
upon them as a temptation against the faith. Always resist them; then they will leave you, and
cease, for they have little strength of their own.[3]

6. Now let us return to the first point—whether
these communications come from the inferior or

[2] Antonius a Sp. S. *l.c.* tr. iii. n. 323. St. John of the Cross, *Ascent
of Mount Carmel*, bk. ii. ch. xxvii.
[3] *Life*, ch. xxv. 13, 18.

the superior part of the soul, or from without, does not affect their originating from God.

7. In my opinion these are the most certain signs of their being divine. The first and truest is the power and authority they carry with them, for these words are operative.[4] For example: a soul is suffering all the sorrow and disquiet I have described: the mind is darkened and dry; but it is set at peace, freed from all trouble and filled with light merely by hearing the words: 'Be not troubled.' These deliver it from all its pains, although it felt as though, if the whole world and all its theologians had united in trying to persuade it there was no cause for grief, it could not, in spite of all their efforts, have been delivered from its affliction.[5]

8. Again, a person is troubled and greatly terrified at being told by her confessor and other people that her soul is under the influence of the evil one: she hears a single sentence which says, 'It is I, be not afraid,'[6] and is at once freed from all fears and filled with consolation; indeed, she believes it would be impossible for any one to disturb her confidence.[7]

9. Again, when exceedingly anxious about important business, not knowing whether or not it will be successful, on hearing words bidding her

[4] Ps. cxlviii. 5: 'Ipse dixit et facta sunt.' *Life*, ch. xxv. 5. Anton. a Sp. S. *l.c.* tr. iii. n. 353. St. John of the Cross, *Ascent of Mount Carmel*, bk. ii. ch. xxxi. calls these 'substantial words.'

[5] *Life*, ch. xxvi. 6; xxx. 17. *Rel*. i. 26.

[6] St. Luke xxiv. 36.

[7] *Life*, ch. xxv. 22; xxxiii. 10. *Rel*. vii. 22. St. John of the Cross, *Ascent of Mount Carmel*, bk. ii. ch. xxxi. 1.

'Be at peace; all will go well,' she feels reassured
and free from all care in the matter.[8] Many other
instances of the same sort could be mentioned.

(2) 10. The second sign is a great calm and a devout
and peaceful recollection which dwell in the soul
together with a desire to praise God. They say
that communications, at any rate in this mansion,
are not uttered directly by God but are transmitted
by an angel.[9] Then, O my God, if a word sent
to us by Thee through Thy messenger has such
force, what effects wilt Thou not leave in the soul
united to Thee in a mutual bond of love?[10]

(3) 11. The third proof is that these words do not
pass from the memory but remain there for a very
long time; sometimes they are never forgotten.
This is not the case with what *men* may utter,
which, however grave and learned they may be,
is not thus impressed on our memory. Neither, if
they prophesy of things to come, do we believe
them as we do these divine locutions which leave
us so convinced of their truth that, although their
fulfilment sometimes seems utterly impossible and
we vacillate and doubt about them, there still

---

[8] *Life*, ch. xxxv. 7. *Rel.* ix. 6. St. John of the Cross, *Ascent of Mount
Carmel*, bk. iii. ch. ii. 7.

[9] *Rel.* v. 14.

[10] *Life*, ch. xxv. 23-25. See also Schram, *Instit. theol. myst.* 528 schol.;
529 schol. ii. and iii.; 531 schol. ii.; 532 schol. ii. Exterior locutions
may proceed direct from God, but generally are due to the ministry
of angels; the same holds good with regard to the imaginary ones.
Intellectual locutions, in which the words are merely impressed upon
the substance of the soul without intervention of the imagination, can
only proceed from God, Who alone is able to act upon the substance
of the soul. See also *Life*, ch. xxvii. 7 (end), 8, 9, and 10, and the
corresponding chapters in St. John's *Ascent of Mount Carmel*.

remains in the soul a certainty of their verity which cannot be destroyed. Perhaps everything may seem to militate against what was heard and years pass by, yet the spirit never loses its belief that God will make use of means unknown to men for the purpose and that finally what was foretold must surely happen; as indeed it does."

12. Still, as I said, the soul is troubled at seeing many obstacles in the way of the accomplishment of the prophecy. The words, their effects, and the assurance they carry with them convinced the soul at the moment that they came from God. Afterwards, however, doubts arise as to whether the locutions came from the devil or from the imagination, although while hearing them the person would have died to defend their truth." But, as I said, these misgivings must be suggested by the evil one to afflict and intimidate her, especially if by carrying out a command thus given great good will result to souls and some work be done conducing notably to the honour and service of God, concerning which great difficulties have to be overcome. In such cases, where will Satan stop short? At least, he weakens faith, and it is a terrible evil to doubt that God has power to work in a way far beyond our understanding.

13. Despite all these difficulties and although the confessors consulted on these matters say the words were but fancies, while events take such an unfavourable turn as to make the realization of these predictions seem impossible, yet there remains so

---

[11] *Life*, ch. xxv. 3, 10. *Rel.* ii. 17.
[12] *Ibid*, ch. xxv. 10.

lively a spark of certainty in the mind (I know not whence it comes) that, although all other hopes die out, it cannot, if it would, quench this ardent spark of confidence. At last, as I said, our Lord's words are accomplished, at which the soul is so satisfied and joyful that it can do nothing but praise His Majesty—more because it sees His words prove true than on account of the thing itself, even though it may be of consequence to the person concerned.

14. I know not why the soul attaches such importance to these communications being verified. I think that if the person herself were detected in telling falsehoods, she would not be so grieved as at these locutions proving untrue—as if she could do anything in the matter beyond repeating what has been said to her! A certain person was frequently reminded in such a case of the Prophet Jonas, when he found Ninive was not to be destroyed.[13]

15. In fact, as these words come from the Spirit of God, it is right thus to trust them and to desire that He Who is supreme truth should not be thought a deceiver. Justly, therefore, does their hearer rejoice when, after a thousand delays and enormous difficulties, they are accomplished. Although this success may entail great suffering on herself, she prefers it to the nonfulfilment of what she knows our Lord most certainly foretold. Possibly every one is not so weak as this, if indeed it

---

[13] Jonas iv. 1: 'Et afflictus est Jonas afflictione magna et iratus est; et oravit ad Dominum et dixit: Obsecro, Domine, numquid non hoc est verbum meum cum adhuc essem in terra mea?'

is a weakness, though I cannot myself condemn it as an evil.

16. If these locutions proceed from the imagination[14] they show no such signs, bringing neither conviction, peace, nor interior joy with them. But in some cases I have come across, on account of a very weak constitution or vivid imagination or of other causes I do not know, persons while absorbed in the prayer of quiet and in spiritual slumber are so entirely carried out of themselves by their deep state of recollection as to be unconscious of anything external. All their senses being thus dormant, as if asleep—as indeed, at times they really are—they thus, in a sort of dream, fancy they are spoken to or see things they imagine come from God, but which leave no more effect than dreams.

17. Again, one who very lovingly asks something of our Lord may fancy that an answer comes from Him.[15] This often occurs, but I think that no one accustomed to receive divine communications could be deceived on this point by the imagination.

18. The devil's deceptions are more dangerous; but if the foregoing signs are present, we may feel fairly confident that these locutions are from God, though not so certain but that, if they refer to some weighty matter in which we are called upon to act or if they concern a third person, we should consult some confessor who is both learned and a servant of God, before attempting or thinking of acting on them, although we may have heard them repeated several times and are convinced of their

[14] *Life*, ch. xxv. 4 (end) and 5 (beginning).
[15] *Ibid.* ch. xxv. 4 (beginning).

truth and divine origin.[16] His Majesty wishes us to take this course; it is not disobedience to His commands, for He has bidden us hold our confessor as His representative even where there is no doubt that the communications come from Him: thus we shall gain courage if the matter is a very difficult one. Our Lord will reassure our confessor, whom, when He so chooses, He will inspire with faith that these locutions are from the Holy Ghost.[17] If not, we are freed from all further obligations in the matter. I think it would be very dangerous to act against our confessor's advice and to prefer our own opinions in such a matter. Therefore, sisters, I admonish you in the name of our Lord, never to do anything of the sort.

19. God speaks to the soul in another way by a certain intellectual vision which I think undoubtedly proceeds from Him; it will be described later on.[18] It takes place far within the innermost depths of the soul which appears to hear distinctly in a most mysterious manner, with its spiritual hearing, the words spoken to it by our Lord Himself. The way in which the spirit perceives these words and the results produced by them, convince us that they cannot in any way come from the devil. Their powerful after-effects force us to admit this and plainly show they do not spring from the imagination.[19] Careful consideration will assure us of this for the following reasons;—

20. Firstly, the clearness of the language varies

[16] *Way of Perf.* ch. xxxix. 6. *Life*, ch. xxvi. 4, 5. St. John of the Cross, *Ascent of Mount Carmel*, bk. ii. ch. xxii. 14-18.
[17] *Rel.* vii. 15. [18] *Infra.* ch. viii. [19] *Life*, ch. xxvii. 8.

in the different kinds of locutions. Those that are divine are so distinct that the hearer remembers if there were a syllable missing, and what words were made use of even though a whole sentence was spoken. But if the speech were only a freak of fancy, it would not be so audible nor would the words be so distinct but would be only half articulated.[20]

21. The second reason is that often the person was not thinking of what is heard; sometimes the locution even comes unexpectedly during conversation, though at times it refers to some thought that passed quickly through the mind or to a subject it was before engaged upon. Frequently it concerns things of whose existence the hearer knew nothing nor even imagined such events could ever come to pass; therefore it is impossible for the imagination to have framed such speeches and deceived the mind by fancies about what it had never wished, nor sought for, nor even thought about.[21]

22. The third reason is that in a genuine case the soul seems to listen to the words, whereas when the imagination is at work, little by little it composes what the person wishes to hear.[22]

23. The fourth reason is because divine locutions differ immensely from others, a single word comprising a depth of meaning which our understanding could not thus quickly condense into one phrase.[23]

24. Fifthly because, in a manner I cannot explain, these communications, without any further explanations, frequently give us to understand far

---

[20] *Life*, ch. xxv. 6 and 10 (end).   [21] *Ibid*. ch. xxv. 9, 16.
[22] *Ibid*. ch. xxv. 4, 6.   [23] *Ibid*, ch. xxv. 12 (beginning).

more than is implied by the words themselves. I shall speak farther on of this way of understanding hidden things which is very subtle and a favour for which we should thank God. Some people are exceedingly suspicious about these and other communications of the same kind. I speak particularly of some one[24] who experienced them herself, though there may be others who cannot understand them. I know that she has considered the subject very carefully, God having often bestowed this grace on her. Her principal difficulty was to discover whether the locutions were merely fancied. It is easier to know when they come from the devil although being so wily, he can with facility imitate the spirit of light. However, he would do this in a form of words pronounced so distinctly that there would be no more doubt as to their reality than if they came from the spirit of truth, while those coming from the imagination leave us uncertain whether we heard the words or not. But Satan could never counterfeit the effects I spoke of;[25] he leaves neither peace nor light in the soul, only anxiety and confusion. In any case, he can do little or no harm to one who is humble and who, as I advised, does not act on what is heard.

25. If the soul receives favours and caresses from our Lord, let it examine carefully whether it rates itself more highly in consequence; unless self-abasement increases with God's expressions of love,

[24] The whole of this chapter as well as chapter xxv. of the *Life* prove clearly that the Saint speaks about herself and that she investigated the subject with the greatest care.

[25] *Life*, ch. xxv. 15.

they do not come from the Holy Spirit. Inevitably, when they are divine, the greater the favours, the less the soul esteems itself and the more keenly it remembers its sins.[26] It becomes more oblivious of self-interest: the will and memory grow more fervent in seeking solely God's honour with no thought of self. It also becomes unceasingly careful not to deviate deliberately from the will of God and feels a keener conviction that instead of meriting such favours, it deserves hell.

26. When these results follow, no graces or gifts received during prayer need alarm the soul which should rather trust in the mercy of God, Who is faithful and will not allow the devil to deceive it; but it is always well to be on one's guard.

27. Those our Lord does not lead by this path may suppose that the soul can avoid listening to these locutions and that even if they are interior it is at least possible to distract the attention from them so as not to hear them and thus escape danger. This cannot be done: I am not speaking of freaks of fancy which may be prevented by ceasing to desire certain things or by paying no attention to its inventions. This is not feasible when these communications come from the Holy Ghost Who, when He speaks, stops all other thoughts and compels the mind to listen.[27] Mark this: that I believe it would be easier for a person with very keen ears to avoid hearing a loud voice, for he could occupy

[26] *Life*, ch. xii. 5: 'The nearer we draw unto God the more this virtue (humility) should grow'; xv. 16; xix. 2; xx. 38. *Rel.* ii. 15; vii. 17; viii. 7, 9. *Way of Perf.* ch. xvii. 3.

[27] *Life*, ch. xxv. 21.

his thoughts and mind in other things. Not so here;
the soul can do nothing, nor has it ears to stop, nor
power to think of aught but what is said to it. For
He Who could stay the sun on its course (at the
prayer of Josue,[28] I believe) can so quiet the faculties and the interior of the spirit as to make it
perceive that another and a stronger Lord than
itself governs this castle; it is thus affected with profound devotion and humility, seeing that it cannot
but listen. May the divine Majesty vouchsafe that,
forgetting ourselves, our only aim may be to please
Him, as I said. Amen. God grant I have succeeded in explaining what I wished and that it may
be some guide to those who may experience such
favours.

[28] Josue x. 12. 13: 'Tunc locutus est Josue: ... sol contra Gabaon
ne movearis; steteruntque sol et luna.'

CHAPTER IV.

TREATS OF HOW GOD SUSPENDS THE SOUL IN PRAYER BY A
TRANCE, ECSTASY OR RAPTURE, WHICH I BELIEVE ARE ALL
THE SAME THING. GREAT COURAGE REQUIRED TO RECEIVE
EXTRAORDINARY FAVOURS FROM HIS MAJESTY.

1. Courage required by the soul for the divine espousals. 2. Raptures. 3. Rapture caused by the spark of love. 4. The powers and senses absorbed. 5. Mysteries revealed during ecstasies. 6. These mysteries are unspeakable. 7. Moses and the burning bush. 8. Simile of the museum. 9. St. Teresa's visit to the Duchess of Alva. 10. Joy of the soul during raptures. 11. No imaginary vision. 12. True and false raptures. 13. Revelations of future bliss. 14. The soul's preparation. 15. The soul blinded by its faults. 16. God ready to give these graces to all. 17. Faculties lost during ecstasy. 18. Spiritual inebriation. 19. Fervour and love of suffering left in the soul. 20. Scandal caused to spectators by such favours. 21. Our Lord's predeliction for such a soul. 22. Illusionary raptures.

1. WHAT rest can the poor little butterfly find, with all the trials I have told you of and many more? They serve to make her desire the Bridegroom more ardently. His Majesty, well aware of our weakness, fortifies her by these and other means in order that she may obtain courage for union with a Lord so great and may take Him for her Spouse. Perhaps you will laugh and think I am talking foolishly: there can be no call for courage here; there is no woman, however low her class, who would not dare to wed a king. So I think, were he an earthly monarch, but there is need of more fortitude than you suppose in order to espouse the King of heaven.[1] Our nature appears too timid and base for anything so high; without doubt, unless God gave us the grace it would be

[1] *Life*, ch. xxxix. 30.

impossible for us, however much we might appreciate its benefits. You will learn how His Majesty ratifies these espousals; probably this is done when He ravishes the soul by ecstasies, thus depriving it of its faculties; if the use of these were retained, I think the sight of its close vicinity to so mighty a Sovereign would probably deprive the body of life. I am speaking of genuine raptures, not fancies that come from women's weakness—which so often occur nowadays—making them imagine everything to be a rapture or an ecstasy. As I think I said, some are so feebly constituted as to die of a single prayer of quiet.[2]

2. I should like to describe here several kinds of raptures of which I have learnt from spiritual persons with whom I have discussed the subject, but I am not sure whether I shall succeed in explaining them as I did elsewhere.[3] It has been decided that it will not be amiss to repeat what was said about these and other things that happen in this state, if only that I may treat of all the mansions contain in proper order.

3. In one sort of rapture the soul, although perhaps not engaged in prayer at the time, is struck by some word of God which it either remembers or hears.[4] His Majesty, touched with pity by what He has seen it suffer for so long past in its longing for Him, appears to increase the spark I described in the interior of the spirit until it entirely inflames the soul which rises with new life like a phœnix from the flames. Such a one may piously believe

[2] *Castle*, M. iv. ch. iii. 11.   [3] *Life*, ch. xx. *passim.*
[4] Philippus a SS. Trinitate, *l.c.* p. iii. tr. i. disc. iii. art. 3.

her sins are now forgiven,[5] supposing that she is in the disposition and has made use of the means required by the Church. The soul being thus purified, God unites it to Himself in a.way known only to Him and the spirit, nor does even the latter so understand what happens as to be able to explain it to others afterwards. Yet the mind had not lost the use of its faculties, for this ecstasy does not resemble a swoon or a fit in which nothing either interior or exterior is felt.

4. What I do understand is that the soul has never been more alive to spiritual things nor so full of light and of knowledge of His Majesty as it is now. This might seem impossible; if the powers and senses were so absorbed that we might call them dead, how does the soul understand this mystery? I cannot tell; perhaps no one but the Creator Himself can say what passes in these places —I mean this and the following mansions which may be treated as one, the door leading from one to the other being wide open. However, as some things in the last rooms are only shown to those who get thus far, I thought it better to treat the mansions separately.

5. While the soul is in this suspension, our Lord favours it by discovering to it secrets such as heavenly mysteries and imaginary visions, which admit of description afterwards because they remain so imprinted on the memory that it never forgets them. But when the visions are intellectual they are not thus easily related, some of those received at such

[5] *Rel.* ix. 4.　*Way of Perf.* ch. xix. 8.

a time being so sublime that it is not fitting for man, while living in this world, to understand them in a way that can be told, although when the use of the faculties returns much can be described of of what was seen in intellectual vision. Possibly you do not know what a vision is, especially an intellectual one. Since I have been bidden by one who has authority, I will tell you at the proper time. Although seemingly superfluous, it may prove useful to certain people.

6. 'But,' you will ask me, 'if the very sublime favours our Lord bestows in this mansion cannot afterwards be remembered, what profit do they bring?'[6] O daughters! their value cannot be over-rated; for though the recipient is incapable of des-cribing them, they are deeply imprinted in the centre of the soul and are never forgotten. 'How can they be remembered if no image is seen and the powers of the soul do not comprehend them?' I, too, do not understand this, but I know that certain truths of the greatness of God remain so impressed on the spirit by this favour that, did not faith teach Who He is and that it is bound to believe He is God, the soul would henceforth worship Him as such, as did Jacob when he saw the ladder.[7] Doubtless the Patriarch learnt other secrets he was unable to reveal, for unless he had received more interior light he could never have discovered such sublime mysteries merely by watch-ing angels ascending and descending the steps. I am not certain whether this quotation is correct;

[6] Philippus a SS. Trinitate, *l.c.*
[7] Gen. xxviii. 12.

although I have heard the passage, I cannot feel
sure of recalling it exactly.

7. Neither was Moses able to relate more than
God willed of what he had seen in the burning
bush;[8] but unless the Almighty had clearly revealed
certain mysteries to his soul, causing it to see and
know its God was present, the lawgiver could
never have undertaken so many and such great
labours. Such sublime revelations were shown him
amidst the thorns of the bush as to give him the
needful courage for his great deeds on behalf of
the Children of Israel. We must not, sisters, search
out reasons for understanding the hidden things
of God, but, believing Him to be Almighty, we
should be convinced that such worms as ourselves,
with our limited power of intelligence, are unable
to comprehend His wonders. Let us praise Him
fervently for allowing us to understand something
of them.

8. I wish I could find some simile for my subject:
none seem to suit the purpose, but I will make use
of the following. Imagine that you are in an apart-
ment—I fancy it is termed *camarin* (or private
museum)—belonging to a king or a great nobleman,
in which are placed numberless kinds of articles of
glass, porcelain, and other things, so arranged that
most of them are at once seen on entering the room.

9. While on a visit to the house of the Duchess
of Alva (where at her request I was bidden by
obedience to stay during a journey)[9] I was taken

[8] Exod. iii. 2.

[9] Doña Maria Enriquez, wife of Ferdinand de Toledo, Duke of
Alva. This visit took place in February, 1574, and lasted two days

into such a room. I stood amazed on entering it
and wondered what could be the use of such a
jumble of knick-knacks; then I thought that the
sight of so many different things should lead one
to praise God. It is fortunate I saw them, for they
offer me a suitable comparison in this case. Although I was in the room some time, there were
so many objects in it that I forgot what I had seen
and could no more remember each object, nor of
what it was made, than if I had never seen it,
though I recalled the sight of the whole collection.

10. Something of this sort occurs when the spirit
is very closely united to God. It is introduced into
this mansion of the empyrean heaven which must
be in the centre of our souls—for since God resides
in them, He must own one of the mansions. While
the soul is in ecstasy, our Lord does not appear to
wish it to apprehend these mysteries and its inebriation of joy in Him suffices it. But sometimes
He is pleased to withdraw it from this rapture
when it at once perceives what the mansion contains. On returning to itself, the mind can recall
what has been seen but is unable to describe it,
nor can it, by its natural abilities, attain to see more
of the supernatural than God has chosen to show
it.

11. Do I seem to own that the soul really sees
something and that this is an imaginary vision? I
mean nothing of the sort: I am speaking of an intellectual vision, but being so ignorant and dull I
can explain nothing and am well aware that if any-

the Saint being then on her journey from Salamanca to Alva de Tormes.
(*Found.* ch. xxi.)

thing is rightly stated, it does not come from myself.

12. I think that if the soul learns no mysteries at any time during raptures, they are no true raptures but some natural weakness that may occur to people of delicate constitutions, such as women, when by its strenuous efforts the spirit overpowers physical nature, and produces stupor, as I think I said in connection with the prayer of quiet.[10]

13. This is not so in genuine raptures, for then I believe God ravishes the soul wholly to Himself, as being His very own and His bride, and shows her some small part of the kingdom she has thus won. However little this may be, all is great that is in this great God. He will allow of no obstacle from the powers or the senses but bids that the doors of all the mansions should be closed at once, only leaving open the one He is in, so that we may enter it. Blessed be such mercy—well may men be accursed who do not seek to profit by it, but who forfeit it!

14. O, my sisters! what nothingness is all we have given up, or that we do, or ever could do for a God who thus wills to communicate Himself to a worm! If we hope to enjoy this favour even during our mortal life, what are we doing? Why do we delay? What can repay the loss of the time of a 'Memento'[11] in searching for this Lord, like the

---

[10] *Castle*, M. iv. ch. iii. 2.

[11] The Saint wrote here and elsewhere *Memento*, and not *momento* as is commonly printed. It refers, of course, to that short interruption at Mass when the priest makes a Memento of those for whom he intends to pray. Likewise St. Teresa often speaks of the 'space of a Credo or an Ave Maria' always implying a very short duration.

bride through the streets and squares?"[12] Oh, what a mockery is everything in this world that does not lead towards and help us to attain to this state! Even though all the earthly pleasures, riches, and happiness that can be imagined could last for eternity, they would be disappointing and base contrasted with the treasures which are to be enjoyed for ever—and yet even *these* are nothing compared with the possession for our own of the Lord of all treasures in heaven and earth.

15. Oh, human blindness! When, oh, when shall this dust be taken from our eyes? Although we think it insufficient to blind us, yet I see some little motes or grains of dust which, if left to spread, will suffice to harm us greatly. At least, for the love of God, my sisters, let these faults convince us of our misery, serving to clear our sight as did the clay the eyes of the blind man who was cured by the Spouse.[13] Then, realizing our imperfections, we shall beg Him more fervently to let us benefit by our defects so as to please Him in all things.

16. I have unconsciously wandered far from my subject: forgive me, sisters. Believe me, when I come to these wonders of God's greatness (I mean when I come to speak of them) I cannot but feel keenly grieved at seeing what we lose by our own fault. It is true that His Majesty grants such favours to whom He chooses; yet if we sought Him as He seeks us, He would give them to us all. He only longs for souls on whom He may bestow them, for His gifts do not diminish His riches.

[12] Cant. iii. 2: 'Per vicos et plateas quæram quem diligit anima mea.'
[13] St. John ix. 6.

17. To return to what I was describing. By the commands of the Bridegroom, the doors of the mansions and even those of the keep and of the whole castle are closed; for when He intends ravishing the soul He takes away the power of speech, and although occasionally the other faculties are retained rather longer, no word can be uttered.[14] Sometimes the person is at once deprived of all the senses, the hands and body becoming as cold as if the soul had fled; occasionally no breathing can be detected.[15] This condition lasts but a short while; I mean in the same degree,[16] for when this profound suspension diminishes the body seems to come to itself and gain strength to return again to this *death* which gives more vigorous *life* to the soul.

18. This supreme state of ecstasy never lasts long, but although it ceases, it leaves the will so inebriated,[17] and the mind so transported out of itself that for a day, or sometimes for several days, such a person is incapable of attending to anything but what excites the will to the love of God;

[14] *Life*, ch. xx. 18. 'Like a person who, having a rope around his neck and being strangled, tries to breathe.'

[15] *Life*, ch. xx 23, 29. *Way of Perf.* ch. xxxii. *Rel.* viii. 8, 11. 'The first effect of ecstatic prayer concerns the body, which remains as if the soul had departed; it grows cold from a deficiency of natural heat, the eyes close gently, and the other senses are suspended; and yet a weak body recovers health in this prayer.' (Anton. a Spiritu Sancto, *Direct. Mystic.* tr. iv. d. 2, § 4, n. 150).

[16] 'Digo para estar in un ser.'

[17] Christusque nobis sit cibus,
Potusque noster sit fides;
Læti bibamus sobriam
Ebrietatem Spiritus.
Hymn for Lauds, Feria secunda, old version.
(Compare Anton. a Sp. S. *l.c.* tr. iv. n. 30.)

although wide awake enough to this, she seems asleep as regards all earthly matters.

19. Oh, when the soul wholly returns to itself, how abashed does it feel at having received this favour and how passionate are its desires of serving God in any way He asks of it! If the former states of prayer caused the powerful effects described, what will not such a signal grace as this do? Such a person wishes she had a thousand lives[18] to spend for God; she would have all earthly creatures changed into as many tongues to praise Him on her account. She longs to perform most severe penances,[19] nor do they cost her much, for the power of her love almost prevents their being felt. She realizes how little the martyrs suffered during their tortures, for pain is easy when our Lord thus aids us: therefore such a soul complains to His Majesty when He gives her no suffering.[20]

20. She considers it a great favour when God sends her this rapture in secret, for when others see it the shame and confusion she feels are so great as somewhat to diminish her transport. Knowing the malice of the world, she fears her ecstasy will not be attributed to its proper cause but may give rise to rash judgment instead of the praise due for it to God. Although this pain and distress are unavoidable, they seem to me to show a certain want of humility, for if she wished to be despised, what would she care?[21]

[18] *Life*, ch. xx. 30.
[19] *Castle*, M. vii. ch. iii. 4. *Way of Perf.* ch. xxxviii. 1. *Excl.* xiv. 3. *Life*, ch. xl. 27.
[20] *Life*, ch. xvi. 6. *Rel.* i. 4.
[21] *Ibid.* ch. xx. 5, 6.

21. Our Lord once said to some one who was troubled by such thoughts: Do not be disturbed; people will either praise Me or condemn thee; in either case thou wilt be the gainer.'[22] I learnt afterwards that she was greatly encouraged and comforted by this speech; I speak of it in case others may suffer in the same way. Apparently our Lord would have all men know that this soul is His own and that none may molest it, for it is all His. Men are welcome to attack, if they will, the body, the honour, and the possessions of such a person, for glory will accrue to His Majesty from all they do; but the soul they may not assail; unless by a most culpable presumption it withdraws from the protection of its Spouse, He will defend it against the whole world and against all hell besides.

22. I do not know whether I have succeeded in teaching you what a rapture is; to explain it fully would, as I said, be impossible. Still I do not think time has been lost in describing a genuine rapture. The effects in false raptures are very different. I do not call them 'false' because people who experience them intentionally deceive others, but because they are themselves unwittingly deceived. As the signs and effects do not correspond with this great grace,

[22] *Life*, ch. xxxi. 15. St. John of the Cross in stanza xiii. 8. of the *Spiritual Canticle*, refers to this and the following chapters. 'This,' he says, 'is an appropriate opportunity for discussing the difference between raptures, ecstasies, and other elevations and subtle flights of the spirit, to which spiritual persons are liable; but as my object is to do nothing more than explain this canticle, I leave the subject for those who are better qualified than I am. I do this the more readily because our mother, the blessed Teresa of Jesus, has written admirably on this matter, whose writings I hope to see soon published.'

the favour itself becomes so discredited that natur-
ally, when our Lord afterwards bestows it on any
soul, nobody believes in it. May He be for ever
blessed and praised! Amen, Amen!

CHAPTER V.

TREATS OF THE SAME SUBJECT AS THE LAST CHAPTER AND
DESCRIBES THE FLIGHT OF THE SPIRIT, WHICH IS ANOTHER
WAY BY WHICH GOD ELEVATES THE SOUL : THIS REQUIRES
GREAT COURAGE IN ONE EXPERIENCING IT. THIS FAVOUR, BY
WHICH GOD GREATLY DELIGHTS THE SOUL IS EXPLAINED.
THIS CHAPTER IS VERY PROFITABLE.

*1. The flight of the spirit. 2. Self-control completely lost. 3. Symbol
of the two cisterns. 4. Obligations following these favours. 5. Humility produced by them. 6. How our crucified Lord comforted
such a soul. 7. A humble soul fears these favours. 8. Mysteries
learnt during the flight of the spirit. 9. Imaginary visions sometimes accompany intellectual ones. 10. How the flight of the
spirit takes place. 11. The soul fortified by it. 12. Three great
graces left in the soul. 13. The third grace. 14. Fear caused by
this favour.*

1. THERE is another form of rapture, which, though
essentially the same as the last, yet produces very
different feelings in the soul. I call it the 'flight
of the spirit,'[1] for the soul suddenly feels so rapid
a sense of motion that the spirit appears to hurry
it away with a speed which is very alarming, especially at first. Therefore I said that the soul on
whom God bestows this favour requires strong
courage, besides great faith, trust, and resignation,
so that God may do what He chooses with it.

2. Do you suppose a person in perfect possession
of her senses feels but little dismay at her soul's
being drawn above her, while sometimes, as we

[1] *Rel.* viii. 10, 11. *Life*, ch. xviii. 8; xx. 3.

read, even the body rises with it?[2] She does not know where the spirit is going, who is raising her, nor how it happens; for at the first instant of this sudden movement one does not feel sure it is caused by God. Can it possibly be resisted? No; resistance only accelerates the motion, as some one told me. God now appears to be teaching the soul, which has so often placed itself absolutely in His hands and offered itself entirely to Him, that it no longer belongs to itself; thus it is snatched away more vehemently in consequence of its opposition. Therefore this person resolved to resist no more than does a straw when attracted by amber (a thing you may have seen); she yielded herself into the hands of Him who is Almighty, seeing it is best to make a virtue of necessity. Speaking of straw, doubtless it is as easy for a stalwart, strapping fellow to lift a straw as for our mighty and powerful Giant to elevate our spirit.[3]

3. It seems that the cistern of water of which I spoke (but I cannot quite remember where) in the fourth mansion,[4] was formerly filled gently and

---

[2] *Life*, ch. xx. 9. St. John of the Cross, *Spiritual Canticle*, stanzas xiv.-xv. 23 *sqq.* Philippus a SS. Trinit. *l.c.* p. iii. tr. i. disc. iii. art. 3. 'This prayer of rapture is superior to the preceding grades of prayer, as also to the ordinary prayer of union, and leaves much more excellent effects and operations in many other ways.' St. Catherine of Siena *(Dialogue*, ch. lxxix . 1) says : 'Wherefore, oftentimes, through the perfect union which the soul has made with Me, she is raised from the earth almost as if the heavy body became light. But this does not mean that the heaviness of the body is taken away, but that the union of the soul with Me is more perfect than the union of the body with the soul ; wherefore the strength of the spirit, united with Me, raises the body from the earth.' (Transl. by Algar Thorold.)

[3] *Life*, ch. xxii. 20.

[4] *Castle*, M. iv. ch. ii. 3.

quietly, without any movement; but now this great
God Who restrains the springs and the waters and
will not permit the ocean to transgress its bounds,[5]
lets loose the streams, which with a powerful rush
flow into the cistern and a mighty wave rises, strong
enough to uplift on high the little vessel of our
soul. Neither the ship herself nor her pilot and
sailors can at their choice control the fury of the
sea and stop its carrying the boat where it will:
far less can the interior of the soul now stay where
it chooses or force its senses or faculties to act more
than He Who holds them in His dominion decrees;
as for the exterior powers, they are here quite
useless.

4. Indeed I am amazed, sisters, while merely
writing of this manifestation of the immense power
of this great King and Monarch. Then what must
be felt by those who actually experience it? I am
convinced that if His Majesty were to reveal Himself thus to the greatest sinners on earth, they
would never dare to offend Him again—if not
through love at least through fear of Him. What
obligations bind those taught in so sublime a manner to strive with all their might not to displease
such a Master! In His Name I beg of you, sisters,
who have received these or the like favours, not
to rest content with merely receiving them but to
remember that she who owes much has much to
pay![6]

5. This thought terrifies the soul exceedingly:

[5] Prov. viii. 29,

[6] St. Luke xii. 48: 'Cui multum datum est, multum quaeretur ab
eo, et cui commendaverunt multum, plus petent ab eo,'

unless the great courage needed was given it by our Lord, it would suffer great and constant grief; for looking first at what His Majesty has done for it and then upon itself, it sees how little good it has performed compared with what it was bound to do, and that the paltry service it has rendered was full of faults, failures and tepidity. To efface the remembrance of the many imperfections of all its good deeds (if indeed it has ever performed any) it thinks best to forget them altogether and to be ever mindful of its sins, casting itself on the mercy of God since it cannot repay its debt to Him and begging for the pity and compassion He ever shows to sinners.

6. Perhaps He will answer as He did to some one who was kneeling before a crucifix in great affliction on this account, for she felt she had never had anything to offer God nor to sacrifice for His sake. The Crucified One consoled her by saying that He gave her for herself all the pains and labours He had borne in His passion, that she might offer them as her own to His Father.[7] I learnt from her that she at once felt comforted and enriched by these words which she never forgets but recalls whenever she realizes her own wretchedness and feels encouraged and consoled. I could relate several other incidents of the same kind learnt in conversation with many holy people much given to prayer, but I will not recount them lest you might imagine they relate to myself.

7. I think this example is very instructive; it

[7] *Rel.* ix. 8. This happened at Seville in 1575 or 1576.

shows that we please our Lord by self-knowledge, by the constant recollection of our poverty and miseries, and by realizing that we possess nothing but what we have received from Him.[8] Therefore courage is needed, sisters, in order to receive this and many other favours which come to a soul elevated to this state by our Lord; I think that if the soul is humble it requires more valour than ever for this last mercy. May God grant us humility for His Name's sake.

8. To return to this sudden rapture of the spirit. The soul really appears to have quitted the body, which however is not lifeless, and though, on the other hand, the person is certainly not dead, yet she herself cannot, for a few seconds, tell whether her spirit remains within her body or not.[9] She feels that she has been wholly transported into another and a very different region from that in which we live, where a light so unearthly is shown[10] that, if during her whole lifetime she had been trying to picture it and the wonders seen, she could not possibly have succeeded. In an instant her mind learns so many things at once that if the imagination and intellect spent years in striving to enumerate them, it could not recall a thousandth part of them.

9. This vision is not intellectual but imaginary and is seen by the eyes of the soul more clearly

---

[8] 1 Cor. iv. 7: 'Quid autem habes quod non accepisti?'

[9] 2 Cor. xii. 2: 'Sive in corpore nescio, sive extra corpus nescio, Deus scit.'

[10] This is called 'lumen prophetiæ' and is a transient form of the 'lumen gloriæ.' See St. Thomas Aquinas, *Sum. theol.* 2a 2æ, q. 175, art. 3 ad 2.

than earthly things are seen by our bodily eyes. Although no words are pronounced, the spirit is taught many truths; for instance, if it beholds any of the saints, it knows them at once as well as if intimately acquainted with them for years.[11] Occasionally, besides what the eyes of the soul perceive in intellectual vision, other things are shown it. In an imaginary vision it usually sees our Lord accompanied by a host of angels; yet neither the bodily eyes nor the eyes of the soul[12] see anything, for these visions and many other things impossible to describe, are revealed by some wonderful intuition that I cannot explain. Perhaps those who have experienced this favour and possess more ability than myself may be able to describe it, although it seems to me a most difficult task.

10. I cannot tell whether the soul dwells in the body meanwhile or not: I would neither affirm that it does nor that the body is deprived of it. I have often thought that as, though the sun does not leave his place in the heavens yet his rays have power to reach the earth instantaneously, so the soul and the spirit, which make one and the same thing (like the sun and its rays) may, while remaining in its own place, through the strength of the ardour coming to it from the true Sun of Justice, send up some higher part of it above itself. In fact I do not understand what I am talking about, but the truth is that, with the swiftness of a bullet fired

[11] The same thing is related of some Saints while on earth, e.g. St Paul the first hermit and St. Anthony, who greeted each other by name though neither knew nor had heard of the other.

[12] These words, though necessary for the context, were only begun, but not completed by St. Teresa.

from a gun, an upward flight takes place in the interior of the soul. (I know no other name for it but 'flight.') Although noiseless, it is too manifest a movement to be any illusion[13] and the soul is quite outside itself; at least that is the impression made upon it. Great mysteries are revealed to it meanwhile, and when the person returns to consciousness she is so greatly benefited that she holds all this world's goods as filth compared with what she has seen. Henceforth earthly life is grievous to her and what used to please her now remains uncared for and unnoticed.[14]

11. Those children of Israel who were sent on first to the Land of Promise brought back tokens from it;[15] so here our Lord seems to seek to show the soul something of the land to which it is travelling, to give it courage to pass through the trials of its painful journey, now that it knows where it must go to find rest. You may fancy that such profit could not thus quickly be obtained, yet only those who have experienced what signal benefits

---

[13] *Life*, ch. xx. 32. *Castle*, M. iv. ch. i. 10.

[14] Compare §§ 8-10 with Philippus a SS. Trinitate, *l.c.* p. iii. tr. i. disc. iii. art. 3.

'Muchas veces he pensado, si como el sol estándose en el cielo, que sus rayos tienen tanta fuerza, que no mudándose él de allí, de presto llegan acá ; si el alma y el espíritu (que son una misma cosa, como le es el sol y sus rayos) puede, quedándose ella en su puesto, con la fuerza de calor que le viene del verdadero Sol de justicia, alguna parte superior salir sobre sì misma. En fin, yo no sé lo que digo, lo que es verdad es, que con la presteza que sale la pelota de un arcabuz, cuando le ponen el fuego, se levanta en lo interior un vuelo (que yo no sé otro nombre que le poner) que aunque no hace ruido, hace movimiento tan claro, que no puede ser antojo en ninguna manera; y muy fuera de sì misma, á todo lo que puede entender, se le muestran grandes cosas.'

[15] Num. xiii. 24.

this favour leaves in the soul can realize its value.
12. This clearly shows it to be no work of the devil;
neither the imagination nor the evil one could
represent what leaves such peace, calm, and good
fruits in the soul, and particularly the following
three graces of a very high order.[16] The first of
these is a perception of the greatness of God which
becomes clearer to us as we witness more of it.
Secondly, we gain self-knowledge and humility
from seeing how creatures so base as ourselves in
comparison with the Creator of such wonders have
dared to offend Him in the past or venture to gaze
on Him now.

13. The third grace is a contempt for all earthly
things unless they are consecrated to the service of
so great a God. With such jewels the Bridegroom
begins to deck His Bride; they are too valuable for
her to keep them carelessly.[17] These visions are so
deeply engraved in her memory that I believe she
can never forget them until she enjoys them for
evermore, for to do so would be the greatest
misfortune.[18] But the Spouse Who gave her these
gifts has power to give her grace not to lose them.

14. I told you that courage was required by the
soul, for do you think it is a trifling matter for the
spirit to feel literally separated from the body, as it
does when perceiving that it is losing its senses without understanding the reason? There is need that

[16] *Life*, ch. xx. 31. The same distinctions with respect to divine and
diabolical locutions may be found in *Life*, ch. xxv. 5.

[17] 'Dexteram meam et collum meum cinxit lapidibus pretiosis; tradi-
dit auribus meis inestimabiles margaritas.' From the Office of St. Agnes.

[18] This is undoubtedly the correct rendering of this difficult and
obscure passage.

He Who gives all the rest should include fortitude.
You will say this fright is well rewarded, and so say
I. May He Who can bestow such graces be for ever
praised and may His Majesty vouchsafe that we
may be worthy to serve Him. Amen.

CHAPTER VI.

DESCRIBES AN EFFECT WHICH PROVES THE PRAYER SPOKEN
OF IN THE LAST CHAPTER TO BE GENUINE AND NO DECEPTION.
TREATS OF ANOTHER FAVOUR OUR LORD BESTOWS ON THE
SOUL TO MAKE IT PRAISE HIM FERVENTLY.

*1. The soul longs for death. 2. The soul cannot help desiring these
favours. 3. St. Teresa bewails her inability to serve God.
3. Fervour resulting from ecstasies. 5. Excessive desires to see
God should be restrained. 6. They endanger health. 7. Tears
often come from physical causes. 8. St. Teresa's own experience.
9. Works, not tears, are asked by God. 10. Confide entirely in
God. 11. The jubilee of the soul. 12. Impossibility of concealing
this joy. 13. The world's judgment of this jubilee. 14. Which is
often felt by the nuns of St. Joseph's. 15. The Saint's delight in
this jubilee.*

1. THESE sublime favours leave the soul so desirous
of fully enjoying Him Who has bestowed them
that life becomes a painful though delicious torture,
and death is ardently longed for. Such a one often
implores God with tears to take her from this
exile where everything she sees wearies her.[1] Solitude alone brings great alleviation for a time, but
soon her grief returns and yet she cannot bear to
be without it. In short, this poor little butterfly
can find no lasting rest. So tender is her love that
at the slightest provocation it flames forth and the
soul takes flight. Thus in this mansion raptures

---

[1] *Excl.* ii. See poem 4, 'Cuan triste es, Dios mio'; and the two
versions of 'Vivir sin vivir en mi.' (Poems 3 and 4. *Minor Works.*)

occur very frequently, nor can they be resisted even in public. Persecutions and slanders ensue;[2] however she may try, she cannot keep free from the fears suggested to her by so many people, especially by her confessors.

2. Although in one way she feels great confidence within her soul, especially when alone with God, yet on the other hand, she is greatly troubled by misgivings lest she is deceived by the devil and so should offend Him Whom she deeply loves. She cares little for blame, except when her confessor finds fault with her as if she could help what happens. She asks every one to pray for her[3] since she has been told to do so, and begs His Majesty to direct her by some other way than this which is so full of danger. Nevertheless, so great are the benefits left by these favours that she cannot but see that they lead her on the way to heaven,[4] of which she has read and heard and learnt in the law of God. As, strive how she may, she cannot resist desiring to receive these graces, she resigns herself into God's hands. Yet she is grieved at finding herself forced to wish for these favours which appears to be disobedience to her confessor, for she believes that in obedience, and in avoiding any offence against God, lies her safeguard against deception. Thus she feels she would prefer to be cut in pieces rather than wilfully commit a venial sin, yet is greatly grieved at seeing that she cannot avoid unwittingly falling into a great number.

[2] *Life*, ch. xxv. 18.
[3] *Ibid.* ch. xxv. 20. *Rel.* vii. 7.
[4] *Ibid.* ch. xxvii. 1, 2.

God bestows on such people so intense a desire neither ever to displease Him in however small a matter, nor to commit any avoidable imperfection, that, were there no other reason, they would try to avoid society and they greatly envy those who live in deserts.[5]   On the other hand, they seek to live amidst men in the hopes of helping if but one soul to praise God better.[6] In the case of a woman, she grieves over the impediment offered by her sex[7] and envies those who are free to proclaim aloud to all Who is this mighty God of hosts.[8]

3. O poor little butterfly! chained by so many fetters that stop thee from flying where thou wouldst! Have pity on her, O my God, and so dispose her ways that she may be able to accomplish some of her desires for Thy honour and glory! Take no account of the poverty of her merits, nor of the vileness of her nature, Lord, Thou Who hast the power to compel the vast ocean to retire, and didst force the wide river Jordan to draw back so that the Children of Israel might pass through![9] Yet spare her not, for aided by Thy strength she can endure many trials. She is resolved to do so—she desires to suffer them. Stretch forth Thine arm, O Lord, to help her lest she waste her life on trifles! Let Thy greatness appear in this Thy creature, womanish and weak as she is, so that men, seeing the good in her is not her own, may praise Thee

[5] *Rel.* i. 6.

[6] *Life*, ch. xxxii. 14; xxxv. 13.   *Castle*, M. vii. ch. iv. 21.   *Found.* ch. i 6, 7.

[7] *Way of Perf.* ch. i.

[8] III Reg. xix. 10.

[9] Ps. cxiii. 3; Exod. xiv. and Jos. iii.

for it! Let it cost her what it may and as dear as she desires, for she longs to lose a thousand lives to lead one soul to praise Thee but a little better. If as many lives were hers to give, she would count them well spent in such a cause, knowing as a truth most certain that she is unworthy to bear the lightest cross, much less to die for Thee.

4. I cannot tell why I have said this, sisters, nor what made me do so; indeed I never intended it. You must know that these effects are bound to follow from such trances or ecstasies: they are not transient, but permanent desires; when opportunity occurs of acting on them, they prove genuine. How can I say that they are permanent, when at times the soul feels cowardly in the most trivial matters and too timorous to undertake any work for God?

5. I believe it is because our Lord, for its greater good, then leaves the soul to its natural weakness, which at once convinces it so thoroughly that any strength it possessed came from His Majesty as to destroy its self-love, enduing it with a greater knowledge of the mercy and greatness of God which He deigned to show forth in one so vile. However, the soul is usually in the former state. Beware of one thing, sisters; these ardent desires to behold our Lord are sometimes so distressing as to need rather to be checked than to be encouraged —that is, if feasible, for in another kind of prayer of which I shall speak later, it is not possible as you will see.

6. In the state I speak of these longings can sometimes be arrested, for the reason is at liberty

to conform to the will of God and can quote the words of St. Martin;[10] should these desires become very oppressive, the thoughts may be turned to some other matter. As such longings are generally found in persons far advanced in perfection, the devil may excite them in order to make us think we are of their number—in any case it is well to be cautious. For my part, I do not believe he could cause the calm and peace given by this pain to the soul, but would disturb it by such uneasiness as we feel when afflicted concerning any worldly matter. A person inexperienced in both kinds of sorrow cannot understand the difference, but thinking such grief an excellent thing, will excite it as much as possible which greatly injures the health, as these longings are incessant or at least very frequent.

7. You must also notice that bodily weakness may cause such pain, especially with people of sensitive characters who cry over every trifling trouble.[11] Times without number do they imagine they are mourning for God's sake when they are doing no such thing. If for a considerable space of time, whenever such a person hears the least mention of God or thinks of Him at all, these fits of uncon-

---

[10] 'When St. Martin was dying, his brethren said to him: 'Why, dear Father, will you leave us? Or to whom can you commit us in our desolation? We know, indeed, that you desire to be with Christ, but your reward above is safe and will not be diminished by delay; rather have pity on us whom you are leaving desolate.' Then Martin, always pitiful, moved by these lamentations, is said to have burst into tears. Turning to God, he replied to the mourners around him only by crying: 'O Lord, if I am still necessary to Thy people, I do not shrink from toil; Thy will be done.' (Sulpitius Severus, *Life of St. Martin*, letter 3.)

[11] *Way of Perf.* ch. xvii. 4; xix. 6.

trollable weeping occur,"¹² the cause may be an accumulation of humour round the heart, which has a great deal more to do with such tears than has the love of God. Such persons seem as if they would never stop crying: believing that tears are beneficial, they do not try to check them nor to distract their minds from the subject, but encourage them as much as possible. The devil seizes this opportunity of weakening nuns so that they become unable to pray or to keep their Rule.

8. I think you must be puzzling over this and would like to ask what I would have you do, as I see danger in everything. If I am afraid of delusions in so good a thing as tears, perhaps I myself am deluded, and may be I am! But believe me, I do not say this without having witnessed it in other people although not in my own case, for there is nothing tender about me and my heart is so hard as often to grieve me.¹³ However, when the fire burns fiercely within, stony as my heart may be, it distils like an alembic.¹⁴ It is easy to know when tears come from this source, for they are soothing and gentle rather than stormy and rarely do any harm. This delusion, when it is one, has the advantage, with a humble person, of only injuring the body and not the soul. But if one is not humble, it is well to be ever on one's guard.

9. Let us not fancy that if we cry a great deal we have done all that is needed—rather we must

¹² *Life*, ch. xxix. 12.

¹³ Compare with this what we have said in note 1 to the second chapter of the Fourth Mansions. *Rel.* ii. 12.

¹⁴ *Life*, ch. xix. 1-3.

work hard and practise the virtues: that is the
essential—leaving tears to fall when God sends
them, without trying to force ourselves to shed
them. Then, if we do not take too much notice
of them, they will leave the parched soil of our
souls well watered, making it fertile in good fruit;
for this is the water which falls from heaven.[15]
However we may tire ourselves in digging to reach
it, we shall never get any water like this; indeed,
we may often work and search until we are exhausted without finding as much as a pool, much
less a springing well!

10. Therefore, sisters, I think it best for us to
place ourselves in the presence of God, contemplate
His mercy and grandeur and our own vileness and
leave Him to give us what He will, whether
water or drought, for He knows best what is good
for us; thus we enjoy peace and the devil will
have less chance to deceive us.

11. Amongst these favours, at once painful and
pleasant, Our Lord sometimes causes in the soul a
certain jubilation[16] and a strange and mysterious
kind of prayer. If He bestows this grace on you,
praise Him fervently for it; I describe it so that
you may know that it is something real. I believe
that the faculties of the soul are closely united to
God but that He leaves them at liberty to rejoice
in their happiness together with the senses, although
they do not know what they are enjoying nor how
they do so. This may sound nonsense but it really

---

[15] *Way of Perf.* ch. xix. 6. *Life*, ch. xviii. 12 *sqq.*
[16] Philippus a SS. Trinit. *l.c.* p. iii. tr. i. disc. iv. art. 5. Antonius
a Sp. S. *l.c.* tr. iv. n.156.

happens. So excessive is its jubilee that the soul will not enjoy it alone but speaks of it to all around so that they may help it to praise God, which is its one desire.[17]

12. Oh, what rejoicings would this person utter and what demonstrations would she make, if possible, so that all might know her happiness! She seems to have found herself again and wishes, like the father of the prodigal son, to invite all her friends to feast with her[18] and to see her soul in its rightful place, because (at least for the time being) she cannot doubt its security. I believe she is right, for the devil could not possibly infuse a joy and peace into the very centre of her being which make her whole delight consist in urging others to praise God. It requires a painful effort to keep silent and to dissemble such impulsive happiness. St. Francis must have experienced this when, as the robbers met him rushing through the fields crying aloud, he told them in answer to their questions that he was the 'herald of the great King.'[19] So felt other saints who retired into the deserts so that, like St. Francis, they might proclaim the praises of their God.

[17] *Rel.* ii. 12.   [18] St. Luke xv. 23.

[19] 'He plunged into a large forest, and there in a loud voice and in French, he made the echoes resound with the praises of God. Some robbers, attracted by his singing, rushed out upon him. But the sight of so poor a man destroyed their hopes of booty. They questioned him, and Francis gave them no answer beyond saying in allegorical language : 'I am the herald of the great King !' The robbers considered themselves insulted by these words. They threw themselves upon him, beat him severely, and went off after having thrown him into a ditch full of snow. This treatment only added fire to the zeal of Francis. He sang his holy canticles with greater love than before.' (Rev. Father Léon, *Lives of the Saints of the Order of St. Francis*, vol. 1, ch. i.)

13. I knew Fray Peter of Alcantara who used to do this. I believe he was a saint on account of the life he led, yet people often took him for a fool when they heard him.[20] Oh happy folly, sisters! Would that God might let us all share it! What mercy He has shown you in placing you where, if He gave you this grace and it were perceived by others, it would rather turn to your advantage than bring on you contempt as it would do in the world, where men so rarely hear God praised that it is no wonder they take scandal at it.

14. Oh miserable times and wretched life spent in the world! How blest are those whose happy lot it is to be freed from them![21] It often delights me, when in my sisters' company to see how the joy of their hearts is so great that they vie with one another in praising our Lord for placing them in this convent: it is evident that their praises come from the very depths of their souls. I should like you to do this often, sisters, for when one begins she incites the rest to imitate her. How can your tongues be better employed when you are together than in praising God, Who has given us so much cause for it?

15. May His Majesty often grant us this kind of prayer which is most safe and beneficial; we cannot acquire it for ourselves as it is quite superna-

[20] 'St. Peter of Alcantara, in the jubilation of his soul through the impetuosity of divine love, was occasionally unable to refrain from singing the divine praises aloud in a wonderful manner. To do this more freely, he sometimes went into the woods where the peasants who heard him sing took him for one who was beside himself.' (Rev. Alban Butler, *Lives of the Saints*.)

[21] *Way of Perf.* ch. ii. 8; iii. 1; viii. 1.

tural. Sometimes it lasts for a whole day and the soul is like one inebriated, although not deprived of the senses;[22] nor like a person afflicted with melancholia,[23] in which, though the reason is not entirely lost, the imagination continually dwells on some subject which possesses it and from which it cannot be freed. These are coarse comparisons to make in connection with such a precious gift, yet nothing else occurs to my mind. In this state of prayer a person is rendered by this jubilee so forgetful of self and everything else that she can neither think nor speak of anything but praising God, to which her joy prompts her. Let us all of us join her, my daughters, for why should we wish to be wiser than she? What can make us happier? And may all creatures unite their praises with ours for ever and ever. Amen, amen, amen!

[22] Compare with this what has been said in the fourth chapter of this Mansion, § 17, note 17.

[23] Melancholia here as elsewhere means hysteria.

CHAPTER VII.

DESCRIBES THE GRIEF FELT ON ACCOUNT OF THEIR SINS BY SOULS ON WHOM GOD HAS BESTOWED THE BEFORE-MENTIONED FAVOURS. SHOWS THAT HOWEVER SPIRITUAL A PERSON MAY BE, IT IS A GREAT ERROR NOT TO KEEP BEFORE OUR MIND THE HUMANITY OF OUR LORD AND SAVIOUR JESUS CHRIST AND HIS SACRED PASSION AND LIFE, AS ALSO THE GLORIOUS MOTHER OF GOD AND THE SAINTS. THE BENEFITS GAINED BY SUCH A MEDITATION. THIS CHAPTER IS MOST PROFITABLE.

1. Sorrow for sin felt by souls in the Sixth Mansion. 2. How this sorrow is felt. 3. St. Teresa's grief for her past sins. 4. Such souls, centred in God, forget self-interest. 5. The remembrance of divine benefits increases contrition. 6. Meditation on our Lord's Humanity. 7. Warning against discontinuing it. 8. Christ and the saints our models. 9. Meditation of contemplatives. 10. Meditation during aridity. 11. We must search for God when we do not feel His presence. 12. Reasoning and mental prayer. 13. A form of meditation on our Lord's Life and Passion. 14. Simplicity of contemplatives' meditation. 15. Souls in every state of prayer should think of the Passion. 16. Need of the example of Christ and the saints. 17. Faith shows us our Lord as both God and Man. 18. St. Teresa's experience of meditation on the sacred Humanity. 19. Evil of giving up such meditation.

1. IT may seem to you, sisters, that souls to whom God has communicated Himself in such a special manner may feel so sure of enjoying Him for ever as no longer to require to fear or to mourn over their past sins. Those of you will be most apt to hold this opinion who have never received the like favours; souls to whom God has granted these

216

graces will understand what I say. This is a great mistake, for sorrow for sin increases in proportion to the divine grace received and I believe will never quit us until we come to the land where nothing can grieve us any more. Doubtless we feel this pain more at one time than at another and it is of a different kind. A soul so advanced as that we speak of does not think of the punishment threatening its offences but of its great ingratitude towards Him to Whom it owes so much[1] and Who so justly deserves that it should serve Him, for the sublime mysteries revealed have taught it much about the greatness of God.

2. This soul wonders at its former temerity and weeps over its irreverence; its foolishness in the past seems a madness which it never ceases to lament as it remembers for what vile things it forsook so great a Sovereign. The thoughts dwell on this more than on the favours received, which, like those I am about to describe, are so powerful that they seem to rush through the soul at times like a strong, swift river. Yet the sins remain like the mire in the river bed and dwell constantly in the memory, making a heavy cross to bear.

3. I know some one who, though she had ceased to wish for death in order to see God,[2] yet desired it that she might be freed from her continual regret for her past ingratitude towards Him to Whom she owed, and always would owe, so much. She thought no one's guilt could be compared to her own, for she felt there could be none with whom

---

[1] *Life*, ch. vi. 7.

[2] *Excl.* vi. 4, 5. *Supra*, M. v. ch. ii, 5. *Poems* 2, 3, 4. *Minor Works*.

God had borne so patiently nor on whom He had
bestowed such graces.

4. Souls that have reached the state I speak of
have ceased to fear hell. At times, though very
rarely, they grieve keenly over the possibility of
their losing God; their sole dread is lest He should
withdraw His hand, allowing them to offend Him,
and so they might return to their former miserable
condition. They care nothing for their own pain
or glory; if they are anxious not to stay long in
Purgatory, it is more on account of its keeping them
from the Presence of God than because of its torments. Whatever favours God may have shown a
soul, I think it is dangerous for it to forget the
unhappy state it was once in; painful as the remembrance may be, it is most beneficial.

5. Perhaps I think so because I have been so
wicked and that may be the reason why I never
forget my sins; people who have led good lives
have no cause for grief; yet we always fall at times
whilst living in this mortal body. This pain is not
lessened by reflecting that our Lord has already
forgiven and forgotten our faults; our grief is rather
increased at seeing such kindness and favours bestowed on one who deserves nothing but hell. I
think St. Paul and the Magdalen must thus have
suffered a cruel martyrdom;[3] their love was intense,
they had received many mercies and realized the
greatness and the majesty of God and so must
have found it very hard to bear the remembrance

[3] *Life*, ch. xxi. 9. All editions have 'Peter'. St. Teresa only wrote
'P⁰' but the parallel passage proves she meant Pablo, and not Pedro.
See also M. i. ch. i. 5.

of their sins, which they must have regretted with a most tender sorrow.

6. You may fancy that one who has enjoyed such high favours need not meditate on the mysteries of the most sacred Humanity of our Lord Jesus Christ but will be wholly absorbed in love. I have written fully about this elsewhere.[4] I have been contradicted and told that I was wrong and did not understand the matter; that our Lord guides souls in such a way that after having made progress it is best to exercise oneself in matters concerning the Godhead and to avoid what is corporeal; yet nothing will make me admit that this latter is a good way.

7. I may be mistaken; we may all really mean the same thing but I found the devil was trying to lead me astray in this manner. Having been warned by experience in this respect, I have decided to speak again about it here although I have very often done so elsewhere.[5] Be most cautious on the subject; attend to what I venture to say about it and do not believe any one who tells you the contrary. I will endeavour to explain myself more clearly than I did before. If the person who undertook to write on the matter had treated it more explicitly he would have done well, for it may do much harm to speak of it in general terms to us women, who have scanty wits.

8. Some souls imagine they cannot meditate even on the Passion, still less on the most blessed Virgin or on the saints, the memory of whose lives greatly

[4] *Life*, ch. xxii. 9-11.
[5] *Ibid.* ch. xxii. 1; xxiii. 18; xxiv. 2.

benefits and strengthens us.[6] I cannot think what
such persons are to meditate upon, for to withdraw
the thoughts from all corporeal things like the
angelic spirits who are always inflamed with love,
is not possible for us while in this mortal flesh;
we need to study, to meditate upon and to imitate
those who, mortals like ourselves, performed such
heroic deeds for God. How much less should we
wilfully endeavour to abstain from thinking of our
only good and remedy, the most sacred Humanity
of our Lord Jesus Christ? I cannot believe that
any one really does this; they misunderstand their
own minds and so harm both themselves and others.
Of this at least I can assure them: they will never
thus enter the last two mansions of the castle. If
they lose their Guide, our good Jesus, they cannot
find the way and it will be much if they have
stayed safely in the former mansions. Our Lord
Himself tells us that He is 'the Way'; He also
says that He is 'the Light'; that no man cometh
to the Father but by Him ; and that 'He that seeth
Me, seeth the Father also.'[7]

[6] 'Deliberate forgetfulness and rejection of all knowledge and of
form must never be extended to Christ and His sacred Humanity.
Sometimes, indeed, in the height of contemplation and pure intuition
of the Divinity the soul does not remember the Sacred Humanity,
because God raises the mind to this, as it were, confused and most
supernatural knowledge; but for all this, studiously to forget it is by
no means right, for the contemplation of the sacred Humanity and
loving meditation upon it will help us up to all good, and it is by it
we shall ascend most easily to the highest state of union. It is evident
at once that, while all visible and bodily things ought to be forgotten,
for they are a hindrance in our way, He, Who for our salvation became
man, is not to be accounted among them, for He is the truth, the
door, and the way, and our guide to all good.' (St. John of the Cross
Ascent of Mount Carmel, bk. iii. ch. i. 12-14.)

[7] St. John viii. 12; xiv. 6, 9.

9. Such persons tell us that these words have some other meaning; I know of no other meaning but this, which my soul has ever recognized as the true one and which has always suited me right well. Some people (many of whom have spoken to me on the subject) after our Lord has once raised them to perfect contemplation, wish to enjoy it continually. This is impossible; still, the grace of this state remains in their souls in such a way that they cannot reason as before on the mysteries of the Passion and the Life of Christ. I cannot account for it but it is very usual for the mind thus to remain less apt for meditation. I think it must be because, as the one end of meditation is to seek God, after He has once been found and the soul is accustomed to seek Him again by means of the will, it no longer wearies itself by searching for Him with the intellect.

10. It also appears to me that as the will is already inflamed with love, this generous faculty would, if it could, cease to make use of the reason. This would be well, were it not impossible, especially before the soul has reached the last two mansions.[8] Time spent in prayer would thus be lost as the will often needs the use of the understanding to rekindle its love. Notice this point, sisters, which as it is important I will explain more fully. Such a soul

[8] *Life*, ch. xv. 20. St. John of the Cross treats the subject most carefully. He shows how and when meditation becomes impossible : *Ascent of Mount Carmel*, bk. ii. ch. xii. *(circa finem)* ch. xiii. *(per totum)*. *Living Flame of Love*, stanza iii. 35. *Obscure Night*, bk. i. ch. x. 8, and bk. ii. ch. viii. That it should be procured whenever possible : *Ibid.* bk. i. ch. x. *(in fine)*; that it should be resumed : *Ascent of Mount Carmel*, bk. ii. ch. xv.

desires to spend all its time in loving God and
wishes to do nothing else; but it cannot succeed,
for though the will is not dead yet the flame which
kindled it is dying out and the spark needs fanning
into a glow. Ought the soul to remain quiescent
in this aridity, waiting like our father Elias for fire
to descend from heaven[9] to consume the sacrifice
which it makes of itself to God? Certainly not; it
is not right to expect miracles; God will work
them for this soul when He chooses. As I have told
you already and shall do again, His Majesty wishes
us to hold ourselves unworthy of their being
wrought on our account and desires us to help
ourselves to the best of our abilities.

11. In my opinion we ought during our whole
life, to act in this manner, however sublime our
prayer may be. True, those whom our Lord admits into the seventh mansion rarely or never need
thus to help their fervour, for the reason I will tell
you of, if I recollect it when I come to write of this
room where, in a wonderful manner, souls are constantly in the company of Christ our Lord both in
His Humanity and His Divinity.[10] Thus, when
the fire in our hearts, of which I spoke does not
burn in the will, nor do we feel the presence
of God, we must search for Him as He would
have us do, like the Bride in the Canticles,[11] and
must ask all creatures 'who it was that made them;'
as St. Augustine (either in his *Soliloquies* or his

[9] III Reg. xviii. 30-39.

[10] Continual sense of the presence of God : *Life*, ch. xxvii. 6. *Rel.*
xi. 3: 'The intellectual vision of the Three Persons and of the Sacred
Humanity seems ever present.' *Castle*, M. vii. ch. iv. 15.

[11] Cant. iii. 3: 'Num quem diligit anima mea, vidistis ?'

Confessions) tells us that he did.[12] Thus we shall not stand like blockheads, wasting our time in waiting for what we before enjoyed. At first, it may be that our Lord will not renew His gift again for a year or even for many years; His Majesty knows the reason which we should not try to discover since there is no need for us to understand it.

12. As most certainly the way to please God is to keep the commandments and counsels, let us do so diligently, while meditating on His life and death and all we owe Him; then let the rest be as God chooses. Some may answer that their mind refuses to dwell on these subjects; and for the above causes, this to a certain extent is true. You know that it is one thing to reason and another thing for the memory to bring certain truths before the mind. Perhaps you may not understand me; possibly I fail to express myself rightly but I will do my

[12] 'I asked the earth, and it answered me: 'I am not He'; and whatsoever it contains confessed the same. I asked the sea and the depths, and the living, creeping things, and they answered : 'We are not thy God, seek above us.' I asked the heavens, I asked the moving air ; and the whole air with its inhabitants answered : 'Anaximenes was deceived, I am not God.' I asked the heavens, sun, moon, stars. 'Nor,' say they, 'are we the God Whom thou seekest.' And I replied unto all things which encompass the door of my flesh: 'Ye have told me of my God, that ye are not He; tell me something of Him.' And they cried out with a loud voice: 'He made us.' By my thought of them I questioned them, and their beauty gave their answer.' (*St. Augustine's Confessions*, bk. x. ch. 6.)

St. Teresa may have read this in St. Augustine's *Confessions*, (see above, p. 78), or in the *Soliloquies*, a collection of extracts from St. Augustine, St. Bernard, St. Anselm, etc., which was printed in Latin at Venice in 1512, translated into Spanish and brought out at Valladolid in 1515, and again at Medina del Campo in 1553, and at Toledo in 1565. The words quoted by St. Teresa occur in chapter xxxi. See *Life*, ch. xl. 10.

best. Using the understanding much in this manner is what I call meditation.

13. Let us begin by considering the mercy God showed us by giving us His only Son; let us not stop here but go on to reflect upon all the mysteries of His glorious life; or let us first turn our thoughts to His prayer in the garden, then allow them to continue the subject until they reach the crucifixion. Or we may take some part of the Passion such as Christ's apprehension and dwell on this mystery, considering in detail the points to be pondered and thought over, such as the treachery of Judas, the flight of the Apostles, and all that followed. This is an admirable and very meritorious kind of prayer.[13]

14. Souls led by God in supernatural ways and raised to perfect contemplation are right in declaring they cannot practise this kind of meditation. As I said, I know not why, but as a rule they are unable to do so. Yet they would be wrong in saying that they cannot dwell on these mysteries nor frequently think about them, especially when these events are being celebrated by the Catholic Church. Nor is it possible for the soul which has received so much from God to forget these precious proofs of His love which are living sparks to inflame the heart with greater love for our Lord, nor can the mind fail to understand them. Such a soul comprehends these mysteries, which are brought before the mind and stamped on the memory in a more perfect way than with other people, so that the mere sight of our Lord prostrate

[13] *Life*, ch. xiii. 17-23.

in the garden, covered with His terrible sweat, suffices to engross the thoughts not merely for an hour but for several days. The soul looks with a simple gaze upon Who He is and how ungratefully we treat Him in return for such terrible sufferings. Then the will, although perhaps without sensible tenderness, desires to render Him some service for such sublime mercies and longs to suffer something for Him Who bore so much for us, employing itself in similar considerations in which the memory and understanding also take their part.

15. I think this is why such souls cannot reason connectedly about the Passion and fancy they are unable to mediate on it. Those who do not meditate on this subject had better begin to do so; for I know that it will not impede the most sublime prayer nor is it well to omit practising this often. If God then sees fit to enrapture them, well and good; even if they are reluctant, He will make them cease to meditate. I am certain that this way of acting is most helpful to the soul and not the hindrance it would become were great efforts made to use the intellect. This, as I said, I believe cannot be done when a higher state of prayer is attained. It may be otherwise in some cases, for God leads souls in many different ways. Let not those be blamed, however, who are unable to discourse much in prayer, nor should they be judged incapable of enjoying the great graces contained in the mysteries of Jesus Christ, our only Good, which no one, however spiritual he may be, can persuade me it is well to omit contemplating.

16. There are souls who, having made a beginning, or advanced half-way, when they begin to experience the prayer of quiet and to taste the sweetness and consolations God gives, think it is a great thing to enjoy these spiritual pleasures continually. Let them, as I advised elsewhere, cease to give themselves up so much to this absorption. Life is long and full of crosses and we have need to look on Christ our pattern, to see how He bore His trials, and even to take example by His Apostles and saints if we would bear our own trials perfectly. Our good Jesus and His most blessed Mother are too good company to be left and He is well pleased if we grieve at His pains, even though sometimes at the cost of our own consolations and joys.[14] Besides, daughters, consolations are not so frequent in prayer that we have no time for this as well. If any one should tell me she continually enjoys them, and that she is one of those who can never meditate on the divine mysteries, I should feel very doubtful about her state. Be convinced of this; keep free from this deception and to the utmost of your power stop yourselves from being constantly immersed in this intoxication. If you cannot do so, tell the Prioress so that she may employ you too busily for you to think of the matter; thus you will be free from this danger which, if it does no more, when it lasts long, greatly injures the health and brain. I have said enough to prove to those who require it that, however spiritual their state, it is an error so to avoid thinking of corporeal things

[14] *Way of Perf.* ch. xxv. 7.

as to imagine that meditation on the most sacred Humanity can injure the soul.

17. People allege, in defence, that our Lord told His disciples that it was expedient for them that He should go from them.[15] This I cannot admit. He did not say so to His blessed Mother, for her faith was firm. She knew He was both God and man; and although she loved Him more dearly than did His disciples, it was in so perfeét a way that His bodily presence was a help to her. The faith of the Apostles must have been weaker than it was later on, and than ours has reason to be. I assure you, daughters, that I consider this a most dangerous idea whereby the devil might end by robbing us of our devotion to the most blessed Sacrament.

18. The mistake I formerly made[16] did not lead me as far as this, but I did not care so much about meditating on our Lord Jesus Christ, preferring to remain absorbed, awaiting spiritual consolations. I recognized clearly that I was going wrong, for as I could not always keep in this state, my thoughts wandered hither and thither and my soul seemed like a bird, ever flying about and finding no place for rest. Thus I lost much time and did not advance in virtue nor make progress in prayer.

19. I did not understand the reason, and as I believed that I was aéting wisely I think I should never have learnt it but for the advice of a servant

[15] St. John xvi. 7: 'Expedit vobis ut ego vadam; si enim non abiero, Paraclitus non veniet ad vos.' *Life*, ch. xxii. 1, 2 and note.

[16] *Life*, ch. xxii. 11. Although the Saint defends herself against the charge of self-contradiction, there can be no doubt from this avowal that she too was at one time mistaken on this point.

of God whom I consulted about my mode of prayer. Then I perceived plainly how mistaken I had been and I have never ceased regretting that there was a time when I did not realize how difficult it would be to gain by so great a loss. Even if I could, I would seek for nothing save by Him through Whom comes all the good we possess. May He be for ever praised! Amen.

CHAPTER VIII.

SPEAKS OF THE MANNER IN WHICH GOD COMMUNICATES WITH THE SOUL BY INTELLECTUAL VISION AND GIVES ADVICE UPON THE SUBJECT. OF THE EFFECTS PRODUCED BY THIS VISION WHEN GENUINE. SECRECY ABOUT THESE FAVOURS IS ENJOINED.

1. Our Lord's presence accompanying the soul. 2. St. Teresa's experience of this. 3. Confidence and graces resulting from this vision. 4. Its effects. 5. It produces humility. 6. And prepares the soul for other graces. 7. Consciousness of the presence of the saints. 8. Obligations resulting from this grace. 9. Signs that this favour is genuine. 10. A confessor should be consulted. 11. Our Lord will enlighten our advisers. 12. Cautions about this vision.

1. To prove to you more clearly, sisters, the truth of what I have been saying and to show that the more the soul advances, the closer does this good Jesus bear it company, it would be well for me to tell you how, when He so chooses, it cannot withdraw from His presence. This is clearly shown by the manners and ways in which His Majesty communicates Himself to us, manifesting His love by wonderful apparitions and visions which, if He is pleased to aid me, I will describe to you so that you may not be alarmed if any of these favours are granted you. We ought, even if we do not receive

them ourselves, to praise Him fervently for thus communing with creatures, seeing how sovereign are His majesty and power.

2. For example, a person who is in no way expecting such a favour nor has ever imagined herself worthy of receiving it, is conscious that Jesus Christ stands by her side although she sees Him neither with the eyes of the body nor of the soul.[1] This is called an intellectual vision; I cannot tell why. I knew a person to whom God granted both this grace and others I shall describe later on. At first it distressed her, for she could not understand it; she could see nothing, yet so convinced did she feel that Jesus Christ was thus in some way manifesting Himself that she could not doubt that it was some kind of vision, whether it came from God or no. Its powerful effects were a strong argument that it was from Him; still she was alarmed, never having heard of an intellectual vision, nor was she aware that such a thing could be. She however felt certain of our Lord's presence,[2] and He spoke to her several times in the way that I described. Before she had received this favour, she had heard words spoken but had never known who uttered them.

3. She was frightened by this vision which, unlike an imaginary one, does not pass away quickly but lasts for several days and even sometimes for more than a year. She went, in a state of great anxiety, to her confessor[3] who asked her how, if she saw

[1] *Life*, ch. xxvii. 3, 5. *Rel.* vii. 26.
[2] *Life*, ch. xxvii. 7.
[3] *Ibid. l.c.* 4. Father Juan de Pradanos was then the Saint's confessor.

nothing, she knew that our Lord was near her, and bade her describe His appearance. She said that she was unable to do so, nor could she see His face nor tell more than she had already done, but that she was sure it was the fact that it was He Who spoke to her and it was no trick of her imagination. Although people constantly cautioned her against this vision, as a rule she found it impossible to disbelieve in it, especially when she heard the words: 'It is I, be not afraid'[4]

4. The effect of this speech was so powerful that for the time being she could not doubt its truth. She felt much encouraged and rejoiced at being in such good company, seeing that this favour greatly helped her to a constant recollection of God and an extreme care not to displease in any way Him Who seemed ever by her side, watching her. Whenever she desired to speak to His Majesty in prayer, or even at other times, He seemed so close that He could not fail to hear her though He did not speak to her whenever she wished, but unexpectedly, when necessity arose. She was conscious of His being at her right hand, although not in the way we know an ordinary person to be beside us but in a more subtle manner which cannot be described. Yet this presence is quite as evident and certain, and indeed far more so, than the ordinary presence of other people about which we may be deceived; not so in this, for it brings with it graces and spiritual effects which could not come from melancholia. Nor could the devil thus fill the soul with peace,

---

[4] *Life*, ch. xxv. 22; xxx. 17. *Supra*, M. vi. ch. iii. 5. *Rel.* vii. 22. St. John of the Cross, *Ascent of Mount Carmel*, bk. ii. ch. xxxi. 1.

with a constant desire to please God, and such utter contempt of all that does not lead to Him. As time went on, my friend recognized that this was no work of the evil one, as our Lord showed her more and more clearly.

5. However, I know that she often felt great alarm and was at times overcome with confusion, being unable to account for so high a favour having been granted her. She and I were so very intimate[5] that I knew all that passed in her soul, hence my account is thoroughly true and reliable. This favour brings with it an overwhelming sense of self-abasement and humility; the reverse would be the case, did it come from Satan.[6] It is evidently divine; no human effort could produce such feelings nor could any one suppose that such profit came from herself, but must needs recognize it as a gift from the hand of God.

6. Although I believe some of the former favours are more sublime, yet this brings with it a special knowledge of God; a most tender love for Him results from being constantly in His company, while the desires of devoting one's whole being to His service are more fervent than any hitherto described. The conscience is greatly purified by the knowledge of His perpetual and near presence, for although we know that God sees all we do, yet nature inclines us to grow careless and forgetful of it. This is impossible here since our Lord makes the soul conscious that He is close at hand, thus preparing it to receive the other graces men-

[5] In fact, one and the same person.
[6] *Life*, ch. xix. 2; xx. 38. *Way of Perf.* ch. xxxvi. 10.

tioned by constantly making acts of love to Him
Whom it sees or feels at its side. In short, the
benefits caused by this grace prove how great and
how valuable it is. The soul thanks our Lord for
bestowing it on one unworthy of it, but who would
refuse to exchange it for any earthly riches or delight.

7. When our Lord chooses to withdraw His
presence, the soul in its loneliness makes every
possible effort to induce Him to return. This avails
but little, for this grace comes at His will and not
by our endeavours. At times we may enjoy the
company of some saint,[7] which also brings us great
profit. You will ask me, if we see no one, how can
we know whether it is Christ, or His most glorious
Mother, or a saint? Such a person cannot answer
this question or know how she distinguishes them,
but the fact remains undoubted. It seems easy to
recognize our Lord when He speaks, but it is
surprising how the soul can, without hearing a
word from him, recognize which saint has been
sent by God to be its companion and helper.

8. There are other spiritual matters which cannot
be explained. Our inability to grasp them should
teach us how incapable is our nature of understanding the sublime mysteries of God. Those on whom
these favours are bestowed should marvel at and
praise God's mercy for them. As these particular
graces are not granted to everybody, any one who
receives them should esteem them highly and strive
to serve God more zealously, since He has given
her such special aid. Therefore such a person does

[7] *Life*, ch. xxix 6.

not rate herself more highly on this account, but rather thinks she serves Him less than any one else in the world; feeling herself to be under greater obligations to Him than others, any fault she commits pierces her to the heart, as indeed it ought under the circumstances.

9. When the effects described are felt, any of you whom our Lord leads by this way may be certain that it is neither deception nor fancy in her case. I believe it to be impossible for the devil to produce an illusion lasting so long, neither could he benefit the soul so remarkably nor cause such interior peace. It is not his custom, nor, if he would, could such an evil creature bring about so much good; the soul would soon be clouded by self-esteem and the idea that it was better than others. The mind's continual keeping in the presence of God[8] and the concentration of its thoughts on Him would so enrage the fiend that, although he might try the experiment once, he would not often repeat it. God is too faithful to permit him so much power over one whose sole endeavour is to please His Majesty and to lay down her life for His honour and glory; He would soon unmask the demon's artifices.

10. I contend, as I always shall, that if the soul reaps the effects described from these divine graces, although God may withdraw these special favours, His Majesty will turn all things to its advantage; even should He permit the devil to deceive it at any time, the evil spirit will only reap his own confusion. Therefore, as I told you, daughters,

[8] Gen. xvii. 1: 'Ambula coram me et esto perfectus.'

none of you who are led by this way need feel
alarm. Fear is good and we should be cautious and
not over-confident, for if such favours made you
careless, it would prove they were not from God
as they did not leave the results I described. It
would be well at first to tell your case, under the
seal of confession, to a thoroughly qualified theologian (for that is the source whence we must
obtain light) or to some highly spiritual person.
If your confessor is not very spiritual, a good theologian would be preferable;[9] best of all, one who
unites both qualities.[10] Do not be disturbed if he
calls it mere fancy; if it is, it can neither harm nor
benefit your soul much. Recommend yourself to
the divine Majesty and beg Him not to allow you
to be misled.

11. It would be worse should he tell you the
devil is deceiving you, although no learned man
would say so if he sees in you the effects described.
Even should your adviser say this, I know that the
same Lord Who is beside you will comfort and
reassure you and will go to your counsellor and
give him light that he may impart it to you.[11] If
the director, though given to prayer, has not been
led by God in this way, he will at once take fright
and condemn it. Therefore I advise you to choose

[9] 'Magni doctores scholastici, si non sint spirituales, vel omni rerum
spiritualium experientia careant, non solent esse magistri spirituales
idonei—nam theologia scholastica est perfectio intellectus; mystica,
perfectio intellectus et voluntatis: unde bonus theologus scholasticus
potest esse malus theologus mysticus. In rebus tamen difficilibus, dubiis,
spiritualibus, praestat mediocriter spiritualem theologum consulere quam
spiritualem idiotam.' (Schram, *Theol. Myst.* § 483.)

[10] *Life*, ch. v. 6.

[11] *Ibid.* ch. xxv. 18 *sqq. Way of Perf.* ch. iv. 11; v. 3.

a qualified theologian and, if possible, one who is also spiritual. The Prioress ought to allow you this, for although she may feel sure that you are safe from delusion because you lead a good life, yet she is bound to permit you to consult some one for your mutual security. When you have conferred with these persons, be at peace; trouble yourself no more about the matter, for sometimes when there is no cause for fear, the demon gives rise to such immoderate scruples that the person cannot be satisfied with consulting her confessor only once on the subject, especially if he is inexperienced and timid or if he bids her consult him again.

12. Thus that which should have been kept strictly private becomes public; [12] such a person is persecuted and tormented and finds that what she believed to be her own secret has become public property. Hence she suffers many troubles which may even devolve upon the Order in such times as these. Consequently I warn all Prioresses that great caution is required in such matters; also they must not think a nun more virtuous than the rest because such favours are shown her. Our Lord guides every one in the way He knows to be best. This grace, if made good use of, prepares one receiving it to become a great servant of God, but sometimes our Lord bestows it on the weakest souls; therefore in itself it is neither to be esteemed nor condemned. We must look to the virtues; she who is most mortified, humble and single-minded in serving God is the most holy. However, we can never feel very certain about such matters until the true

[12] *Life*, ch. xxiii. 14-15. *Rel.* vii. 17.

Judge rewards each one according to his merits. Then we shall be surprised to find how very different is His judgment from that of this world. May He be for ever praised. Amen.

CHAPTER IX.

THIS CHAPTER SPEAKS OF THE MANNER IN WHICH GOD COMMUNICATES WITH THE SOUL BY IMAGINARY VISIONS. STRONG REASONS ARE GIVEN FOR NOT DESIRING TO BE LED IN THIS WAY; THIS IS VERY PROFITABLE READING.

1. The jewel in the locket. 2. The simile explained. 3. The apparition explained. 4. Awe produced by this vision. 5. False and genuine visions. 6. Illusive visions. 7. Effects of a genuine vision. 8. Conviction left by a genuine vision. 9. Its effects upon the after conduct. 10. A confessor should be consulted. 11. How to treat visions. 12. Effects of seeing the face of Christ. 13. Reasons why visions are not to be sought. 14. The second reason. 15. Third reason. 16. Fourth reason. 17. Fifth reason. 18. Sixth reason. 19. Additional reasons. 20. The virtues more meritorious than consolations. 21. Fervent souls desire to serve God for Himself alone.

1. Now we come to treat of imaginary visions, whereby it is held that the devil is more liable to deceive people than by the other visions I have already described. This is probably true. Yet when imaginary visions are divine, they seem, in a certain manner, more profitable for us than the others, as being more suited to our nature—with the exception of the visions sent by our Lord in the seventh mansion which far surpass all others. The presence of our Lord described in the last chapter may thus be symbolized. Let us suppose that we have in our possession a gold locket containing a precious stone of the highest value and powers, which, though we have not seen it, we are certain

is in the case, and its virtues benefit us when we wear the pendant. Although we have never gazed on it we value it highly, knowing by experience that it has cured us of maladies for which it is remedial. However, we dare not look at it nor open the locket nor could we do so even if we wished, for the owner of the jewel alone knows the secret of unfastening its casket. Although he lent it us for our use, yet he kept the key for himself; he will open the trinket when he chooses to show us its contents and close it again when he sees fit to do so.

2. Our Lord treats us here in this way. Now, suppose the owner of this locket suddenly opened it at times for the benefit of the person to whom he has entrusted it; doubtless the latter would value the diamond more highly through remembering its wonderful lustre. This may be compared to what happens when our Lord is pleased to caress the soul. He shows it in vision His most sacred Humanity under whatever form He chooses; either as He was during His life on earth[1] or after His resurrection.[2] The vision passes as quickly as a flash of lightning, yet this most glorious picture makes an impression on the imagination that I believe can never be effaced until the soul at last sees Christ to enjoy Him for ever. Although I call it a 'picture,' you must not imagine that it looks like a painting; Christ appears as a living Person Who sometimes speaks and reveals deep mysteries. You must understand that though the soul sees this for a certain space of time, it is no more possible to continue

[1] *Life*, ch. vii. 11.   [2] *Ibid.* xxix. 4.

looking at it than to gaze for a very long time on
the sun; therefore this vision passes very quickly,
although its brightness does not pain the interior
sight in the same way as the sun's glare injures
our bodily eyes.

3. The image is seen by the interior sight alone;
but of bodily apparitions I can say nothing, for the
person I know so intimately never having experienced anything of the kind herself could not speak
about them with certainty.[3] The splendour of Him
Who is revealed in the vision resembles an infused
light like that of the sun covered with a veil as
transparent as a diamond, if such a texture could
be woven, while His raiment looks like fine linen.
The soul to whom God grants this vision almost
always falls into an ecstasy, nature being too weak
to bear so dread a sight. I say 'dread,' though this
apparition is more lovely and delightful than anything that could be imagined even though any
one should live a thousand years and spend all that
time in trying to picture it, for it far surpasses our
limited imagination and understanding; yet the
presence of such surpassing majesty inspires the
soul with great fear.

4. There is no need to ask how the soul knew
Who He was or who declared with absolute certainty that He was the Lord of heaven and earth.
This is not so with earthly kings; unless we were
told their names or saw their attendant courtiers,
they would attract little notice. O Lord, how little
do we Christians know Thee! What will that day
be in which Thou comest as our Judge, since now,

[3] *Life*, ch. vii. 11, 12.

when Thou comest as a Friend to Thy spouse, the sight of Thee strikes us with such awe? O daughters! what will it be when He says in wrath: 'Go, accursed of my Father?'[4] Let this impression be the result of this favour granted by God to the soul and we shall reap no little benefit from it, since St. Jerome, saint as he was, ever kept the thought of the last judgment before his eyes.[5] Thus we shall care nothing what sufferings we endure from the austerities of our Rule, for long as they may last, the time is but a moment compared to this eternity of pain. I sincerely assure you that, wicked as I am, I have never feared the torments of hell[6] for they have seemed to me as nothing when I remembered that the lost would see the beautiful, meek and pitiful eyes of our Lord turned on them in wrath.[7] I have thought all my life that this would be more than my heart could bear.

5. How much more must any one fear this to whom our Lord so revealed Himself in vision here as to overcome her feelings and produce unconsciousness! This must be the reason that the soul remains in a rapture: our Lord strengthens its weakness so as to unite it to His greatness in this sublime communion with God. When any one

---

[4] St. Matt. xxv. 41: 'Discedite a me, maledicti, in ignem æternum.'

[5] 'Whenever I ponder on the Day of Judgment I am overwhelmed by the thought and tremble from head to foot.' (St. Jerome). The following saying is by some attributed to St. Jerome, though not to be found in his works: 'Whether I eat or drink, or whatever else I do, the dreadful trumpet of the last day seems always sounding in my ears: Arise, ye dead, and come to judgment.' (Alban Butler, *Life of St. Jerome*). The *Life of Christ* by Ludolf of Saxony gives this quotation with the word *vox* instead of *tuba* (part ii. ch. lxxxvii. 9).

[6] *Life*, ch. iii. 7.   [7] *Excl.* xiii. 3.

can contemplate this sight of our Lord for a long time, I do not believe it is a vision but rather some overmastering idea which causes the imagination to fancy it sees something; but this illusion is only like a dead image in comparison with the living reality of the other case.

6. As not only three or four, but a large number of people have spoken to me on the subject, I know by experience that there are souls which, either because they possess vivid imaginations or active minds, or for some other reason of which I am ignorant, are so absorbed in their own ideas as to feel certain they see whatever their fancy imagines. If they had ever beheld a genuine vision, they would recognize the deception unmistakably. They themselves fabricate, piece by piece, what they fancy they see: no after effects are produced on the mind, which is less moved to devotion than by the sight of a sacred picture. It is clear that no attention should be paid to such fancies, which pass more quickly than dreams from the memory.

7. In the favour of which I speak, the case is very different. A person is far from thinking of seeing anything, no idea of which has crossed the mind, when suddenly the vision is revealed in its entirety, causing within the powers and senses of the soul a fright and confusion soon changed into a blissful peace. Thus, after St. Paul was thrown to the ground, a great tempest and noise followed from heaven;[8] so, in the interior world of the soul, there is a violent tumult followed instantly, as I said, by

[8] Acts ix. 3, 4.

perfect calm. Meanwhile certain sublime truths have been so impressed on the mind that it needs no other master, for with no effort of its own, Wisdom Himself has enlightened its former ignorance.

8. The soul for some time afterwards possesses such certainty that this grace comes from God that whatever people may say to the contrary it cannot fear delusion. Later on, when her confessor suggests doubts to her, God may allow such a person to waver in her belief for a time and to feel misgivings lest, in punishment for her sins, she may possibly have been left to go astray. However, she does not give way to these apprehensions, but (as I said in speaking of other matters)[9] they only affect her in the same way as the temptations of the devil against faith, which may disturb the mind but do not shake the firmness of belief. In fact, the more severe the assault,[10] the more certain is she that the evil one could never have produced the great benefits she is conscious of having received, because he exercises no such power over the interior of the soul. He may present a false apparition but it does not possess such truth, majesty, and efficacy.

9. As confessors cannot see these effects, which perhaps the person to whom God has shown the vision is unable to explain, they are afraid of deception, as indeed they have good reason to be. Therefore caution is necessary and time should be allowed to see what effects follow. Day by day, the progress of the soul in humility and in the virtues should be watched: if the devil is concerned in the matter, he will soon show signs of himself and will

---

[9] *Castle*, M. vi. ch. iii. 12.   [10] *Way of Perf.* ch. xl. 4.

be detected in a thousand lies. If the confessor is
experienced and has received such favours himself,
he will not take long in discovering the truth. In
fact, he will know immediately, on being told of
the vision, whether it is divine or comes from the
imagination or the demon: more especially if he
has received the gift of discerning spirits—then, if
he is learned, he will understand the matter at
once even though he has not personally experienced the like.

10. The great point is, sisters, that you should
be perfectly candid and straightforward with your
confessor: I do not mean in declaring your sins—
that is evident enough—but in giving him an
account of your prayer." Unless you do this, I cannot assure you of your safety nor that you are led
by God. Our Lord desires that we should be as
truthful and open with those who stand in His
place as we should with Himself; that we should
wish them to know not only our thoughts but
especially all relating to our actions, however insignificant. Then you need feel no trouble nor anxiety"
because even if your vision were not from God, it
could do you no harm if you are humble and possess
a good conscience, for His Majesty knows how to
glean good from evil. What the devil intended to
injure you will benefit you instead: believing that
God has granted you such signal favours, you will
strive to please Him better and will keep His
image ever before your memory.

¹¹ *Life*, ch. xxvi. 5 ; xxviii. 21.
¹² *Way of Perf.* ch. xl. 3.

11. A great theologian[13] once said that he should not trouble himself though the devil, who is a clever painter, should present before his eyes the living image of Christ, which would only kindle his devotion and defeat the evil one with his own weapons. However wicked an artist may be, we should reverence his picture if it represents Him Who is our only good. This great scholar held that it was very wrong to advise any one who saw a vision of our Lord to offer it signs of scorn,[14] because we are bound to show respect to the portrait of our King wherever we see it. I am sure that he was right, for even in the world any one who was on friendly terms with a person would take it as an offence were his portrait treated with contempt. How much more should we always show respect to a crucifix or a picture of our heavenly Sovereign wherever it meets our gaze! Although I have written about this elsewhere, I am glad of the opportunity of saying it now for I know some one who was deeply pained at being bidden to behave in this way. I know not who can have invented such a torture for one who felt bound to obey the counsel given by her confessor, for she would have thought her soul was at stake had she disobeyed him. My advice is, if you are given such an order, that humbly alleging the reasons I have set before you to your confessor, you should not carry it out. I am perfectly satisfied with the motives given for doing so by him who counselled me on this subject.

[13] This was Father Dominic Bañez. *Found.* ch. viii. 3. *Life*, ch. xxix. 6, 7 and note.

[14] *Letters of Blessed John of Avila* (translated by the Benedictines of Stanbrook), i. 5, p. 19.

12. One great advantage gained by the soul from this favour shown by our Lord is that when thinking of Him or of His life and Passion, the remembrance of His most meek and beautiful face brings with it the greatest consolation. In the same way, we feel happier after having seen a benefactor than if we had never known him personally. I can assure you that the remembrance of the joy caused by this vision gives us the greatest comfort and assistance.

13. Many other advantages result; but as I have written elsewhere [15] at length about the effect these visions produce, and must do so again later on, I will say no more now lest I weary us both. But I most earnestly advise you, when you know or hear of God's bestowing these graces on others, never to pray nor desire to be led by this way yourself though it may appear to you to be very good; indeed, it ought to be highly esteemed and reverenced, yet no one should seek to go by it for several reasons. Firstly, as it is a want of humility to desire what you have never deserved, I do not think any one who longs for these graces can be really humble: a common labourer never dreams of wishing to be made a king—the thing seems impossible and he is unfit for it; a lowly mind has the same feeling about these divine favours. I do not believe God will ever bestow these gifts on such a person, as before doing so He always gives thorough self-knowledge. How can that soul, while filled with such lofty aspirations, realize the truth that He has shown it great mercy in not casting it into hell?

14. The second reason is that such a one is certain

[15] *Life*, ch. xxviii. 13, 14.

to be deceived or at least is in great danger of delusion, for an entrance is thus left open to the devil, who only needs to see the door left ajar to slip in at once and play us a thousand tricks.

15. Thirdly: when people strongly desire a thing, the imagination makes them fancy they see or hear it, just as when a man's mind is set upon a subject all day he dreams of it at night.

16. Fourthly: it would be very presumptuous of me to choose a way for myself without knowing what is good for me.[16] I should leave our Lord, Who knows my soul, to guide me as is best for me so that His will may be done in all things.

17. Fifthly: do you think people on whom our Lord bestows these favours have little to suffer? No, indeed! their trials are most severe and of many kinds. How can you tell whether you would be able to bear them?

18. Sixthly: perhaps what you think would be your gain might prove your loss, as happened to Saul when he was made king.[17] In short, sisters, there are other reasons besides these; believe me, it is safer to wish only what God wishes, Who knows us better than we know ourselves and Who loves us. Let us place ourselves entirely in His hands so that His will may be done in us; we can never go astray if our will is ever firmly fixed on this.

19. Know that for having received many favours of this kind, you will not merit more glory but will

---

[16] St. Teresa, when led in this way, always asked to be delivered from favours so dangerous as visions, etc. See *Life*, ch. xxv. 20; xxvii. 3.

[17] I. Reg. xv. 26-28.

be the more stringently obliged to serve, since you have received more. God does not deprive us of anything by which we merit more, for this remains in our own control. There are many saints who never knew what it was to receive one such favour, while others who have received them are not saints at all. Do not imagine that these gifts are continually bestowed; indeed, for one that is granted, the soul bears many a cross, so that instead of longing to receive more favours, it only strives to use them better.

20. True, such a grace is a most powerful aid towards practising the virtues in their highest perfection, but it is far more meritorious to gain them at the cost of one's own toil. I was acquainted with some one,[18] indeed with two people (of whom one was a man), on whom our Lord had bestowed some of these gifts. They were both so desirous of serving His Majesty at their own cost without these great consolations and so longed to suffer for His sake, that they remonstrated with Him for giving them these favours, and if it had been possible would have refused to receive them. When I say 'consolations,' I do not mean these visions which greatly benefit the soul and are highly to be esteemed, but the delights given by God during contemplation.

21. I believe that these desires are supernatural and proper to very fervent souls who wish to prove to God that they do not serve Him for pay; so as I said, such people do not urge themselves to work

---

[18] *Life*, ch. xl. 27. She herself was one, and the other, no doubt, was St. John of the Cross.

harder for Him by the thought of the glory they will gain, but rather labour to satisfy their love, of which the nature is to toil for the Beloved in a thousand ways. Such souls would fain find a way to consume themselves in Him, and were there need that, for the sake of God's greater glory, they should be annihilated for ever, they would count it great gain. May He be for ever praised Who, in abasing Himself to hold converse with us miserable creatures, vouchsafes to manifest His greatness! Amen.

CHAPTER X.

SPEAKS OF VARIOUS OTHER GRACES GOD BESTOWS ON THE SOUL IN DIFFERENT WAYS, AND OF THE GREAT BENEFITS CONFERRED BY THEM.

1. Reasons for speaking of these supernatural favours. 2. An intellectual vision. 3. God compared to a palace in which His creatures dwell. 4. Forgive as we are forgiven. 5. The vision shows God to be Truth itself. 6. We should imitate God by truthfulness. 7. Why God reveals these truths.

1. OUR Lord communicates with the soul by means of these apparitions on many occasions—sometimes when it is afflicted, at other times when it is about to receive some heavy cross, and again for the sake of the mutual delight of Himself and His beloved. There is no need for me to specify each different case nor do I intend to do so. I only wish to teach you (as far as I am acquainted with them myself) what are the different favours God shows a soul in this state so that you may understand their characteristics and the effects they produce.

Thus you will not mistake every idle fancy for a vision and if you really see one, knowing that such a thing is possible, you will not be disturbed nor unhappy. The devil, who gains greatly by it, is delighted to see a soul troubled and distressed, knowing how this hinders it from employing itself wholly in loving and serving God.

2. His Majesty has far higher ways of communicating Himself to the soul; they are less dangerous for I do not think the evil spirit can imitate them. They are more difficult to explain, being more abstruse; therefore imaginary visions are easier to describe. God is sometimes pleased, while a person is engaged in prayer and in perfeᵭt possession of her senses, to suspend them and to discover sublime mysteries to her which she appears to see within God Himself. This is no vision of the most sacred Humanity nor can I rightly say the soul 'sees,' for it sees nothing; this is no imaginary vision but a highly intelleᵭtual one, wherein is manifested how all things are beheld in God and how He contains them within Himself.[1] It is of great value, for although passing in an instant, it remains deeply engraved in the memory, producing a feeling of great shame in the mind which perceives more clearly the malice of offences against God, since these most heinous sins are committed within His very being since we dwell within Him. I will try to explain this truth to you by a comparison, for although it is obvious and has been often told us, we either never refleᵭt upon it or do not wish to

[1] *Life*, ch. xl. 13-16.

understand it. If we realized it, we could not possibly behave with such audacity.

3. Let us compare God to a very spacious and magnificent mansion or palace and remember that this edifice is God Himself. Can the sinner withdraw from it in order to carry out his crimes? No, certainly not, for within this very palace, that is, within God Himself, are perpetrated all the abominations, impurities and evil deeds that sinners commit. Oh awful thought, well worthy to be pondered over! What profit it would bring to us, who know so little and understand these truths but partially or how could we possibly be so reckless in our daring? Let us, sisters, meditate on the infinite mercy and patience of God in not casting us down to hell at once and let us render Him hearty thanks. Surely we should be ashamed of resenting anything done or said against us—*we* who are the scum of the earth—when we see what outrages are offered to *God* our *Creator* within His very being, by us His creatures; yet we are wounded whenever we hear of an unkind word having been spoken of us in our absence, although perhaps with no evil intention.

4. Oh misery of mankind! When, daughters, shall we imitate Almighty God in any way? Oh, let us not think we are doing great things if we suffer injuries *patiently:* rather let us bear them with *alacrity;* let us love our enemies, since this great God has not ceased to love us in spite of our many sins! This is indeed the chief reason that all should forgive any harm done them. I assure you, daughters, that though this vision passes very quickly,

our Lord has bestowed signal grace on her to whom
He grants it, if she seeks to profit by keeping it
constantly in mind.

5. Short as the time lasts, yet, in a manner impossible to describe, God also manifests that in
Him there is a verity which makes all truth in
creatures seem obscure. He convinces the soul
that He alone is that Truth which cannot lie, thus
demonstrating the meaning of David's words in
the psalm: 'Every man is a liar,'² which could
never be thus realized by any other means, however often we might hear that God is truth infal-
lible. As I recall Pilate and how he besought our
Lord in His Passion to answer his question: 'What
is truth?'³ I realize how little mortals know of
that sublime veracity.

6. I wish I could explain this better but am unable
to do so. Let us learn from it, sisters, that if we
would bear any resemblance to our God and our
Spouse, we must strive to walk ever in the truth.
I do not merely mean that we should not tell falsehoods—thank God, I see that in these convents you
are most careful never to do so on any account—
but I desire that as far as possible we should act
with perfect truth before God and man and above
all that we should not wish to be thought better
than we are; that in all our deeds we should ascribe
to God what is His and attribute what is ours to
ourselves, and that we should seek for verity in all
things. Thus we shall care little for this world,
which is but deception and falsehood, and there-

² Ps. cxv. 11. 'Omnis homo mendax.'
³ St. John xviii. 38: Quid est veritas?

fore cannot last. Once, while I was wondering why our Lord so dearly loves the virtue of humility, the thought suddenly struck me, without previous reflection, that it is because God is the supreme Truth and humility is the *truth*, for it is most true that we have nothing good of ourselves but only misery and nothingness: whoever ignores this, lives a life of falsehood. They that realize this fact most deeply are the most pleasing to God, the supreme Truth, for they walk in the truth. God grant, sisters, that we may have the grace never to lose this self-knowledge! Amen.

7. Our Lord shows the soul these favours because she is now indeed His bride, resolute to do His will in all things; therefore He wishes to give her some idea how to accomplish it and to manifest to her some of His divine attributes. I need say no more about it, but I believe the two points above mentioned will prove very useful. These favours should cause no fear but lead us to praise God for bestowing these graces. I think neither the devil nor our own imaginations can have much to do with them, therefore the soul may rest in perfect peace.

CHAPTER XI.

1. WILL all these graces bestowed by the Spouse upon the soul suffice to content this little dove or butterfly (you see I have not forgotten her after all!) so that she may settle down and rest in the place where she is to die? No indeed: her state is far worse than ever; although she has been receiving these favours for many years past, she still sighs and weeps because each grace augments her pain. She sees herself still far away from God, yet with her increased knowledge of His attributes her longing and her love for Him grow ever stronger as she learns more fully how this great God and Sovereign deserves to be loved. As, year by year her yearning after Him gradually becomes keener, she experiences the bitter suffering I am about to describe. I speak of 'years' because relating what happened to the person I mentioned, though I know well that with God time has no limits and in a single moment He can raise a soul to the most sublime state I have described. His Majesty has the power to do all He wishes and He wishes to do much for us. These longings, tears, sighs, and

violent and impetuous desires and strong feelings, which seem to proceed from our vehement love, are yet as nothing compared with what I am about to describe and seem but a smouldering fire, the heat of which, though painful, is yet tolerable.

2. While the soul is thus inflamed with love, it often happens that, from a passing thought or spoken word of how death delays its coming, the heart receives, it knows not how or whence, a blow as from a fiery dart.[1] I do not say that this actually is a 'dart,' but, whatever it may be, decidedly it does not come from any part of our being.[2] Neither is it really a 'blow' though I call it one, but it wounds us severely—not, I think, in that part of our nature subject to physical pain but in the very depths and centre of the soul, where this thunder-bolt, in its rapid course, reduces all the earthly part of our nature to powder. At the time we cannot even remember our own existence, for in an instant, the faculties of the soul are so fettered as to be incapable of any action except the power they retain of increasing our torture. Do not think I am exaggerating; indeed I fall short of explaining what happens which cannot be described.

3. This is a trance of the senses and faculties except as regards what helps to make the agony more intense. The understanding realizes acutely what cause there is for grief in separation from God and His Majesty now augments this sorrow by a vivid manifestation of Himself. This increases the anguish to such a degree that the sufferer gives vent

[1] *Life*, ch. xxix. 17. (Transverberation.)
[2] *Ibid.* ch. xxix. 13, 14.   *Rel.* viii. 16-19.

to loud cries which she cannot stifle, however
patient and accustomed to pain she may be, because
this torture is not corporal but attacks the innermost recesses of the soul. The person I speak of
learnt from this how much more acutely the spirit
is capable of suffering than the body; she understood that this resembled the pains of purgatory,
where the absence of the flesh does not prevent
the torture's being far worse than any we can feel
in this world.

4. I saw some one in this condition who I really
thought would have died, nor would it have been
surprising, for there is great danger of death in
this state. Short as is the time it lasts, it leaves the
limbs all disjointed and the pulse as feeble as if
the soul were on the point of departure, which is
indeed the case, for the natural heat fails, while
that which is supernatural so burns the frame that
were it increased ever so little God would satisfy
the soul's desire for death. Not that any pain is
felt by the body at the moment, although, as I
said, all the joints are dislocated so that for two or
three days afterwards the suffering is too severe
for the person to have even the strength to hold
a pen;[3] indeed I believe that the health becomes
permanently enfeebled in consequence. At the
time this is not felt, probably because the spiritual
torments are so much more keen that the bodily
ones remain unnoticed; just as when there is very

[3] St. John of the Cross, *Obscure Night*, bk. ii. ch. i. *(in fine)* ; *Spiritual Canticle*, stanza xiii; xiv-xv. *(in fine)*. When this happened to St.
Teresa she was unable to write for twelve days. Ribera, *Acta SS.* p. 555
(in fine). *Rel.* viii. 13. *Life*, ch. xx. 16.

severe pain in one part, slighter aches elsewhere are hardly perceived, as I know by experience. During this favour there is no physical suffering either great or small, nor do I think the person would feel it were she torn to pieces.

5. Perhaps you will say this is an imperfection, and you may ask why she does not conform herself to the will of God since she has so completely surrendered herself to it. Hitherto she has been able to do so and she consecrated her life to it; but now she cannot because her reason is reduced to such a state that she is no longer mistress of herself, nor can she think of anything but what tends to increase her torment—for why should she seek to live apart from her only Good? She feels a strange loneliness, finding no companionship in any earthly creature; nor could she, I believe, among those who dwell in heaven, since they are not her Beloved: meanwhile all society is a torture to her. She is like one suspended in mid-air, who can neither touch the earth nor mount to heaven; she is unable to reach the water while parched with thirst and this is not a thirst that can be borne, but one which nothing will quench nor would she have it quenched save with that water of which our Lord spoke to the Samaritan woman, but this is not given to her.[4]

6. Alas, O Lord, to what a state dost Thou bring those who love Thee! Yet these sufferings are as nothing compared with the reward Thou wilt give for them. It is right that great riches should be

[4] St. John iv. 15. *Life*, ch. xxx. 24. *Way of Perf.* ch. xix. 4 *sqq.* *Concept.* ch. vii. 7, 8. *Found.* ch. xxxi. 42. See note, *Life*, ch. i. 6.

dearly bought. Moreover, her pains purify her soul so that it may enter the seventh mansion, as purgatory cleanses spirits which are to enter heaven:[5] then indeed these trials will appear like a drop of water compared to the sea. Though this torment and grief could not, I think, be surpassed by any earthly cross (so at least this person said and she had endured much both in body and mind), yet they appeared to her as nothing in comparison with their recompense. The soul realizes that it has not merited anguish which is of such measureless value. This conviction, although bringing no relief, enables the sufferer to bear her trials willingly—for her entire lifetime, if God so wills, —although instead of dying once for all, this would be but a living death, for truly it is nothing else.

7. Let us remember, sisters, how those who are in hell lack this submission to the divine will and the resignation and consolation God gives such a soul and the solace of knowing that their pains benefit them, for the damned will continually suffer more and more; (*more and more*, I mean in regard to accidental pains[6]). The soul feels far more keenly than the body and the torments I have

---

[5] St. John of the Cross, *Obscure Night*, bk. ii. ch. xii.

[6] Marginal note in the Saint's handwriting. The 'substantial' pain of hell consists in the irrevocable loss of God, our last end and supreme Good; this is incurred from the first moment in its fullest intensity and therefore cannot increase. The physical pain with which the bodies will be afflicted when united to the souls after the general resurrection may vary, but will neither increase nor abate. The 'accidental' pain of the damned arises from various causes, for instance from the ever-increasing effects of evil actions, and therefore increases in the same proportion. Thus a heresiarch will suffer keener accidental pain as more and more souls are lost through his false teaching.

just described are incomparably less severe than those endured by the lost, who also know that their anguish will last for ever: what, then, will become of these miserable souls? What can we do or suffer during our short lives which is worth reckoning if it will free us from such terrible and endless torments? I assure you that, unless you have learned by experience, it would be impossible to make you realize how acute are spiritual pangs and how different from physical pain. Our Lord wishes us to understand this, so that we may realize what gratitude we owe Him for having called us to a state where we may hope, by His mercy, to be freed from and forgiven our sins.

8. Let us return to the soul we left in such cruel torment. This agony does not continue for long in its full violence—never, I believe, longer than three or four hours; were it prolonged, the weakness of our nature could not endure it except by a miracle. In one case, where it lasted only a quarter of an hour, the sufferer was left utterly exhausted; indeed, so violent was the attack that she completely lost consciousness. This occurred when she unexpectedly heard some verses to the effect that life seemed unending; she was engaged in conversation at the time, which was on the last day of Easter. All Eastertide she had suffered such aridity as hardly to realize what mystery was being celebrated.[7]

[7] *Rel.* iv. 1. *Concept.* ch. vii. 2. Isabel of Jesus, in her deposition in the Acts of Canonisation (Fuente, *Obras*, vol. vi. 316) declares that she was the singer. The words were:

> Véante mis ojos,
> Dulce Jesús bueno:
> Véante mis ojos,
> Y muérame yo luégo.

9. It is as impossible to resist this suffering as it would be to prevent the flame's having heat enough to burn us if we were thrown into a fire. These feelings cannot be concealed: all who are present recognize the dangerous condition of such a person although they are unable to see what is passing within her. True, she knows her friends are near, but they and all earthly things seem to her but shadows. To show you that, should you ever be in this state, it is possible for your weakness and human nature to be of help to you, I may tell you that at times, when a person seems dying from her desire for death [8] which so oppresses her soul with grief that it appears on the point of leaving her body, yet her mind, terrified at the thought, tries to still its pain so as to keep death at bay. Evidently this fear arises from human infirmity, for the soul's longings for death do not abate meanwhile nor can its sorrows be stilled or allayed until God brings it comfort.[9] This He usually does by a deep trance or by some vision whereby the true Comforter consoles and strengthens the heart, which thus becomes resigned to live as long as He wills.[10]

Fuente, *l.c.* vol. v. 143, note 1. *Œuvres*, ii. 231. (Poem 36, English version.) There is a slight difference in the two relations of this occurrence. In *Rel.* iv. St. Teresa seems to imply that it happened on Easter Sunday evening, but here she says distinctly: 'Pascua de Resurreccion, el postrer dia,' that is, on Easter Tuesday, April 17, 1571, at Salamanca.

[8] Compare the words 'Que muero porque no muero' in the *Glosa* of St. Teresa. *Way of Perf.* ch. xlii . 2. *Castle*, M. vii. ch. iii. 14.

[9] *Way of Perf.* ch. xix. 10. *Excl.* vi.; xii. 2.; xiv.

[10] See the two versions of the poems written by the Saint on her recovery from the trance into which she was thrown, beginning 'Vivir sin vivir in me' and the poem, 'Cuan triste es, Dios mio (Poems 2, 3, and 4, English version). See also St. Teresa's poem, 'Ya toda me

10. This favour entails great suffering but leaves most precious graces within the soul, which loses all fear of any crosses it may henceforth meet with, for in comparison with the acute anguish it has gone through all else seems nothing. Seeing what she has gained, the sufferer would gladly endure frequently the same pains[11] but can do nothing to help herself in the matter. There are no means of reaching that state again until God chooses to decree it, when neither resistance nor escape is possible. The mind feels far deeper contempt for the world than before, realizing that nothing earthly can succour it in its torture; it is also much more detached from creatures, having learnt that no one but its Creator can bring it consolation and strength. It is more anxious and careful not to offend God, seeing that He can torment as well as comfort.[12]

11. Two things in this spiritual state seem to me to endanger life,—one is that of which I have just spoken which is a real peril and no small one; the other an excessive gladness and a delight so extreme that the soul appears to swoon away and seems on the point of leaving the body, which indeed would bring it no small joy.

entregué y dí.' (Poem 7,   English version).

Struck by the gentle Hunter
    And overthrown,
Within the arms of Love
    My soul lay prone.
Raised to new life at last,
This contract 'tween us passed,
That the Beloved should be mine own,
    I His alone.

[11] *Rel.* viii. 17.   [12] *Acta SS.* p. 64, n. 229.

12. Now you see. sisters, whether I had not reason to tell you that courage was needed for these favours and that when any one asks for them from our Lord He may well reply, as He did to the sons of Zebedee: 'Can you drink the chalice that I shall drink?''[13] I believe, sisters, we should all answer 'Yes'—and we should be perfectly right for His Majesty gives strength when He sees it needed: He ever defends such souls and answers for them when they are persecuted and slandered as He did for the Magdalen—if not in words, at least in deeds.[14] At last, ah, at last! before they die He repays them for all they have suffered, as you shall now learn. May He be for ever blessed and may all creatures praise Him! Amen.

[13] St. Matt. xx. 22: 'Potestis bibere calicem quem ego bibiturus sum?'

[14] St. Matt. xxvi. 10: St. Mark xiv. 6; St. John xii. 7. *Way of Perf.* ch. xvi. 7; xvii. 4. *Excl.* v. 2-4.

THE SEVENTH MANSIONS

CHAPTER I.

TREATS OF THE SUBLIME FAVOURS GOD BESTOWS ON SOULS
WHICH HAVE ENTERED THE SEVENTH MANSIONS. THE AUTHOR
SHOWS THE DIFFERENCE SHE BELIEVES TO EXIST BETWEEN
SOUL AND SPIRIT ALTHOUGH THEY ARE BOTH ONE. THIS
CHAPTER CONTAINS SOME NOTEWORTHY THINGS.

*1. Sublime mysteries of these mansions. 2. St. Teresa abashed at
treating such subjects. 3. Our Lord introduces His bride into His
presence chamber. 4. Darkness of a soul in mortal sin. 5. Inter-
cession for sinners. 6. The soul an interior world. 7. The spiritual
nuptials. 8. Former favours differ from spiritual nuptials. 9. The
Blessed Trinity revealed to the soul. 10. Permanence of Its
presence in the soul. 11. The effects. 12. This presence is not always equally realized. 13. It is beyond the soul's control. 14. The
centre of the soul remains calm. 15. The soul and the spirit distinct though united. 16. The soul and its faculties not identical.*

1. You may think, sisters, that so much has been
said of this spiritual journey that nothing remains
to be added. That would be a great mistake: God's
immensity has no limits, neither have His works;
therefore, who can recount His mercies and His
greatness?[1] It is impossible, so do not be amazed
at what I write about them which is but a cipher
of what remains untold concerning God. He has
shown great mercy in communicating these mys-

[1] Ps. cxliv. 3: 'Magnitudinis ejus non est finis.'

teries to one who could recount them to us, for as
we learn more of His intercourse with creatures,
we ought to praise Him more fervently and to
esteem more highly the soul in which He so
delights. Each of us possesses a soul but we do not
realize its value as made in the image of God,
therefore we fail to understand the important
secrets it contains. May His Majesty be pleased
to guide my pen and to teach me to say *somewhat*
of the *much* there is to tell of His revelations to
the souls He leads into this mansion. I have begged
Him earnestly to help me, since He sees that my
object is to reveal His mercies for the praise and
glory of His name. I hope He will grant this
favour, if not for my own sake, at least for yours,
sisters—so that you may discover how vital it is for
you to put no obstacle in the way of the Spiritual
Marriage of the Bridegroom with your soul which
brings, as you will learn, such signal blessings
with it.

2. O great God! surely such a miserable creature
as myself should tremble at the thought of speaking on such a subject so far beyond anything I
deserve to understand. Indeed I felt abashed and
doubted whether it would not be better to finish
writing about this Mansion in a few words, lest
people might imagine that I am recounting my
personal experience. I was overwhelmed with
shame for, knowing what I am, it is a terrible
undertaking. On the other hand, this fear seemed
but a temptation and weakness: even if I should
be misjudged, so long as God is but a little better
praised and known, let all the world revile me.

Besides, I may be dead before this book is seen
May He Who lives and shall live to all eternity
be praised! Amen.

3. When our Lord is pleased to take pity on the
sufferings, both past and present, endured through
her longing for Him by this soul which He has
spiritually taken for His bride, He, before consum-
mating the celestial marriage, brings her into this
His mansion or presence chamber. This is the
seventh Mansion, for as He has a dwelling-place
in heaven, so has He in the soul, where none but
He may abide and which may be termed a second
heaven.

4. It is important, sisters, that we should not
fancy the soul to be in darkness. As we are accustomed to believe there is no light but that which
is exterior, we imagine that the soul is wrapt in
obscurity. This is indeed the case with a soul out
of the state of grace,[2] not, however, through any
defect in the Sun of Justice which remains within
it and gives it being, but the soul itself is incapable
of receiving the light, as I think I said in speaking
of the first Mansion.[3] A certain person was given
to understand that such unfortunate souls are, as it
were, imprisoned in a gloomy dungeon, chained
hand and foot and unable to perform any meritorious action: they are also both blind and dumb.
Well may we pity them when we reflect that we
ourselves were once in the same state and that
God may show them mercy also.

[2] See the Saint's description of a soul in the state of sin, *Rel.* iii. 13.
(towards the end).
[3] *Supra*, M. i. ch. ii. 1.

5. Let us, then, sisters, be most zealous in interceding for them and never neglect it. To pray for a soul in mortal sin is a far more profitable form of almsgiving than it would be to help a Christian whom we saw with hands strongly fettered behind his back, tied to a post and dying of hunger—not for want of food, because plenty of the choicest delicacies lay near him, but because he was unable to put them into his mouth, although he was extremely exhausted and on the point of dying, and that not a temporal death, but an eternal one. Would it not be extremely cruel of us to stand looking at him, and give him nothing to eat? What if by your prayers you could loose his bonds? Now you understand.

6. For the love of God I implore you constantly to remember in your prayers souls in a like case. We are not speaking now of them but of others who, by the mercy of God, have done penance for their sins and are in a state of grace. You must not think of the soul as insignificant and petty but as an interior world containing the number of beautiful mansions you have seen; as indeed it should, since in the centre of the soul there is a mansion reserved for God Himself.

7. When His Majesty deigns to bestow on the soul the grace of these divine nuptials, He brings it into His presence chamber and does not treat it as before, when He put it into a trance. I believe He then united it to Himself, as also during the prayer of union; but then only the superior part was affected and the soul did not feel called to

enter its own centre as it does in this mansion. Here it matters little whether it is in the one way or the other.

8. In the former favours our Lord unites the spirit to Himself and makes it both blind and dumb like St. Paul after his conversion,[4] thus preventing its knowing whence or how it enjoys this grace, for the supreme delight of the spirit is to realize its nearness to God. During the actual moment of divine union the soul feels nothing, all its powers being entirely lost. But now He acts differently: our pitiful God removes the scales from its eyes[5] letting it see and understand somewhat of the grace received in a strange and wonderful manner in this mansion by means of intellectual vision.

9. By some mysterious manifestation of the truth, the three Persons of the most Blessed Trinity reveal themselves, preceded by an illumination which shines on the spirit like a most dazzling cloud of light.[6] The three Persons are distinct from one

[4] Acts ix. 8: 'Surrexit autem Saulus de terra, apertisque oculis nihil videbat.' There is, however, nothing to imply that he was dumb as well as blind.

[5] Acts ix. 18 : 'Et confestim ceciderunt ab oculis ejus tamquam squamæ, et visum recepit.' *Way of Perf.* ch. xxviii. 11.

[6] *Rel.* iii. 6; v. 6-8; viii. 20, 21; ix. 12, 17, 19. Deposition by Fr. Giles Gonzalez, S.J., Provincial of Old Castile, afterwards Assistant-General in Rome : 'While the holy Mother lived at the convent of the Incarnation of Avila [as prioress], I often spoke with her, and once I remember she asked me : "What am I to do, Father? Whenever I recollect myself I realize that already in this life the Three Persons of the Blessed Trinity may be seen, and that They accompany me and assist me in the management of my affairs."' (Fuente, *Obras*, vol. vi. p. 280.)

'Doña Maria Enriquez, Duchess of Alva, said that St. Teresa made known to her many revelations she had received from our Lord, and that she (the duchess) held in her possession three paintings of the

another; a sublime knowledge is infused into the
soul, imbuing it with a certainty of the truth that
the Three are of one substance, power, and knowledge and are one God. Thus that which we hold
as a doctrine of faith, the soul now, so to speak,
understands by sight, though it beholds the Blessed
Trinity neither by the eyes of the body nor of the
soul, this being no imaginary vision. All the Three
Persons here communicate Themselves to the soul,
speak to it and make it understand the words of our
Lord in the Gospel that He and the Father and the
Holy Ghost will come and make their abode with
the soul which loves Him and keeps His commandments.[7]

10. O my God, how different from merely hearing and believing these words is it to realize their
truth in this way! Day by day a growing astonishment takes possession of this soul, for the three
Persons of the Blessed Trinity seem never to depart;
it sees with certainty, in the way I have described,
that They dwell far within its own centre and
depths; though for want of learning it cannot
describe how, it is conscious of the indwelling of
these divine Companions.

11. You may fancy that such a person is beside
herself and that her mind is too inebriated to care
for anything else. On the contrary, she is far more

Blessed Trinity made according to the description of the holy Mother,
who, while they were being done, effaced with her own hand those
portions which the painter failed to design conformably to the vision
she had had.' (Fuente, *l.c.* p. 297.)

[7] St. John xiv. 23: 'Si quis diligit me, sermonem meum servabit,
et Pater meus diliget eum, et ad eum veniemus, et mansionem apud
eum faciemus.'

active than before in all that concerns God's service, and when at leisure she enjoys this blessed companionship. Unless she first deserts God, I believe He will never cease to make her clearly sensible of His presence: she feels confident, as indeed she may, that He will never so fail her as to allow her to lose this favour after once bestowing it; at the same time, she is more careful than before to avoid offending Him in any way.

12. This presence is not always so entirely realized, that is, so distinctly manifest, as at first, or as it is at times when God renews this favour, otherwise the recipient could not possibly attend to anything else nor live in society. Although not always seen by so clear a light, yet whenever she reflects on it she feels the companionship of the Blessed Trinity. This is as if, when we were with other people in a very well lighted room, some one were to darken it by closing the shutters; we should feel certain that the others were still there, though we were unable to see them.[8]

13. You may ask: 'Could she not bring back the light and see them again?'[9] This is not in her

---

[8] One of the Saint's favourite comparisons. See *Life*, ch. xxvii. 7. *Castle*, M. vi. ch. viii. 3. *Rel.* vii. 26.

[9] 'Though the soul be always in the high estate of marriage since God has placed it there, nevertheless, actual union in all its powers is not continuous, though the substantial union is. In this substantial union the powers of the soul are most frequently in union, and drink of His cellar, the understanding by knowledge, the will by love, etc. We are not therefore to suppose that the soul, when saying it went out, has ceased from its substantial or essential union with God, but only from the union of its faculties, which is not, and cannot be, permanent in this life.' (St. John of the Cross, *Spiritual Canticle*, stanza xxvi. 9. On the words: 'In the inner cellar of my Beloved have I drunk, and when I went forth').

power; when our Lord chooses, He will open the
shutters of the understanding: He shows her great
mercy in never quitting her and in making her
realize it so clearly. His divine Majesty seems to
be preparing His bride for greater things by this
divine companionship which clearly helps perfection in every way and makes her lose the fear
she sometimes felt when other graces were granted
her.

14. A certain person so favoured found she had
improved in all virtues: whatever were her trials
or labours, the centre of her soul seemed never
moved from its resting-place. Thus in a manner
her soul appeared divided: a short time after God
had done her this favour, while undergoing great
sufferings, she complained of her soul as Martha
did of Mary,[10] reproaching it with enjoying solitary
peace while leaving her so full of troubles and
occupations that she could not keep it company.

15. This may seem extravagant to you, daughters,
yet though the soul is known to be undivided, it
is fact and no fancy and often happens. Interior
effects show for certain that there is a positive difference between the soul and the spirit, although
they are one with each other.[11] There is an extremely

[10] St. Luke x. 40. *Excl.* v. 2, 3. *Way of Perf.* ch. xv. 4; xxxi. 4.
Rel. viii. 6. *Concept.* ch. vii. 4.

[11] *Life*, ch. xviii. 4. The distinction between soul and spirit, to be
found in the Epistle to the Hebrews, iv. 12, according to Cornelius a
Lapide (*ad loc.*) consists in this, that the term *soul* comprises the faculties,
senses, and passions, whereas the term *spirit* denotes the substance of the
soul independently of its powers. In the inferior degrees of the Mystical
life God operates through the faculties, while in the Mystical marriage
He acts directly on the substance of the soul. St. Teresa is not quite

subtle distinction between them, so that sometimes they seem to act in a different manner from one another, as does the knowledge given to them by God.

16. It also appears to me that the soul and its faculties are not identical. There are so many and such transcendental mysteries within us, that it would be presumption for me to attempt to explain them. If by God's mercy we enter heaven we shall understand these secrets.

CHAPTER II.

TREATS OF THE SAME SUBJECT: EXPLAINS, BY SOME DELICATELY DRAWN COMPARISONS, THE DIFFERENCE BETWEEN SPIRITUAL UNION AND SPIRITUAL MARRIAGE.

1. The spiritual nuptials introduced by an imaginary vision. 2. Spiritual betrothal and marriage differ. 3. Spiritual marriage lasting. 4. Not so spiritual betrothal. 5. Spiritual marriage permanent. 6. St. Paul and spiritual marriage. 7. The soul's joy in union. 8. Its conviction of God's indwelling. 9. Its peace. 10. Christ's prayer for the divine union of the soul. 11. Its fulfilment. 12. Unalterable peace of the soul in the seventh Mansion. 13. Unless it offends God. 14. Struggles outside the seventh Mansion. 15. Comparisons explaining this.

1. WE now come to speak of divine and spiritual nuptials, although this sublime favour cannot be received in all its perfection during our present life, for by forsaking God this great good would be lost. The first time God bestows this grace, He, by an imaginary vision of His most sacred Humanity, reveals Himself to the soul so that it may understand and realize the sovereign gift it is

consistent in the use of these terms, which is not surprising, as she owns that she does not quite understand this subtle distinction.

receiving. He may manifest Himself in a different way to other people; the person I mentioned, after having received Holy Communion beheld our Lord, full of splendour, beauty, and majesty, as He was after His resurrection.[1] He told her that henceforth she was to care for His affairs as though they were her own and He would care for hers: He spoke other words which she understood better than she can repeat them. This may seem nothing new, for our Lord had thus revealed Himself to her at other times;[2] yet this was so different that it left her bewildered and amazed, both on account of the vividness of what she saw and of the words heard at the time, also because it took place in the interior of the soul where, with the exception of the one last mentioned, no other vision had been seen.

2. You must understand that between the visions seen in this and in the former mansions there is a vast difference; there is the same distinction between spiritual espousals and spiritual marriage as between people who are only betrothed and others who are united for ever in holy matrimony. I have told you[3] that though I make this comparison because there is none more suitable, yet this betrothal is no more related to our corporal condition than if the soul were a disembodied spirit. This is even more true of the spiritual marriage, for this secret union takes place in the innermost centre of the soul where God Himself must dwell: I believe that no door is required to enter it. I say, 'no door

---

[1] *Rel.* iii. 20; ix. 8 and 25.   [3] *Castle*, M. v. ch. iv. 1.
[2] *Life*, ch. xxxix. 29.

is required,' for all I have hitherto described seems to come through the senses and faculties as must the representation of our Lord's Humanity, but what passes in the union of the spiritual nuptials is very different. Here God appears in the soul's centre, not by an imaginary but by an intellectual vision far more mystic than those seen before, just as He appeared to the Apostles without having entered through the door when He said: 'Pax vobis.'[4]

3. So mysterious is the secret and so sublime the favour that God thus bestows instantaneously on the soul, that it feels a supreme delight, only to be described by saying that our Lord vouchsafes for the moment to reveal to it His own heavenly glory in a far more subtle way than by any vision or spiritual delight. As far as can be understood, the soul, I mean the spirit of this soul, is made one with God[5] Who is Himself a spirit, and Who has been pleased to show certain persons how far His love for us extends in order that we may praise His greatness. He has thus deigned to unite Himself to His creature: He has bound Himself to her as firmly as two human beings are joined in wedlock and will never separate Himself from her.

4. Spiritual betrothal is different and like the grace of union is often dissolved; for though two things are made one by union, separation is still possible and each part then remains a thing by itself. This favour generally passes quickly, and afterwards the soul, as far as it is aware, remains without His company.

[4] St. John xx. 19.   [5] *Rel.* xi. 1. *sqq.*

5. This is not so in the spiritual marriage with our Lord, where the soul always remains in its centre with its God. Union may be symbolized by two wax candles, the tips of which touch each other so closely that there is but one light; or again, the wick, the wax, and the light become one, but the one candle can again be separated from the other and the two candles remain distinct; or the wick may be withdrawn from the wax. But spiritual marriage is like rain falling from heaven into a river or stream, becoming one and the same liquid, so that the river and rain water cannot be divided; or it resembles a streamlet flowing into the ocean, which cannot afterwards be disunited from it. This marriage may also be likened to a room into which a bright light enters through two windows—though divided when it enters, the light becomes one and the same.

6. Perhaps when St. Paul said, 'He who is joined to the Lord is one spirit,'[6] he meant this sovereign marriage, which presupposes His Majesty's having been joined to the soul by union. The same Apostle says: 'To me, to live is Christ and to die is gain.'[7] This, I think, might here be uttered by the soul, for now the little butterfly of which I spoke dies with supreme joy, for Christ is her life.

7. This becomes more manifest by its effects as time goes on, for the soul learns that it is God Who gives it 'life,' by certain secret intuitions too strong to be misunderstood, and keenly felt, although impossible to describe. These produce such over-

[6] I Cor. vi. 17: 'Qui adhæret Domino únus spiritus est.'
[7] Philip. i. 21: 'Mihi vivere Christus est, et mori lucrum.'

mastering feelings that the person experiencing them cannot refrain from amorous exclamations, such as: 'O Life of my life, and Power which doth uphold me!' with other aspirations of the same kind.[8] For from the bosom of the Divinity, where God seems ever to hold this soul fast clasped, issue streams of milk, which solace the servants of the castle. I think He wishes them to share, in some way, the riches the soul enjoys; therefore from the flowing river in which the little streamlet is swallowed up, some drops of water flow every now and then to sustain the bodily powers, the servants of the bride and Bridegroom.

8. A person who was unexpectedly plunged into water could not fail to be aware of it; here the case is the same, but even more evident. A quantity of water could not fall on us unless it came from some source—so the soul feels certain there must be some one within it who lances forth these darts and vivifies its own life, and that there is a Sun whence this brilliant light streams forth from the interior of the spirit to its faculties.

9. The soul itself, as I said, never moves from this centre, nor loses the peace He can give Who gave it to the Apostles when they were assembled together.[9] I think this salutation of our Lord contains far deeper meaning than the words convey, as

[8] Such exclamations, in considerable number, form the *Book of Exclamations* published by Fray Luis de Leon. De Fuente thinks it was written in 1569, but as St. Teresa's spiritual betrothal took place on November 18, 1572, it seems, at least in parts, of a later date. The spiritual nuptials must be placed between the aforementioned year and May 1575, but it is not possible to ascertain the exact date. (For the *Exclamations*, see *Minor Works*).   [9] St. John xx. 19.

also His bidding the glorious Magdalen to 'go in peace.'[10] Our Lord's words *act* within us,[11] and in these cases they must have wrought their effect in the souls already disposed to banish from within themselves all that is corporal and to retain only what is spiritual, in order to be joined in this celestial union with the uncreated Spirit. Without doubt, if we empty ourselves of all that belongs to the creature, depriving ourselves of it for the love of God, that same Lord will fill us with Himself.

10. Our Lord Jesus Christ, praying for His Apostles, (I cannot remember the reference), asked that they might be made one with the Father and with Himself, as Jesus Christ our Lord is in the Father and the Father in Him![12] I do not know how love could be greater than this! Let none draw back from entering here, for His Majesty also said: 'Not only for them do I pray, but for them also who through their word shall believe in Me';[13] and He declared: 'I am in them.'[14]

11. God help me! how true these words are, and how clearly are they understood by the soul which in this state of prayer finds them fulfilled in itself! So should we all but for our own fault, for the words of Jesus Christ, our King and our Lord, cannot fail. It is *we* who fail by not disposing ourselves fitly, nor removing all that can obstruct this light,

[10] St. Luke vii. 50.

[11] *Supra*, M. vi. ch. iii. 6. *Life*, ch. xxv. 5.

[12] St. John xvii. 21: 'Ut omnes unum sint, sicut tu Pater in me, et ego in te, ut et ipsi in nobis unum sint.'

[13] St. John xvii. 20: 'Non pro eis autem rogo tantum, sed et pro eis, qui credituri sunt per verbum eorum in me.'

[14] St. John xvii. 23: 'Ego in eis.'

so that we do not behold ourselves in this mirror wherein our image is engraved.[15]

12. To return to what I was saying. God places the soul in His own mansion which is in the very centre of the soul itself. They say the empyreal heavens, in which our Lord dwells, do not revolve with the rest: so the accustomed movements of the faculties and imagination do not appear to take place in any way that can injure the soul or disturb its peace.

13. Do I seem to imply that after God has brought the soul thus far it is certain to be saved and cannot fall into sin again?[16] I do not mean this: whenever

[15] This idea is expressed in St. Teresa's poem: 'Alma, buscarte has en Mi' (Poem 10, *Minor Works*).

> Such is the power of love, O soul,
> To paint thee in my heart
> No craftsman with such art
> Whate'er his skill might be, could there
> Thine image thus impart !
> 'Twas love that gave thee life—
> Then, fair one, if thou be
> Lost to thyself, thou'lt see
> Thy portrait in my bosom stamped—
> Soul, seek thyself in Me.

[16] In a letter dated May 1581, addressed to Don Alonso Velasquez, then bishop of Osma, St. Teresa writes as follows:

'She [herself] has received such an assurance of coming one day to the fruition of God that she almost imagines she has already come into possession of Him, without, however, the joy that will accompany it. She is in the same position as one who by legal contract has received a splendid property which will become his, and whose fruit he will enjoy at a given date. Until then he only holds the title-deeds, without being able to take possession of the property. Nevertheless my soul would not like to come immediately into the possession of God, for it does not believe that it has deserved such a grace. It only desires to continue in His service, even at the cost of terrible sufferings. It would not mind thus serving Him to the end of the world, after having received such a pledge.' St. John of the Cross, in treating of this subject (*Spir.*

I say that the soul seems in security, I must be understood to imply for as long as His Majesty thus holds it in His care and it does not offend Him. At any rate I know for certain that though such a person realizes the high state she is in and has remained in it for several years, she does not consider herself safe, but is more careful than ever to avoid committing the least offence against God. As I shall explain later on, she is most anxious to serve Him and feels a constant pain and confusion at seeing how little she can do for Him compared with all she ought.ᐧ This is no light cross but a severe mortification, for the harder the penances she can perform, the better is she pleased. Her greatest penance is to be deprived by God of health and strength to perform any. I told you elsewhere what keen pain this caused her, but now it grieves her far more. This must be because she is like a tree grafted on a stock growing near a stream which makes it greener and more fruitful.[17] Why marvel at the longings of this soul whose spirit has truly become one with the celestial water I described?

14. To return to what I wrote about. It is not intended that the powers, senses and passions should continually enjoy this peace. The soul does so, indeed, but in the other mansions there are still times of struggle, suffering, and fatigue, though as a general rule, peace is not lost by them. This 'centre of the soul' or 'spirit' is so hard to describe

Cant. stanza xxii. 3) says: 'I believe that no soul ever attains to this state without being confirmed in grace in it.' See also Ribera, in the *Acta Ss.* p. 554, *circa finem.*

[17] Ps. i. 3: 'Et erit tamquam lignum quod plantatum est secus decursus aquarum, quod fructum suum dabit in tempore suo.'

or even to believe in, that I think, sisters, my inability to explain my meaning saves your being tempted to disbelieve me; it is difficult to understand how there can be crosses and sufferings and yet peace in the soul.

15. Let me give you one or two comparisons—God grant they may be of use; if not, I know that what I say is true. A king resides in his palace; many wars and disasters take place in his kingdom but he remains on his throne. In the same way, though tumults and wild beasts rage with great uproar in the other mansions, yet nothing of this enters the seventh mansions, nor drives the soul from it. Although the mind regrets these troubles, they do not disturb it nor rob it of its peace, for the passions are too subdued to dare to enter here where they would only suffer still further defeat. Though the whole body is in pain, yet the head, if it be sound, does not suffer with it. I smile at these comparisons—they do not please me—but I can find no others. Think what you will about it —I have told you the truth.

CHAPTER III.

1. THE little butterfly has died with the greatest joy at having found rest at last, and now Christ lives in her.[1] Let us see the difference between her present and her former life, for the effects will prove whether what I told you was true. As far as can be ascertained they are these: first, a self-forgetfulness so complete that she really appears not to exist, as I said,[2] for such a transformation has been worked in her that she no longer recognizes herself; nor does she remember that heaven, or life, or glory are to be hers, but seems entirely occupied in seeking God's interests. Apparently the words spoken by His Majesty have done their work: 'that she was to care for His affairs, and He would care for hers.'[3]

2. Thus she recks nothing, whatever happens, but lives in such strange oblivion that, as I stated, she seems no longer to exist, nor does she wish to be of

---

[1] Gal. ii. 20.   [2] *Castle*, M. vii. ch. i. 11 and 15.
[3] *Castle*, M. vii. ch. ii. 1. Compare the references there given.

any account in anything—*anything* ! unless she sees that she can advance, however little, the honour and glory of God, for which she would most willingly die.

3. Do not fancy I mean, daughters, that she neglects to eat and drink, though it brings no small torment to her, or to perform the duties of her state. I am speaking of her interior; as regards her exterior actions there is little to say, for her chief suffering is to see that she has hardly strength to do anything. For nothing in the world would she omit doing all she can which she knows would honour our Lord.

4. The second fruit is a strong desire for suffering, though it does not disturb her peace as before because the fervent wish of such souls for the fulfilment of God's will in them makes them acquiesce in all He does. If He would have her suffer, she is content; if not, she does not torment herself to death about it as she used to do. She feels a great interior joy when persecuted, and is far more peaceful than in the former state under such circumstances: she bears no grudge against her enemies, nor wishes them any ill. Indeed she has a special love for them, is deeply grieved at seeing them in trouble, and does all she can to relieve them,[4] earnestly interceding with God on their behalf. She would be glad to forfeit the favours His Majesty shows her, if they might be given to her enemies instead, to prevent their offending our Lord.

[4] Don Alvaro de Mendoza, Bishop of Avila, used to say that the best means of obtaining St. Teresa's friendship was to injure or insult her, *Acta Ss.* n. 1233. *Rel.* vii. 20.

5. The most surprising thing to me is that the sorrow and distress which such souls felt because they could not die and enjoy our Lord's presence[5] are now exchanged for as fervent a desire of serving Him, of causing Him to be praised, and of helping others to the utmost of their power. Not only have they ceased to long for death, but they wish for a long life and most heavy crosses, if such would bring ever so little honour to our Lord. Thus, if they knew for certain that immediately on quitting their bodies their souls would enjoy God, it would make no difference to them, nor do they think of the glory enjoyed by the saints, and long to share it. Such souls hold that their glory consists in helping, in any way, Him Who was crucified, especially as they see how men offend against Him, and how few, detached from all else, care for His honour alone. True, people in this state forget this at times, and are seized with tender longings to enjoy God and to leave this land of exile, especially as they see how little they serve Him. Then, returning to themselves and reflecting how they possess Him continually in their souls, they are satisfied, offering to His Majesty their willingness to live as the most costly oblation they can make.[6] They fear death no more than they would a delicious trance.

[5] *Rel.* viii. 15.

[6] Compare with the Saint's poem on self-oblation : 'Vuestro soy, para Vos naci' (Poem 1. *Minor Works*).

> Long life bestow, or straightway let me die;
> Let health be mine, or pain and sickness send;
> Honour or foul dishonour—be my path
> Beset by war or peaceful till the end.
> My strength or weakness be as Thou dost choose,
> Since naught Thou askest shall I e'er refuse.
> Say, Lord, what is it Thou dost will for me ?

*
7. Such a soul, thoroughly detached from all things, wishes to be either always alone or occupied on what benefits the souls of others: she feels neither aridity nor any interior troubles, but a constant tender recollection of our Lord Whom she wishes to praise unceasingly. When she grows negligent, the same Lord arouses her in the way that I told you, and it is easy to see that this impulse (I know not what term to use for it) comes from the interior of the soul, like the former impetuous desires.[7] It is now felt very sweetly, but is neither produced by the intellect nor the memory, nor is there reason to believe the soul itself has any share in it. This is so usual and so frequent that whoever has been in this state must have noticed it. However large a fire may be, the flame never burns downwards, but upwards, and so this movement is seen to come from the centre of the soul whose powers it excites. Indeed, were nothing else gained by this way of prayer but the knowledge of the special care God takes to communicate Himself to us and how He entreats us to abide with Him (for indeed I can describe it in no other way) I think that for the sake of these sweet and penetrating touches of His love all our past pains would be well spent.

8. You will have learnt this by experience, sisters, for I think that when our Lord has brought us to the prayer of union, He watches over us in this way unless we neglect to keep His commandments. When these impulses are given you, remember that they come from the innermost mansion, where

[7] *Castle*, M. vi. ch. vi. 6.
* For Paragraph 6, see p. 297.

God dwells in our souls. Praise Him fervently, for it is He Who sends you this message, or love letter, so tenderly written, and in a cipher that only you can understand and know what He asks. By no means neglect to answer His Majesty, even though you may be occupied exteriorly and engaged in conversation. Our Lord may often be pleased to show you this secret favour in public; but it is very easy, as the reply should be entirely interior, to respond by an act of love or to ask with Saint Paul: 'Lord, what wilt Thou have me to do?'[8] Jesus will show you in many ways how to please Him. It is a propitious moment, for He seems to be listening to us and the soul is nearly always disposed by this delicate touch to respond with a generous determination.[9] As I told you, this mansion differs from the rest in that, as I said,[10] the dryness and disturbance felt in all the rest at times hardly ever enter here, where the soul is nearly always calm. It does not fear that this sublime favour can be counterfeited by the devil, but feels a settled conviction that it is of divine origin because, as above stated, nothing is here perceived

[8] Acts ix. 6: 'Domine, quid me vis facere?'

[9] The words from 'know what He asks' to 'as I told you' are not in the original manuscript, but must have been written on a separate slip, as is proved by a marginal note in the handwriting of the Saint: 'Quando dice aqui: os pide, léase luego este papel.' This paper is now lost, but the passage it contained is preserved in the early manuscript copies of Toledo, Cordova and Salamanca, as well as in the first printed edition, and, through this, in the old translations; hence both Woodhead and Dalton have it in its proper place. It is, of course, not to be found in the autograph published in 1882, nor in Fuente's Spanish editions nor in translations based upon these. The Spanish text will be found in Œuvres vi, 297 note.

[10] Supra §§ 1 and 2.

by the senses or faculties but His Majesty reveals Himself to the spirit, which He takes to be with Himself in a place where I doubt not the devil dares not enter, nor would our Lord ever permit him.

9. All the graces here divinely bestowed on the soul come, as I said, through no action of its own except its total abandonment of itself to God. They are given in peace and silence, like the building of Solomon's Temple where no sound was heard.[11] It is thus with this temple of God, this mansion of His where He and the soul rejoice in each other alone in profound silence. The mind need not act nor search for anything, as the Lord Who created it wishes it to be at rest and only to watch through a little chink, what passes within. Though at times it cannot see this, yet such intervals are very short, I believe because the powers are not here lost but only cease to work, being, as it were, dazed with astonishment.

10. I, too, am astonished at seeing that when the soul arrives at this state it does not go into ecstasies except perhaps on rare occasions—even then they are not like the former trances and the flight of the spirit and seldom take place in public as they did before.[12] They are no longer produced by any special calls to devotion, such as by the sight of a religious picture, by hearing a sermon (were it only the first few words), or by sacred music; formerly, like the poor little butterfly, the soul

[11] III Reg. vi. 7.
[12] 'That is, so as to lose the senses' (marginal note in the Saints' handwriting). Rel. iii. 5.

was so anxious that anything used to alarm it and make it take flight. This may be either because the spirit has at last found repose, or that it has seen such wonders in this mansion that nothing can frighten it, or perhaps because it no longer feels solitary since it rejoices in such Company.

11. In short, sisters, I cannot tell the reason, but as soon as God shows the soul what this mansion contains, bringing it to dwell within the precincts, the infirmity formerly so troublesome to the mind and impossible to get over, disappears at once. Probably this is because our Lord has now strengthened, dilated, and developed the soul, or it may be that He wished to make public (for some end known only to Himself) what He was doing in secret within such souls, for His judgments are beyond our comprehension in this life.

12. These effects, with all the other good fruits I have mentioned of the different degrees of prayer, are given by God to the soul when it draws near Him to receive that 'kiss of His mouth' for which the bride asked,[13] and I believe her petition is now granted. Here the overflowing waters are given to the wounded hart: here she delights in the tabernacles of God[14]: here the dove sent out by Noe to see whether the flood had subsided, has plucked the olive branch, showing that she has found firm land amongst the floods and tempests of this world.[15] O Jesus! Who knows how much in Holy Scripture refers to this peace of soul? Since, O my God, Thou dost see of what grave import is this peace

[13] Cant. i. 1.   [14] Ps. xli. 2, 5.   [15] Gen. viii. 10, 11.

to us, do Thou incite Christians to strive to gain it! In Thy mercy do not deprive those of it on whom Thou hast bestowed it, for until Thou hast given them true peace and brought them to where it is unending, they must ever live in fear.

13. I do not mean that peace is unreal on earth because I say 'true peace,' but that such souls might have to begin all their struggles over again if they forsook God. What must these people feel at the thought that it is possible to lose so great a good? Their dread makes them more careful; they try to gather strength from their weakness lest, through their own fault, they should miss any opportunity of pleasing God better. The greater the favours they have received from His Majesty, the more diffident and mistrustful are they of themselves; the marvels they have witnessed having revealed more clearly to them their own miseries and the heinousness of their sins, so that often, like the publican, they dare not so much as lift up their eyes.[16]

14. Sometimes they long to die and be in safety, but then their love at once makes them wish to live in order to serve God, as I told you; therefore they commit all that concerns them to His mercy.[17] At times they are more crushed than ever by the thought of the many graces they have received lest, like an overladen ship, they sink beneath the burden. I assure you, sisters, such souls have their cross to bear, yet it does not trouble them nor rob them of their peace, but is quickly gone like a wave or a storm which is followed by a calm, for God's

---

[16] St. Luke. xviii. 13.   [17] *Rel.* ix. 19.

presence within them soon makes them forget all
else. May He be for ever blessed and praised by all
His creatures! Amen,

CHAPTER IV.

THE CONCLUSION SETS FORTH WHAT APPEARS TO BE OUR LORD'S
PRINCIPAL INTENTION IN CONFERRING THESE SUBLIME FAVOURS
ON SOULS, AND EXPLAINS HOW NECESSARY IT IS FOR MARY AND
MARTHA TO GO TOGETHER. THIS CHAPTER IS VERY PROFITABLE.

*1. Vicissitudes of the Seventh Mansion. 2. Humility produced by
them. 3. Such souls free from mortal and from wilful venial
sins. 4. The fate of Solomon. 5. Holy fear. 6. These favours
strengthen souls to suffer. 7. Crosses borne by the saints.
8. Effect of vision of our Lord on St. Peter. 9. Fruits of these
favours. 10. Why the spiritual marriage takes place. 11. Love
for Christ proved by our deeds. 12. True spirituality. 13. Humility and the virtues must combine with prayer. 14. Zeal of
advanced souls. 15. Strengthened by the divine Presence within
them. 16. Examples of the saints. 17. Both Martha and Mary
must serve our Lord. 18. Christ's food. 19. Mary's mortification.
20. Her grief at the Passion. 21. Can we lead souls to God?
22. How to do so. 23. Love gives value to our deeds. 24. Conclusion.*

1. You must not suppose, sisters, that the effects I
mentioned always exist in the same degree in these
souls, for as far as I remember, I told you that in
most cases our Lord occasionally leaves such persons to the weakness of their nature. The venomous
creatures from the moat round the castle and the
other mansions at once unite to revenge themselves
for the time when they were deprived of their
power.

2. True, this lasts but a short time—a day perhaps
or a little longer—but during this disturbance,
which generally arises from some passing event,
these persons learn what benefits they derive from

the holy Company they are in. Our Lord gives them such great fortitude that they never desert His service nor the good resolutions they have made, which only seem to gather strength by trial, nor do their hearts ever turn from them, even by a slight movement of the will. This trouble rarely happens; our Lord wishes the soul to keep in mind its natural condition so that it may be humble and may better understand how much it owes Him, and how great a grace it has received, and so may praise Him.

3. Do not fancy that in spite of the strong desire and determination of these souls that they do not commit imperfections and even fall into many sins: that is, not *wilfully*; for such people are given special grace from God on this point: I mean venial sins. As far as they are aware, they are free from mortal sins, although they do not feel certain they may not be guilty of some of which they are ignorant.

4. This grieves their hearts sorely, as does the sight of the souls perishing around them; although on the one hand they have strong hopes of not being themselves among the number of the lost, yet remembering what we are told in Holy Scripture of the fate of men who, like Solomon, seemed the special favourites of God[1] and conversed so familiarly with His Majesty, they cannot help fearing for themselves.

5. Let that one among you who feels most confidence on this point fear the most, for: 'Blessed

[1] III. Reg. xi.

is the man who feareth the Lord,' as David said.[2]
May His Majesty ever protect us. Let us beg Him
never to permit us to offend Him: therein lies our
greatest safety. May He be for ever praised. Amen.

6. It would be well to tell you, sisters, the reason
why God bestows such favours on souls in this
world, although you must have learned this by the
effects produced if you have considered the matter.
I return to the matter in order that none of you
may think it is only for the sake of the pleasure
such persons feel, which would be a great mistake
on your part, for His Majesty can bestow no greater
favour on us than to give us a life such as was led
by His beloved Son. Therefore, as I have often told
you, I feel certain that these graces are sent to
strengthen our weakness so that we may imitate
Him by suffering much.

7. We always find that those nearest to Christ
our Lord bear the heaviest cross: think of what
His glorious Mother and the Apostles bore. How
do you think St. Paul went through such immense
labours?[3] We learn from his conduct the fruits of
genuine visions and contemplation which come
from our Lord and not from our own imagination,
or the devil's fraud. Do you suppose that St. Paul
hid himself to enjoy these spiritual consolations at

[2] Ps. cxi. 1 . ' Beatus vir qui timet Dominum.'

[3] Though thou shouldst have been rapt up to the third heaven with
Saint Paul, thou art not thereby secured that thou shalt suffer no ad-
versity. 'I,' said Jesus, 'will shew him how great things he must suffer
for My name's sake' (Acts. ix. 16). To suffer, therefore, is what waits
for thee, if thou wilt love Jesus and constantly serve Him. . . . . For
our merit and the advancement of our state consist not in having many
sweetnesses and consolations, but rather in bearing great afflictions and
tribulations' (*Imitation*, bk. ii. ch. xii. 12).

leisure and did nothing else? You know that he never took a day's rest so far as we can learn, nor could he have slept much since he worked all night to get his living.[4]

8. I am delighted with St. Peter, who when fleeing from prison was met by our Lord, Who told him He was going to Rome to be crucified again. I never recite the Office in which this is commemorated without feeling a special joy.[5] What effect did this vision have on St. Peter, and what did he do? He went at once to meet his death—and our Lord did him no small favour in finding him an executioner!

9. Oh, my sisters, how forgetful of her ease, how unmindful of honours, and how far from seeking men's esteem should she be whose soul God thus chooses for His special dwelling-place! For if her mind is fixed on Him, as it ought to be, she must needs forget herself: all her thoughts are bent on how to please Him better and when and how she can show the love she bears Him.

10. *This* is the end and aim of prayer, my daughters; *this* is the reason of the spiritual marriage whose children are always good works. *Works* are the unmistakable sign which shows these favours come from God, as I told you. It will do me little

[4] I Thess. ii. 9.

[5] The Antiphon of the Magnificat at first Vespers of the Feast of Saints Peter and Paul, June 29, in the Carmelite Breviary used by St. Teresa is: 'Beatus Petrus Apostolus vidit sibi Christum occurrere. Adorans eum ait: "Domine, quo vadis?"—"Venio Romam iterum crucifigi." 'The Blessed Apostle Peter saw Christ come to meet him. Adoring Him, he asked "Lord, where art Thou going?"—"I go to Rome to be crucified anew." The saint at once returned to Rome and was taken by the soldiers and crucified. See *Letter* of Jan. 17. 1577, note 4. Vol. II.

good to be deeply recollected when alone, making
acts of the virtues, planning and promising to do
wonders in God's service, if afterwards, when
occasion offers, I do just the opposite. I did wrong
in saying, 'It will do me *little* good,' for all the
time we spend with God does us *great* good.
Though afterwards we may weakly fail to perform
our good intentions, yet some time or other His
Majesty will find a way for us to practise them
although perhaps much to our regret. Thus when
He sees a soul very cowardly, He often sends it
some great affliction, much against its will, and
brings it through this trial with profit to itself,
When the soul has learnt this, it is less timid in
offering itself to Him.

11. I ought to have said, 'will do us *little* good'
in comparison with the far *greater* good we can
gain when our works fulfil our aspirations and our
promises. She that cannot do all this at once should
do it little by little, gradually dominating her will,
if she wishes to gain fruit from prayer. Even in
this little nook she will find many a chance to
practise this. Remember, this is of far more importance than I know how to express. Fix your
eyes on the Crucified One, and all will seem easy.
If His Majesty proved His love for us by such
stupendous labours and sufferings, how can you
seek to please Him by words alone?

12. Do you know what it is to be truly spiritual?
It is for men to make themselves the *slaves* of God
—branded with His mark, which is the cross. Since
they have given Him their freedom, He can sell

them as slaves to the whole world, as He was, which would be doing them no wrong but the greatest favour. Unless you make up your minds to this, never expect to make much progress,[6] for as I said humility is the foundation of the whole building and unless you are truly humble, our Lord, for your own sake, will never permit you to rear it very high lest it should fall to the ground.

13. Therefore, sisters, take care to lay a firm foundation by seeking to be the least of all and the slave of others, watching how you can please and help them, for it will benefit you more than them. Built on such strong rocks, your castle can never go to ruin. I insist again: your foundation must not consist of prayer and contemplation alone: unless you acquire the virtues and practise them, you will always be dwarfs; and please God no worse may befall you than making no progress, for you know that to *stop* is to go *back*—if you love, you will never be content to come to a standstill.

14. Perhaps you think I am speaking of beginners and that one may rest later on, but, as I told you, the rest such souls feel is within them: they have less outwardly nor do they wish for it. Why, do you think, does the soul send from its centre these inspirations, or rather aspirations, (the messages of which I spoke), to the dwellers in the precincts of the castle and to the surrounding mansions? To send them to sleep? No, no, no! The soul wages a fiercer war from thence to keep the powers,

---

[6] 'If thou wilt stand upon self and wilt not offer thyself freely to My will, thine offering is not perfect, nor will there be entire union between us.' (*Imitation*, bk. iv. ch. viii. 2.)

senses and the whole body from being idle, than ever it did when it suffered in their company. Formerly it did not understand the immense benefit its afflictions brought, though indeed they may have been the means God used to advance it to this state.

15. Besides, the company it enjoys gives it far greater strength than ever before. If, as David says: 'With the holy thou shalt be holy,'[7] doubtless by its becoming one with the Almighty, by this sovereign union of spirit with spirit, the soul must gather strength, as we know the saints did, to suffer and to die. Beyond doubt, with the force thus gained, the soul succours all within the castle and even the very body itself, which often seems to have no feeling left in it. The vigour the soul derives from 'the wine' drunk in the 'cellar'[8] (into which the Bridegroom brought her and would not let her go) overflows into the feeble body, just as the food we eat nourishes both the head and the whole frame.

16. Indeed the body suffers much while alive, for whatever work it does, the soul has energy for far greater tasks and goads it on to more, for all it can perform appears as nothing. This must be the reason of the severe penances performed by many of the saints, especially the glorious Magdalen, who had always spent her life in luxury.[9] This

[7] Ps. xvii. 26: 'Cum sancto sanctus eris.'

[8] Cant. ii. 4.

[9] 'St. Mary Magdalen gave herself up to penance and contemplation in a deep excavation of the rocks at La Baume, near Marseilles. In this wild spot there was neither bread, water, nor even herbage. Thus she lived for more than thirty-two years without any kind of nourishment but that which was celestial, performing meanwhile most severe penances.' (St. Vincent Ferrer.)

caused the zeal felt by our Father Elias for the honour of God,[10] and the desires of St. Dominic,[11] and St. Francis[12] to draw souls to praise the Almighty. I assure you that, forgetful of themselves, they must have passed through no small trials.

17. This, my sisters, is what I would have us strive for—to offer our petitions and to practise prayer, not for our own enjoyment but to gain strength to serve God. Let us seek no fresh path; we should lose ourselves in ways of ease. It would be a strange thing to fancy we should gain these graces by any other road than that by which Jesus and all His saints have gone before. Let us not dream of such a thing: believe me, both Martha and Mary must entertain our Lord and keep Him as their Guest, nor must they be so inhospitable as to offer Him no food. How can Mary do this

---

[10] III Reg. xix. 10.

[11] 'There was one sentiment within him to which may almost be given the name of passion : it was his ceaseless burning thirst for the salvation of souls. As his Divine Master had come into the world to save sinners and loved them even unto death, so he, too, gave up all that was most dear to him in his life to win souls to Christ. He was always giving himself : it was the very key-note of his existence. He would have sold himself as a slave, he would have been cut to pieces by the heretics, he would spare himself neither by day nor by night, if by any means he might save some.' (From the *History of St. Dominic*, by Augusta Theodosia Drane. London, 1891, p. 256).

[12] 'St. Francis of Assisi, at the very beginning of his Order, when he had only seven followers, said to them : "Consider, my brethren, what is our vocation. It is not only for our own salvation that the mercy of God has called us, but for the salvation of many other souls. It is that we may go forth and exhort all men rather by our example than by our words, to do penance and keep the divine commands."' *(The Life of St. Francis of Assisi*, by a religious of the Order of Poor Clares, London, 1861, p. 32).

while she sits at His feet, if her sister does not help her?"[13]

18. His food is that in every possible way we should draw souls to Him so that they may be saved and may praise Him for ever. You may offer two objections—first, that I said that Mary had chosen the better part,[14] for she had already done Martha's work by waiting on our Lord, by washing His feet and by wiping them with her hair.

19. Do you think it was a small mortification for a woman of rank, as she was, to go through the street, perhaps by herself, for in her zeal she never thought of how she went? Then she entered a house where she was a stranger and had to bear the railing of the Pharisee and many other trials.[15] It was strange to see such a woman as she had been thus publicly change her life. With a wicked nation like the Jews, the sight of her love for our Lord Whom they hated so bitterly was enough to make them cast in her face her former life and taunt her with wanting to become a saint. Doubtless she must have changed her rich robes and all the rest. Considering how men talk now of people far less known than she was, what must have been said of her?

20. I assure you, sisters, she won the better part after many crosses and mortifications. Must not the mere sight of men's hatred of her Master have been an intolerable trial? Then, think of what she

[13] St. Luke x. 39, 40. *Life*, ch. xvii. 6. *Rel.* viii. 6. *Way of Perf.* ch. xxxi. 4. *Concep.* ch. vii. 4.

[14] *Ibid.* x. 42: 'Maria optimam partem elegit.'

[15] *Ibid.* vii. 37.

endured afterwards at our Lord's death! I believe, myself, that she did not suffer martyrdom because she was already a martyr by grief at witnessing the crucifixion.[16] Then what terrible pain His absence must have caused her[17] during the long years afterwards! You see, she was not always enjoying contemplation at the feet of our Saviour!

21. Secondly, you may say that you have neither the power nor the means to lead souls to God; though you would willingly do so, you do not know how, as you can neither teach nor preach as did the Apostles. I have often written an answer to this objection though I cannot tell whether I have done so in connection with the Castle. However, as the difficulty probably often crosses your minds on account of the desires our Lord gives you of serving Him, I will now speak of it again.[18] I told you elsewhere how the devil frequently fills our thoughts with great schemes, so that instead of putting our hands to what work we can do to serve our Lord, we may rest satisfied with wishing to perform impossibilities.

22. You can do much by prayer; and then, do not try to help the whole world, but principally your companions; this work will be all the better because you are the more bound to it. Do you think it is a trifling matter that your humility and mortification, your readiness to serve your sisters, your fervent charity towards them, and your love of God, should be as a fire to enkindle their zeal,

[16] Marginal note in the Saint's handwriting.
[17] *Life*, ch. xxi. 9.
[18] *Way of Perf.* ch. i. 1. *Found.* ch. i. 6, 7. *Supra*, M. vi ch. vi. 2.

and that you should constantly incite them to practise the other virtues? This would be a great work and one most pleasing to our Lord: by thus doing all that is in your power, you would prove to His Majesty your willingness to do still more and He would reward you as if you had won Him many souls. Do you answer: 'This would not be converting my sisters, for they are very good already?' What business is that of yours? If they were still better, the praise they render God would please Him more and their prayers would be more helpful to their neighbours.'[9]

23. In short, my sisters, I will conclude with this advice; do not build towers without a foundation, for our Lord does not care so much for the importance of our works as for the love with which they are done. When we do all we can, His Majesty will enable us to do more every day. If we do not grow weary, but during the brief time this life lasts (and perhaps it will be shorter than any of you think) we give our Lord every sacrifice we can, both interior and exterior, His Majesty will unite them with that He offered to His Father for us on the Cross so that they may be worth the value given them by our love, however mean the works themselves may be.

24. May it please His Majesty, my sisters and my daughters, that we may all meet together where we may praise Him for ever, and may He give me grace to practice something of what I have taught you, by the merits of His Son, Who liveth and

[19] *Way of Perf.* ch. vii. 7.

reigneth for ever! Amen. I assure you that I am filled with confusion at myself and I beg you, for the sake of the same Lord, not to forget this poor sinner in your prayers.

Addendum to p. 281 (7th Mansions, Chap. III, par. 6).

6. The fact is, that He Who gave them these torturing desires of death has exchanged them for the others. May He be for ever blessed and praised! Amen. In fact, such persons no longer wish for consolations nor delights, since they bear God Himself within them, and it is He Who lives in them. It is evident that His life was one continual torment: so would He have ours to be, at least in desire, for as to the rest He leads us mercifully as our weakness requires, though when He sees the need He imparts to us His strength.

I H S

ALTHOUGH, as I told you, I felt reluctant to begin this work, yet now it is finished I am very glad to have written it, and I think my trouble has been well spent, though I confess it has cost me but little. Considering your strict enclosure, the little recreation you have, my sisters, and how many conveniences are wanting in some of your convents, I think it may console you to enjoy yourselves in this interior castle which you can enter, and walk about at will, at any hour you please, without asking leave of your superiors. It is true you cannot enter all the mansions by your own power, however great it may appear to you, unless the Lord of the castle Himself admits you. Therefore I advise you to use no violence if you meet with any obstacle, for that would displease Him so much that He would never give you admission to them. He dearly loves humility:[1] if you think yourselves unworthy to enter the third mansion, He will grant you all the sooner the favour of entering the fifth. Then, if you serve Him well there and often repair to it, He will draw you into the mansion where He dwells Himself, whence you need never depart unless called away by the Prioress, whose

[1] *Way of Perf.* ch. xvi. 1.

298

commands this sovereign Master wishes you to obey as if they were His own. If by her orders, you are often absent from His presence chamber, whenever you return He will hold the door open for you. When once you have learnt how to enjoy this castle, you will always find rest, however painful your trials may be, in the hope of returning to your Lord, which no one can prevent. Although I have only mentioned seven mansions, yet each one contains many more rooms, above, below, and around it, with fair gardens, fountains, and labyrinths, besides other things so delightful that you will wish to consume yourself in praising in return the great God Who has created the soul to His own image and likeness. If you find anything in the plan of this treatise which helps you to know Him better, be certain that it is sent by His Majesty to encourage you, and that whatever you find amiss in it is my own. In return for my strong desire to aid you in serving Him, my God and my Lord, I implore you, whenever you read this, to praise His Majesty fervently in my name and to beg Him to prosper His Church, to give light to the Lutherans, to pardon my sins and to free me from purgatory, where perhaps I shall be, by the mercy of God, when you see this book (if it is given to you after having been examined by theologians). If these writings contain any error, it is through my ignorance; I submit in all things to the teachings of the holy Catholic Roman Church, of which I am now a member, as I protest and promise I will be both in life and death. May our Lord God be for ever praised and blessed! Amen, Amen.

I finished writing this book in the convent of St. Joseph of Avila, 1577, on the Vigil of St. Andrew, for the glory of God, Who liveth and reigneth for ever and ever! Amen.

HERE ENDS THE INTERIOR CASTLE
OR THE MANSIONS
TRANSLATED AND PRINTED BY THE
BENEDICTINES OF STANBROOK
A.D. MCMXXI

INDEX

If you have enjoyed this book, consider making your next selection from among the following . . .

Prices subject to change.

Prices subject to change.

Sermons of the Curé of Ars. *Vianney* 12.50
St. Antony of the Desert. *St. Athanasius* 5.00
Is It a Saint's Name? *Fr. William Dunne* 1.50
St. Pius V—His Life, Times, Miracles. *Anderson* 5.00
Who Is Therese Neumann? *Fr. Charles Carty* 2.00
Martyrs of the Coliseum. *Fr. O'Reilly* 18.50
Way of the Cross. *St. Alphonsus Liguori* 1.00
Way of the Cross. *Franciscan version* 1.00
How Christ Said the First Mass. *Fr. Meagher* 18.50
Too Busy for God? Think Again! *D'Angelo* 5.00
St. Bernadette Soubirous. *Trochu* 18.50
Passion and Death of Jesus Christ. *Liguori* 10.00
Treatise on the Love of God. 2 Vols. *St. Francis de Sales* .... O.S.
Confession Quizzes. *Radio Replies Press* 1.00
St. Philip Neri. *Fr. V. J. Matthews* 5.50
St. Louise de Marillac. *Sr. Vincent Regnault* 6.00
The Old World and America. *Rev. Philip Furlong* 18.00
Prophecy for Today. *Edward Connor* 5.50
The Book of Infinite Love. *Mother de la Touche* 5.00
Chats with Converts. *Fr. M. D. Forrest* 10.00
The Church Teaches. *Church Documents* 16.50
Conversation with Christ. *Peter T. Rohrbach* 10.00
Purgatory and Heaven. *J. P. Arendzen* 5.00
Liberalism Is a Sin. *Sarda y Salvany* 7.50
Spiritual Legacy of Sr. Mary of the Trinity. *van den Broek* 10.00
The Creator and the Creature. *Fr. Frederick Faber* 16.50
Radio Replies. *3 Vols. Frs. Rumble and Carty* 36.00
Convert's Catechism of Catholic Doctrine. *Fr. Geiermann* 3.00
Incarnation, Birth, Infancy of Jesus Christ. *St. Alphonsus* 10.00
Light and Peace. *Fr. R. P. Quadrupani* 7.00
Dogmatic Canons & Decrees of Trent, Vat. I. *Documents* 9.50
The Evolution Hoax Exposed. *A. N. Field* 6.00
The Primitive Church. *Fr. D. I. Lanslots* 10.00
The Priest, the Man of God. *St. Joseph Cafasso* 12.50
Blessed Sacrament. *Fr. Frederick Faber* 18.50
Christ Denied. *Fr. Paul Wickens* 2.50
New Regulations on Indulgences. *Fr. Winfrid Herbst* 2.50
A Tour of the Summa. *Msgr. Paul Glenn* 18.00
Spiritual Conferences. *Fr. Frederick Faber* 15.00
Latin Grammar. *Scanlon and Scanlon* 16.50
A Brief Life of Christ. *Fr. Rumble* 2.00
Marriage Quizzes. *Radio Replies Press* 1.00
True Church Quizzes. *Radio Replies Press* 1.00
The Secret of the Rosary. *St. Louis De Montfort* 3.00
Mary, Mother of the Church. *Church Documents* 4.00
The Sacred Heart and the Priesthood. *de la Touche* 9.00
Revelations of St. Bridget. *St. Bridget of Sweden* 3.00
Magnificent Prayers. *St. Bridget of Sweden* 2.00
The Happiness of Heaven. *Fr. J. Boudreau* 8.00
St. Catherine Labouré of the Miraculous Medal. *Dirvin* 13.50
The Glories of Mary. (pocket, unabr.). *St. Alphonsus Liguori* 10.00
The Three Ways of the Spiritual Life. *Garrigou-Lagrange, O.P.* 6.00

Prices subject to change.

Freemasonry: Mankind's Hidden Enemy. *Bro. C. Madden* 5.00
Fourteen Holy Helpers. *Hammer* 5.00
All About the Angels. *Fr. Paul O'Sullivan* 5.00
AA—1025: Memoirs of an Anti-Apostle. *Marie Carré.* 6.00
All for Jesus. *Fr. Frederick Faber.* 15.00
Growth in Holiness. *Fr. Frederick Faber.* 16.50
Behind the Lodge Door. *Paul Fisher.* 18.00
Chief Truths of the Faith. (Book I). *Fr. John Laux* 10.00
Mass and the Sacraments. (Book II). *Fr. John Laux* 10.00
Catholic Morality. (Book III). *Fr. John Laux.* 10.00
Catholic Apologetics. (Book IV). *Fr. John Laux.* 10.00
Introduction to the Bible. *Fr. John Laux.* 16.50
Church History. *Fr. John Laux* 24.00
Devotion for the Dying. *Mother Mary Potter* 9.00
Devotion to the Sacred Heart. *Fr. Jean Croiset.* 15.00
An Easy Way to Become a Saint. *Fr. Paul O'Sullivan* 5.00
The Golden Arrow. *Sr. Mary of St. Peter.* 12.50
The Holy Man of Tours. *Dorothy Scallan.* 10.00
Hell—Plus How to Avoid Hell. *Fr. Schouppe/Nelson* 10.00
History of Protestant Ref. in England & Ireland. *Cobbett.* 18.00
Holy Will of God. *Fr. Leo Pyzalski* 6.00
How Christ Changed the World. *Msgr. Luigi Civardi* 7.00
How to Be Happy, How to Be Holy *Fr. Paul O'Sullivan* 7.50
Imitation of Christ. *Thomas à Kempis. (Challoner transl.)* 10.00
Life & Message of Sr. Mary of the Trinity. *Rev. Dubois* 9.00
Life Everlasting. *Fr. Garrigou-Lagrange, O.P.* 13.50
Life of Mary as Seen by the Mystics. *Compiled by Raphael Brown* 12.50
Life of St. Dominic. *Mother Augusta Drane.* 12.00
Life of St. Francis of Assisi. *St. Bonaventure* 10.00
Life of St. Ignatius Loyola. *Fr. Genelli.* 16.50
Life of St. Margaret Mary Alacoque. *Rt. Rev. Emile Bougaud* 13.50
Mexican Martyrdom. *Fr. Wilfrid Parsons.* 10.00
Children of Fatima. *Windeatt. (Age 10 & up).* 8.00
Cure of Ars. *Windeatt. (Age 10 & up)* 12.00
The Little Flower. *Windeatt. (Age 10 & up).* 8.00
Patron of First Communicants. (Bl. Imelda). *Windeatt. (Age 10 & up)* 6.00
Miraculous Medal. *Windeatt. (Age 10 & up).* 7.00
St. Louis De Montfort. *Windeatt. (Age 10 & up)* 12.00
St. Thomas Aquinas. *Windeatt. (Age 10 & up).* 6.00
St. Catherine of Siena. *Windeatt. (Age 10 & up)* 5.00
St. Rose of Lima. *Windeatt. (Age 10 & up)* 8.00
St. Hyacinth of Poland. *Windeatt. (Age 10 & up).* 11.00
St. Martin de Porres. *Windeatt. (Age 10 & up).* 7.00
Pauline Jaricot. *Windeatt. (Age 10 & up).* 13.00
Douay-Rheims New Testament. *Paperbound* 15.00
Prayers and Heavenly Promises. *Compiled by Joan Carroll Cruz.* 5.00
Preparation for Death. (Unabr., pocket). *St. Alphonsus* 10.00
Rebuilding a Lost Faith. *John Stoddard* 15.00
The Spiritual Combat. *Dom Lorenzo Scupoli* 9.00
Retreat Companion for Priests. *Fr. Francis Havey* 7.50
Spiritual Doctrine of St. Cath. of Genoa. *Maribotti/St. Catherine* 10.00
The Soul of the Apostolate. *Dom Chautard* 10.00

Prices subject to change.

Hail Holy Queen (from *Glories of Mary*). *St. Alphonsus* 8.00
Novena of Holy Communions. *Lovasik* 2.00
Brief Catechism for Adults. *Cogan*................................ 9.00
The Cath. Religion—Illus./Expl. for Child, Adult, Convert. *Burbach*....... 9.00
Eucharistic Miracles. *Joan Carroll Cruz* 15.00
The Incorruptibles. *Joan Carroll Cruz*............................ 13.50
Pope St. Pius X. *F. A. Forbes*.................................... 8.00
St. Alphonsus Liguori. *Frs. Miller and Aubin*....................... 16.50
Self-Abandonment to Divine Providence. *Fr. de Caussade, S.J.*.......... 18.00
The Song of Songs—A Mystical Exposition. *Fr. Arintero, O.P.* 20.00
Prophecy for Today. *Edward Connor*............................. 5.50
Saint Michael and the Angels. *Approved Sources*..................... 7.00
Dolorous Passion of Our Lord. *Anne C. Emmerich*.................... 16.50
Modern Saints—Their Lives & Faces, Book I. *Ann Ball* 18.00
Modern Saints—Their Lives & Faces, Book II. *Ann Ball*............... 20.00
Our Lady of Fatima's Peace Plan from Heaven. *Booklet* .... .75
Divine Favors Granted to St. Joseph. *Père Binet* 5.00
St. Joseph Cafasso—Priest of the Gallows. *St. John Bosco*............. 4.50
Catechism of the Council of Trent. *McHugh/Callan*................... 24.00
The Foot of the Cross. *Fr. Faber*................................. 16.50
The Rosary in Action. *John Johnson* 9.00
Padre Pio—The Stigmatist. *Fr. Charles Carty* 15.00
Why Squander Illness? *Frs. Rumble & Carty*....................... 2.00
The Sacred Heart and the Priesthood. *de la Touche* 9.00
Fatima—The Great Sign. *Francis Johnston* 8.00
Heliotropium—Conformity of Human Will to Divine. *Drexelius* 13.00
Charity for the Suffering Souls. *Fr. John Nageleisen* 16.50
Devotion to the Sacred Heart of Jesus. *Verheylezoon* 15.00
Who Is Padre Pio? *Radio Replies Press* 1.50
Child's Bible History. *Knecht*.................................... 4.00
The Stigmata and Modern Science. *Fr. Charles Carty* 1.25
The Life of Christ. 4 Vols. H.B. *Anne C. Emmerich* 60.00
St. Anthony—The Wonder Worker of Padua. *Stoddard* 5.00
The Precious Blood. *Fr. Faber*................................... 13.50
The Holy Shroud & Four Visions. *Fr. O'Connell*.................... 2.00
Clean Love in Courtship. *Fr. Lawrence Lovasik*..................... 2.50
The Prophecies of St. Malachy. *Peter Bander*....................... 7.00
St. Martin de Porres. *Giuliana Cavallini* 12.50
The Secret of the Rosary. *St. Louis De Montfort*.................... 3.00
The History of Antichrist. *Rev. P. Huchede*........................ 4.00
St. Catherine of Siena. *Alice Curtayne*............................ 13.50
Where We Got the Bible. *Fr. Henry Graham* 6.00
Hidden Treasure—Holy Mass. *St. Leonard*......................... 5.00
Imitation of the Sacred Heart of Jesus. *Fr. Arnoudt* 15.00
The Life & Glories of St. Joseph. *Edward Thompson*.................. 15.00
Père Lamy. *Biver*.. 10.00
Humility of Heart. *Fr. Cajetan da Bergamo* 8.50
The Curé D'Ars. *Abbé Francis Trochu*............................ 21.50
Love, Peace and Joy. (St. Gertrude). *Prévot*........................ 7.00

At your Bookdealer or direct from the Publisher.
Call Toll-Free 1-800-437-5876.

Prices subject to change.

NOTES

NOTES

NOTES

NOTES